IMAGES
of America

MARKESAN

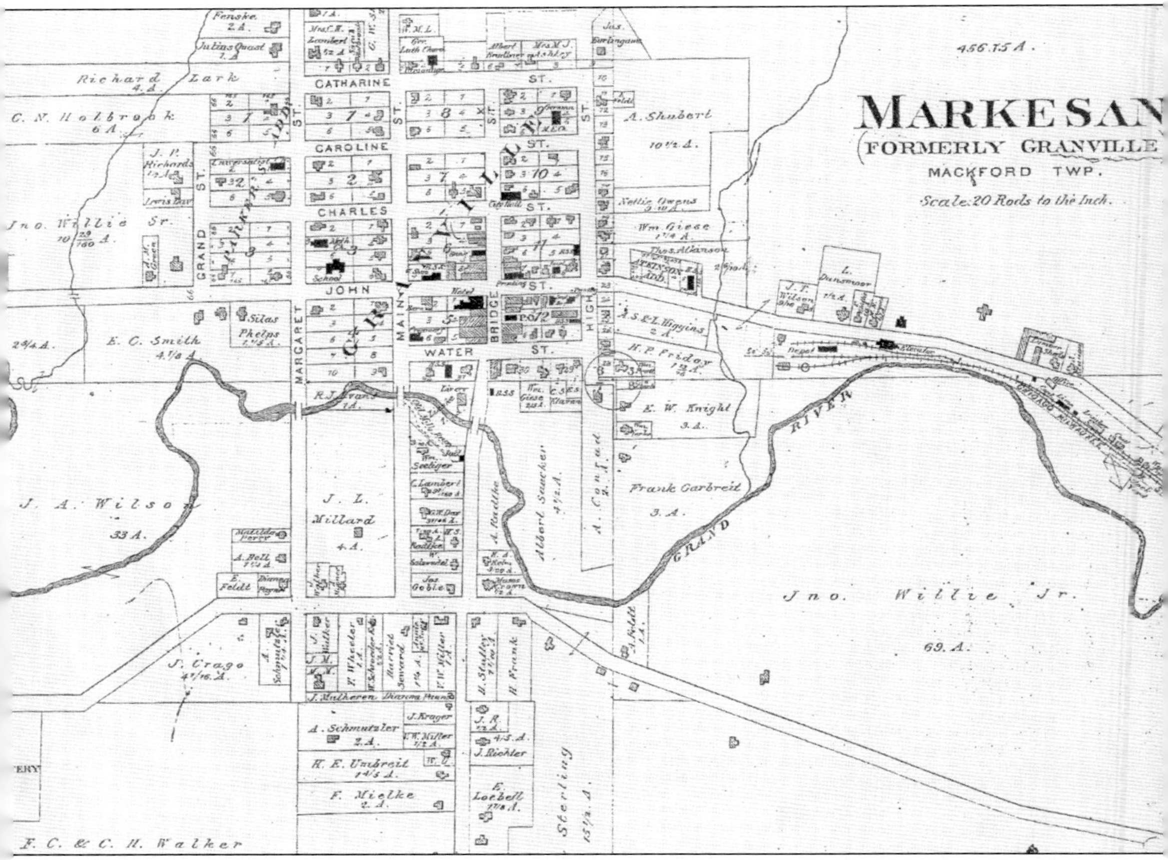

A 1901 map shows the layout of the Markesan community. It depicts the street layouts and names, along with the land holdings of residents of the community. Darker boxes outline landmarks and businesses within the town. (Courtesy of the Markesan Historical Society.)

On the Cover: This is a photograph of Bridge Street between the years 1916 and 1918, the downtown district of Markesan where everyday business activity was carried out. The citizens of Markesan went downtown to fulfill any obligation they might have. Ladies would buy fine jewelry at the Henninger Jewelry Store, men could browse for cars or pianos at Perry's Piano & Auto Store, and a distant traveler could check in at the elegant Yosemite Hotel while visiting a relative in town. (Courtesy of the Markesan Historical Society.)

IMAGES
of America

MARKESAN

Austin Frederick
and the Markesan Historical Society

ARCADIA
PUBLISHING

ISBN 978-0-7385-8250-4

Published by Arcadia Publishing
Charleston, South Carolina

Printed in the United States of America

Library of Congress Control Number: 2011938853

For all general information, please contact Arcadia Publishing:
Telephone 843-853-2070
Fax 843-853-0044
E-mail sales@arcadiapublishing.com
For customer service and orders:
Toll-Free 1-888-313-2665

Visit us on the Internet at www.arcadiapublishing.com

Dedicated to the citizens of Markesan, past and present,
for making Markesan a "Grand Community."

Contents

Acknowledgments 6

Introduction 7

1. The Streets of Markesan 9
2. School and Academic Activities 33
3. Residents and Their Residences 49
4. Bustling Businesses 67
5. Railroad and Industry 89
6. Leisure and Celebrations 109

Acknowledgments

I would like to thank the amazing people who influenced and helped me assemble this insightful book about our community. My first thank-you goes out to my past teachers in the history department of the Markesan School District: Peter James, Paul White, Skip Laper, and Monte Spillane. Your enthusiasm and teaching style sparked my passion and inspired me to further explore history. Thanks goes to the Markesan Historical Society for allowing me to use its wonderful facility in order to make this book possible. I extend a big thank-you to Gayle Schultz and Sue Abendroth for their assistance with identifying some pictures. I would like to thank my fiancée, Molly Guendert, for encouraging me and helping me with this project all along the way.

Unless noted otherwise, all photographs and documents are courtesy of the Markesan Historical Society.

INTRODUCTION

I have called Markesan my home for the past 20 years, growing up on a working farm about six miles northwest of town. My passion for history is what truly sparked this venture of exploring the past of Markesan to learn about the evolution of a small village into a prosperous community.

For years, I thought the expression of Markesan being a "Grand Community" was in reference to its location around the Grand River, but as I began to do my research I realized it meant more than that. I feel it refers to the overall attitude and work ethic its citizens have demonstrated from the past up to the present. It is their determination and toil that built Markesan into what it is today.

Early-19th-century travelers saw Wisconsin Territory as an area of economic opportunity and new beginnings. The first settler in the area was Miller Seward, who traveled up from Illinois in 1843. His father, John Seward, came in 1844 after he purchased 300 acres of land and built the first frame house in what would become Markesan—this home still stands today. By 1849, the village of Granville had been established by John Chapel and Charles E. Russell, who were settlers in the area. In 1854, the US Postal Service issued an urgent notice to the citizens of Granville. A dilemma occurred when it was discovered that there was another Granville in the state of Wisconsin. Mail was getting mixed up, and the name of the town needed to be changed. A decision was made to have citizens submit a potential name for the town, which would be chosen at random; Markesan was selected. History has Henry Wright to thank for the newly selected name. Wright had once served as treasurer of former Granville and also was an important business figure and citizen in town. His idea for the name Markesan derived from a newly discovered chain of Pacific islands known as the Marquesas Islands, known for their spectacular climate and fertile soil. On May 8, 1858, the village of Markesan was officially incorporated.

With the name dilemma solved, Markesan began to grow. By 1859, the population was around 800 people, and the community prospered. There were mills, blacksmiths, a cigar factory, cheese factory, a tailor, slaughterhouse, many farm operations, and much more. The village of Markesan was home to four different church congregations, and in 1850 a school district was established, and classes started the following year. Markesan became an important center of business, and the citizens looked to connect their business with the outside markets.

Steady industry meant the need to expand trade. Markesan somehow had to connect to the outside markets in order to produce trade. Early ways to export goods from the area were by road or river; the Fox River served as an early way to import and export goods from the area. Located about six miles North of Markesan, farmers and merchants would haul their goods by road (on what is now Wisconsin Highway 73) to boat piers built on a channel that connected to the Fox River. The channel had been dug to allow boats to travel through marshy areas and reach piers where goods could be loaded and unloaded and moved along the river. These piers would have been located down what is now Old Ditch Road, just west of present-day Highway 73. The Fox River's need for constant maintenance, from moving sandbars and the boom of railroad transportation, put an end to steamboat travel on the river.

By the end of the American Civil War, massive railroad expansion was underway throughout the country, and Markesan wanted to be connected. The closest railroad line available to merchants was in Brandon, Wisconsin. Wagons and stagecoaches made many trips transporting people and goods to and from the Chicago, Milwaukee, and St. Paul Railroad line (later to be known as the Milwaukee Road) in Brandon. In 1870, an attempt was made to connect a railroad from Ripon to Markesan. Soon after work started, it had come to an abrupt end, as monetary funding ran out. However, with the discovery of excellent quality granite in a nearby area in 1880, the citizens of Markesan saw their chance to get their railroad and open lines of trade. Much debate and resistance happened over whether a line would be extended past the granite quarry and linked to Markesan. Markesan citizen James Densmoor Sr., the same man who headed the channel-digging operation to the Fox River, invested funds and headed a railroad project. With other citizens investing and donating money towards the project, the Markesan and Brandon Railroad Company was formed. Upon completion in 1883, trains made regular runs to Markesan. Seeing as the venture had paid off, the Markesan and Brandon Railroad Company was sold to the Chicago, Milwaukee, and St. Paul Railroad Company, and it became part of that larger rail network.

With the railroad line extending into Markesan, along with telegraph lines, Markesan was now open to outside markets. The train was said to have run to Markesan three times a day on a weekly basis. Farmers were now able to load their grains and livestock and transport them out to bigger markets. Merchants and businessmen were shipping goods and setting up business in Markesan, and passenger transportation brought people in and out of town.

The railroad brought great prosperity to Markesan and promoted growth. Its citizens continued their hard work and dedication to keep Markesan a prosperous area. A sign that there was no shortage of money is seen in the magnificent homes built in town by its wealthy citizens. Business filled the downtown area, and industry took foot on the outskirts. Over the years, people have come and gone, businesses have opened and closed, but the citizens of Markesan have retained their hard work ethic. May residents of the community continue moving forward into the future with this hard work ethic, adding more to Markesan's already 162-year history, and continue to make it a Grand Community.

One

The Streets of Markesan

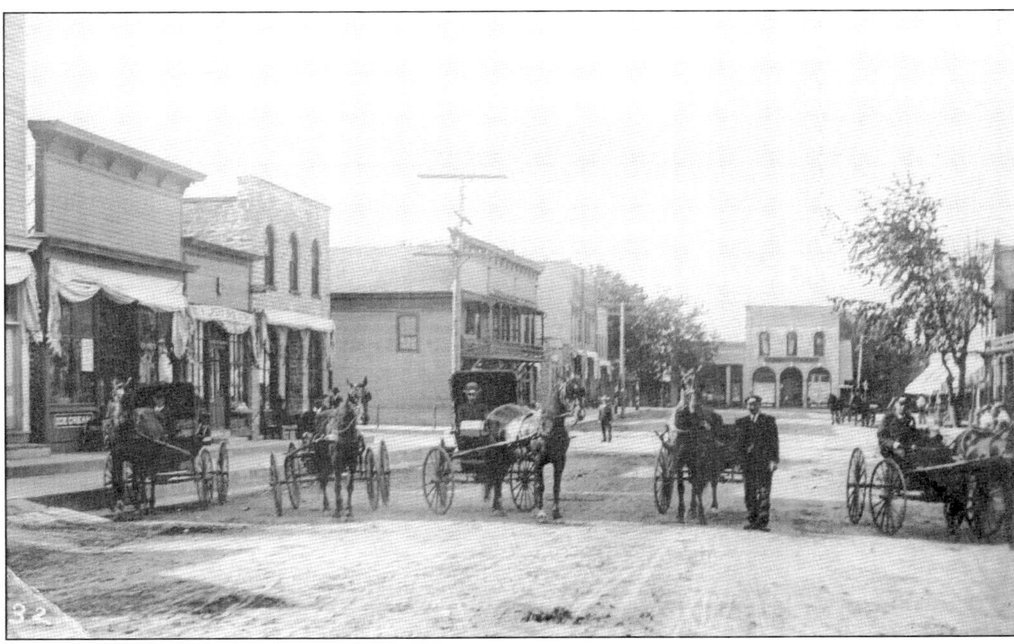

Whether it was downtown or in the residential district, people were out and about carrying on with their work in the community. Downtown was a prime location of activity, where business or pleasure needs could be fulfilled. Here, a group of men poses for a photograph with their buggies on Markesan's downtown portion of Bridge Street.

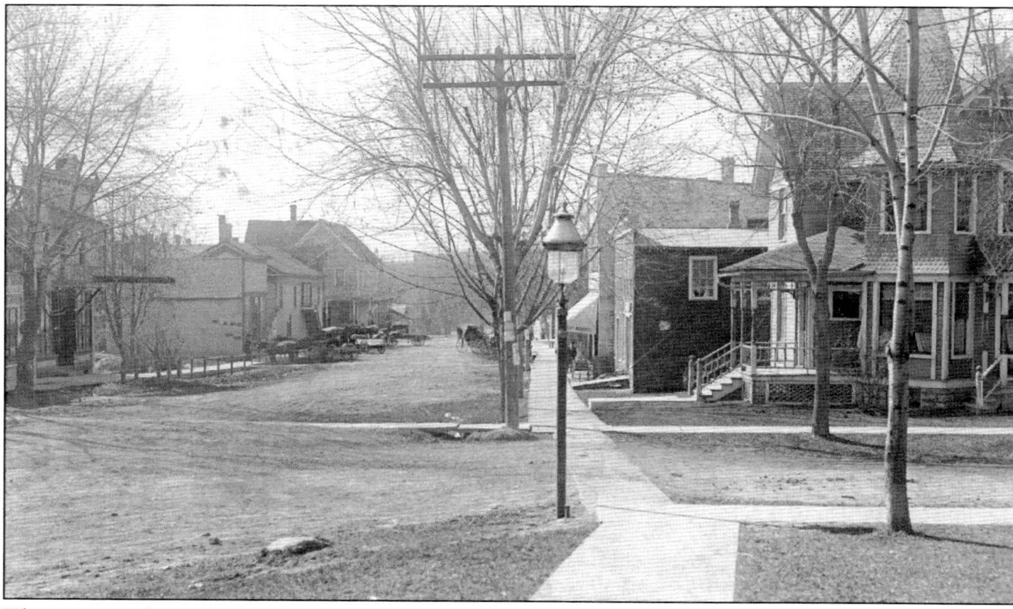

This picture shows a glimpse of the corner on John and High Streets looking west. The Kempton House (front right) is seen, and the electric poles show that Markesan had electricity running to its residents. Markesan's first streetlights were lamps on street corners that were lit at dusk by resident Lewis Day.

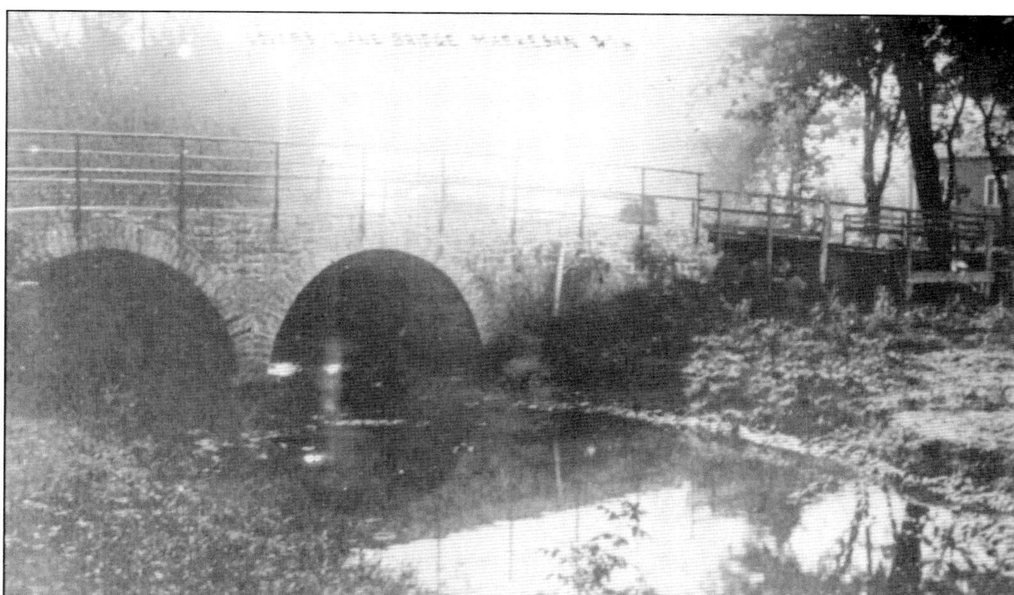

Here, the Lovers Lane double arch bridge is seen spanning the Grand River. This stone bridge is believed to have been built in 1894. Lovers Lane is no longer the name of this stretch of street; it is now known as Main Street, and the old stone bridge was replaced long ago but was rebuilt with the same double arch design as it predecessor. The image of the Grand River flowing under the bridge has become a distinguished symbol of the community.

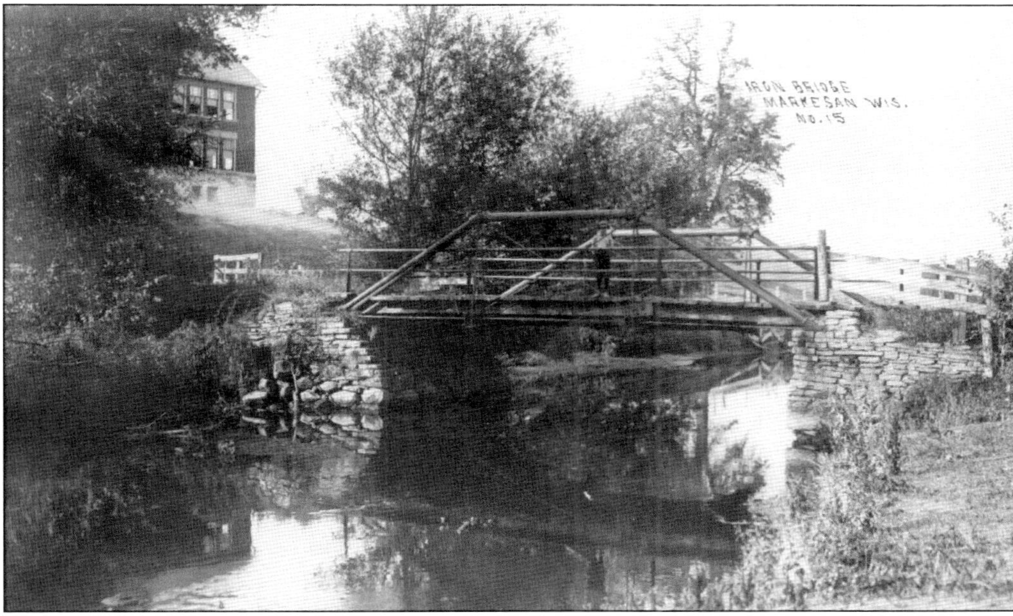

Pictured here is an iron bridge on Margaret Street that crosses the Grand River. The Markesan schoolhouse can be seen in the background, which was built on the high ground near the river in 1906. Also, note the young man standing on the middle of the bridge; perhaps he is on his way to or from school.

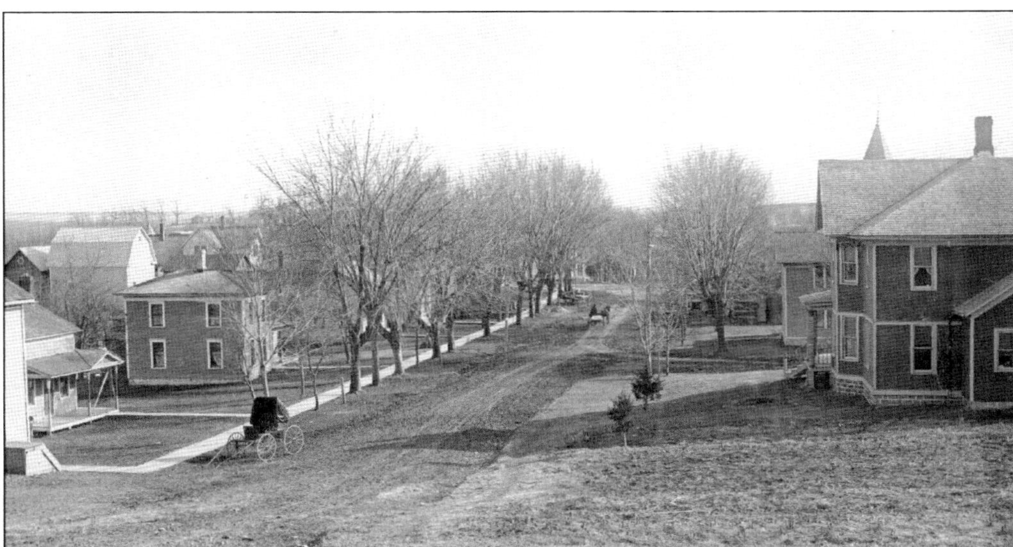

This hill was once the highest point in the community just northeast of town on High Street. It shows the line of homes looking south on High. The Congregationalist Church built its stone church on this hill, and this was also the location of Markesan's first water tower.

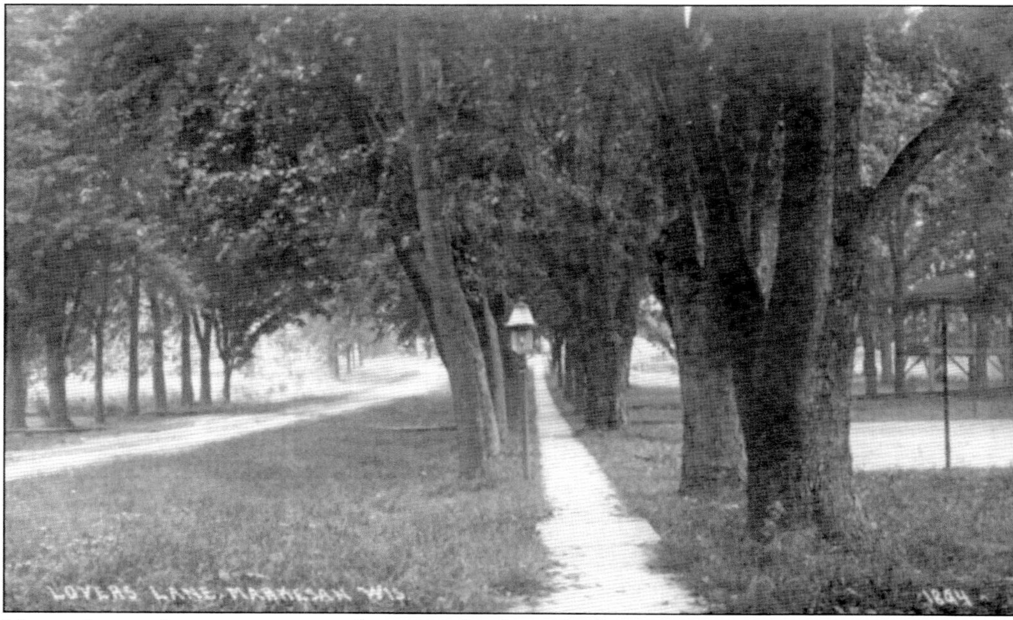

Here is Lovers Lane as it appeared in 1894. In the early days, Lovers Lane was a thinly populated street where courting young men and women took walks down the boarded sidewalk. Some parts of the sidewalk were even suspended on posts to avoid walking on marshy area. Along the road was also a bandstand where the Markesan Town Band would put on performances.

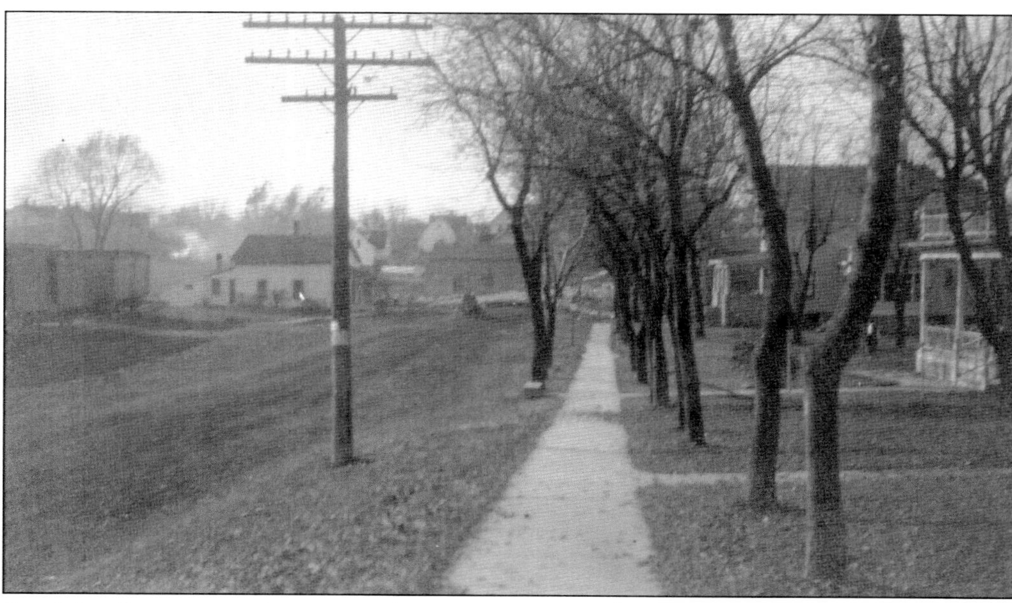

East John Street ran right next to the action going on down by the railroad. Railcars can be seen (left) waiting at the end of the line. A carriage is heading up John Street (center) toward downtown. Maybe a family member has just come to town by train, and he or she was picked up down at the Markesan depot.

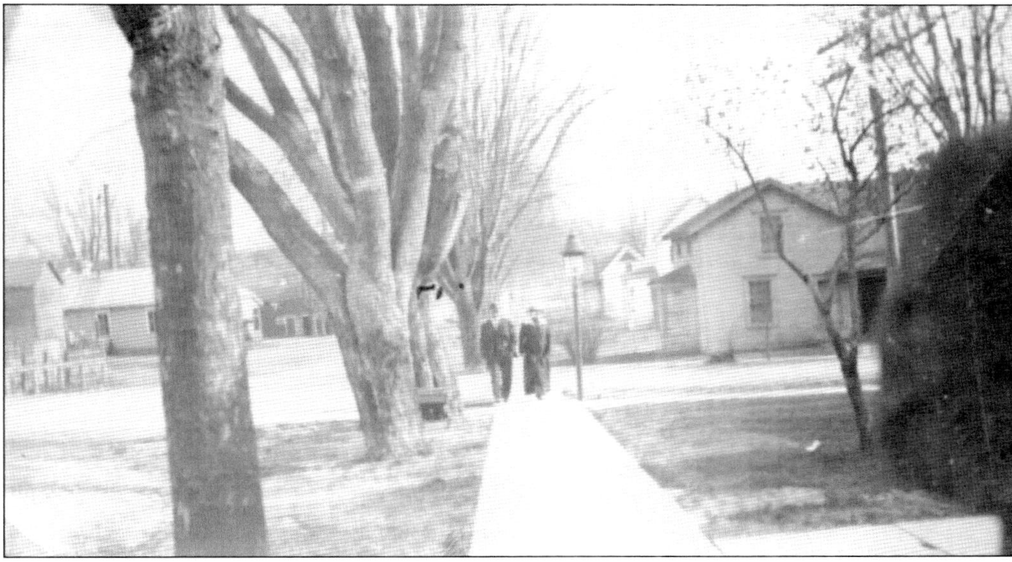

This couple is out for a stroll on Main Street in the days when kerosene lamps lit the streets. On the left, the Markesan Creamery, which was started by Henry P. Friday, can be seen. Starting at the creamery, Main Street ended and Lovers Lane began.

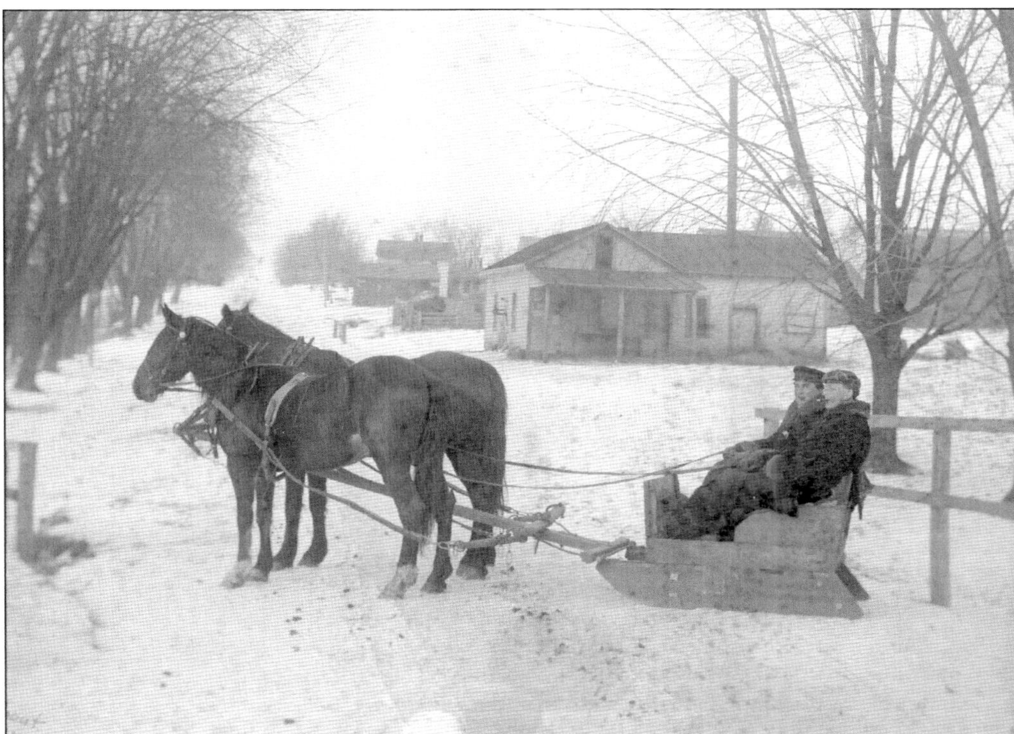

The men in this photograph are identified as Oscar Laper (left) and Louie Pollesch taking a winter sleigh ride on the corner of Main and Water Streets in 1910. The building directly in the background with the large smokestack is the Markesan Creamery.

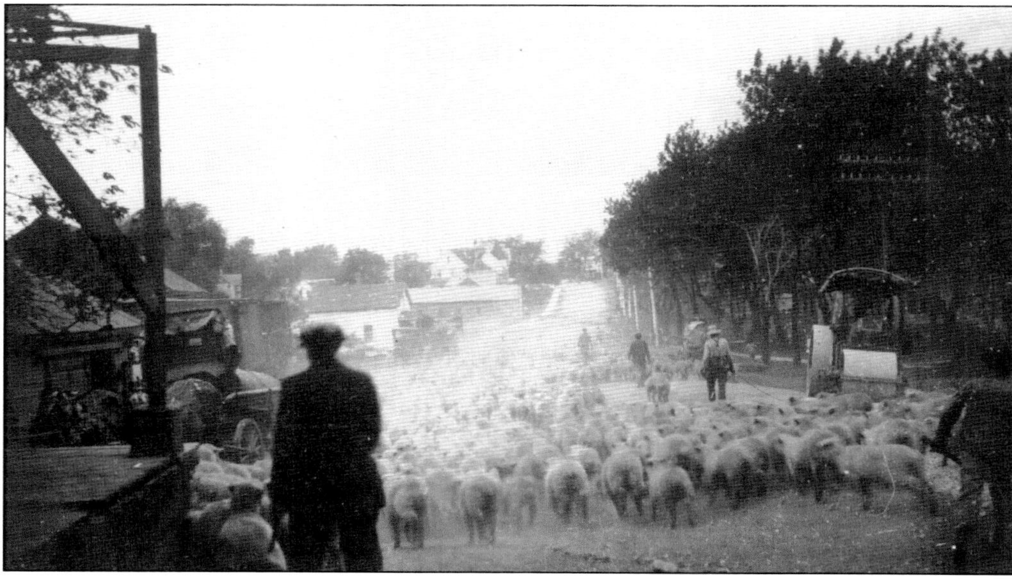

Having livestock on the farm was important to area farmers. When the railroad came to town, it made shipping livestock faster and more efficient. Here is a scene of sheep being moved on John Street. Perhaps a farmer was driving his herd to town to be loaded on the train, where the sheep would be taken to a larger stockyard.

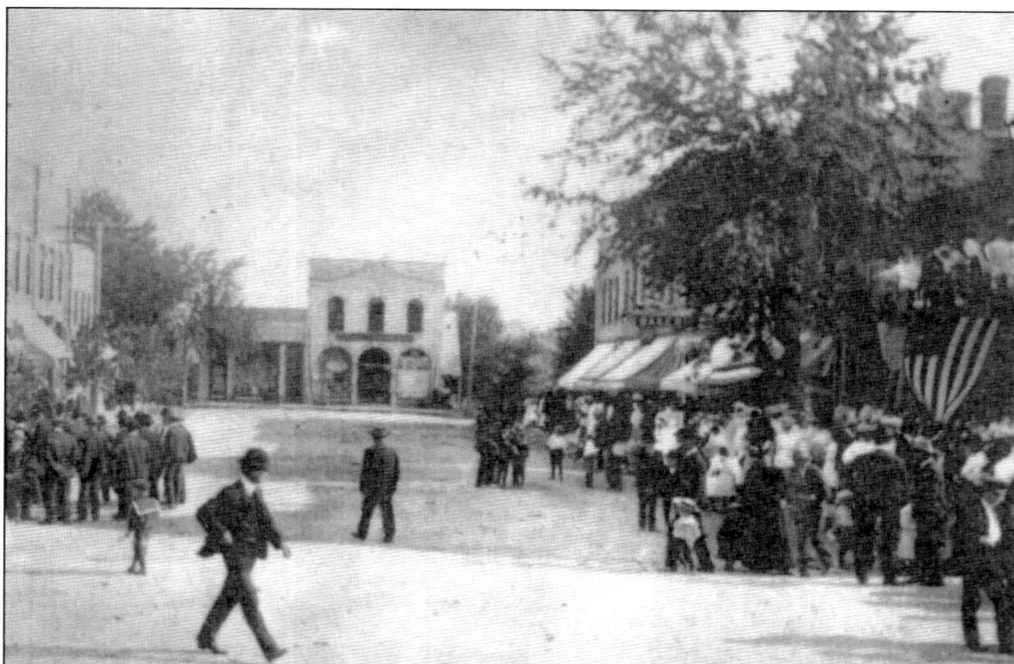

Here a celebration is underway on Bridge Street. Crowds gathered in the main section of Markesan for all different reasons, whether it was for celebrating holidays, parades, or the return home of soldiers from war. Bridge Street remains a beacon of activity for social events to this day.

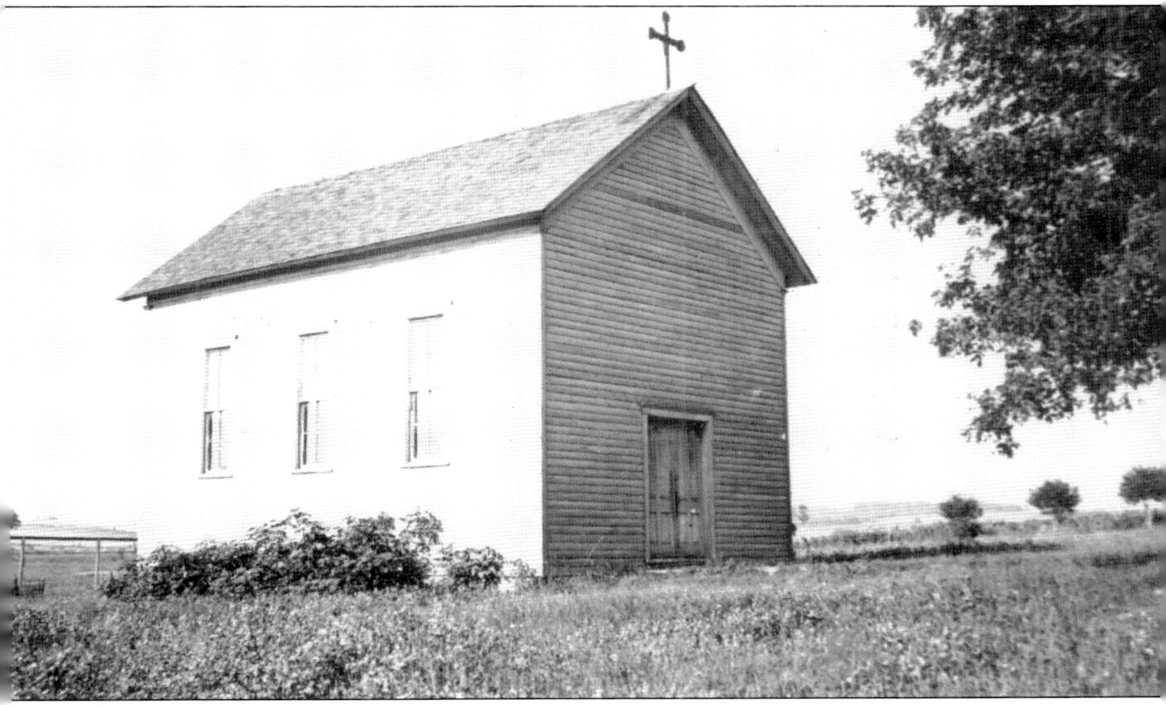

This picture, taken in the late 1930s, is of St. Joseph's Catholic Church located on St. Joseph's Street. The church is recorded as being established in Markesan between 1897 and 1899. Upon the request of local Catholic residents, land was purchased from August Laper, and a wood-frame church was constructed. This original building was used until 1950, when it was demolished and a new brick building constructed in its place. In 1975, an addition was constructed onto the 1950s building to make room for the expanding parish.

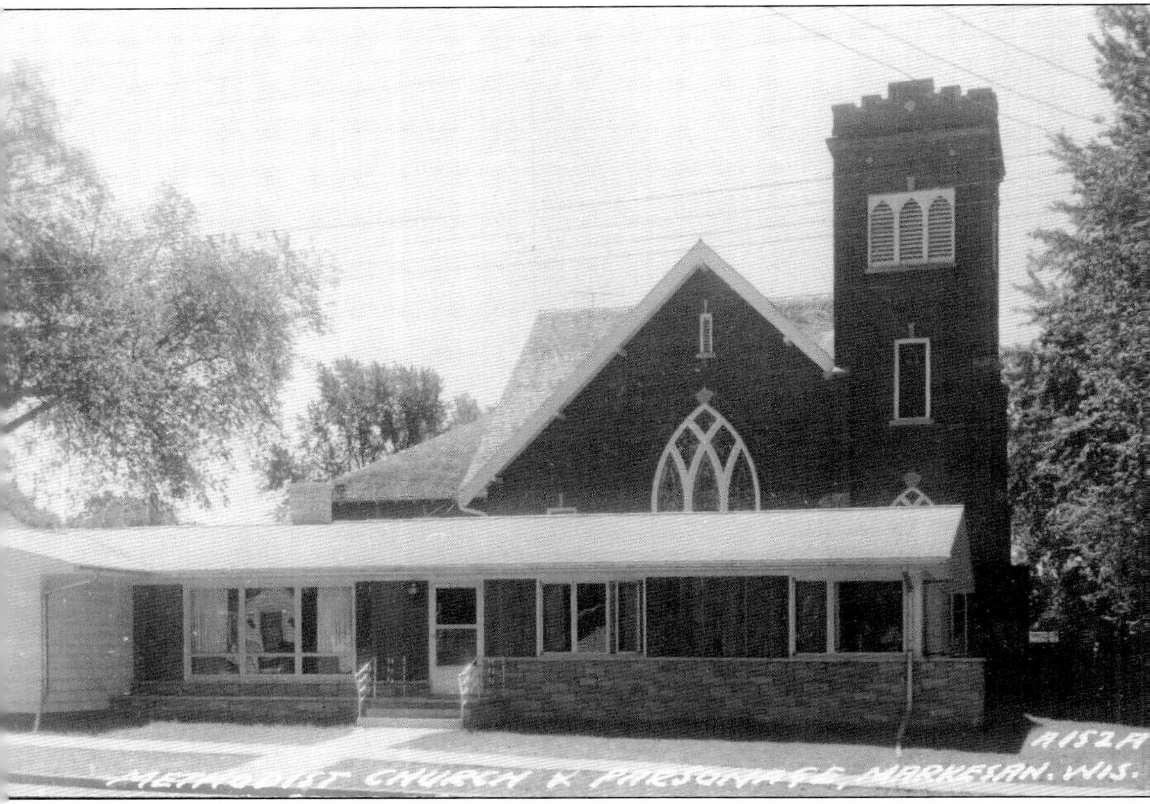

The original Methodist Episcopal Church was built in 1862 on North Margaret Street. By 1915, the congregation had outgrown its building and plans were underway to build a new church in its place. The new brick building was completed in January 1916. The Methodist Episcopal Church remained its own entity until the merger with the Zion Evangelical Church took place in 1970. The services were then moved to the Zion Church on the hill on Catherine Street. This church, seen here with the parsonage in the foreground, is now occupied by the Markesan Bible Church.

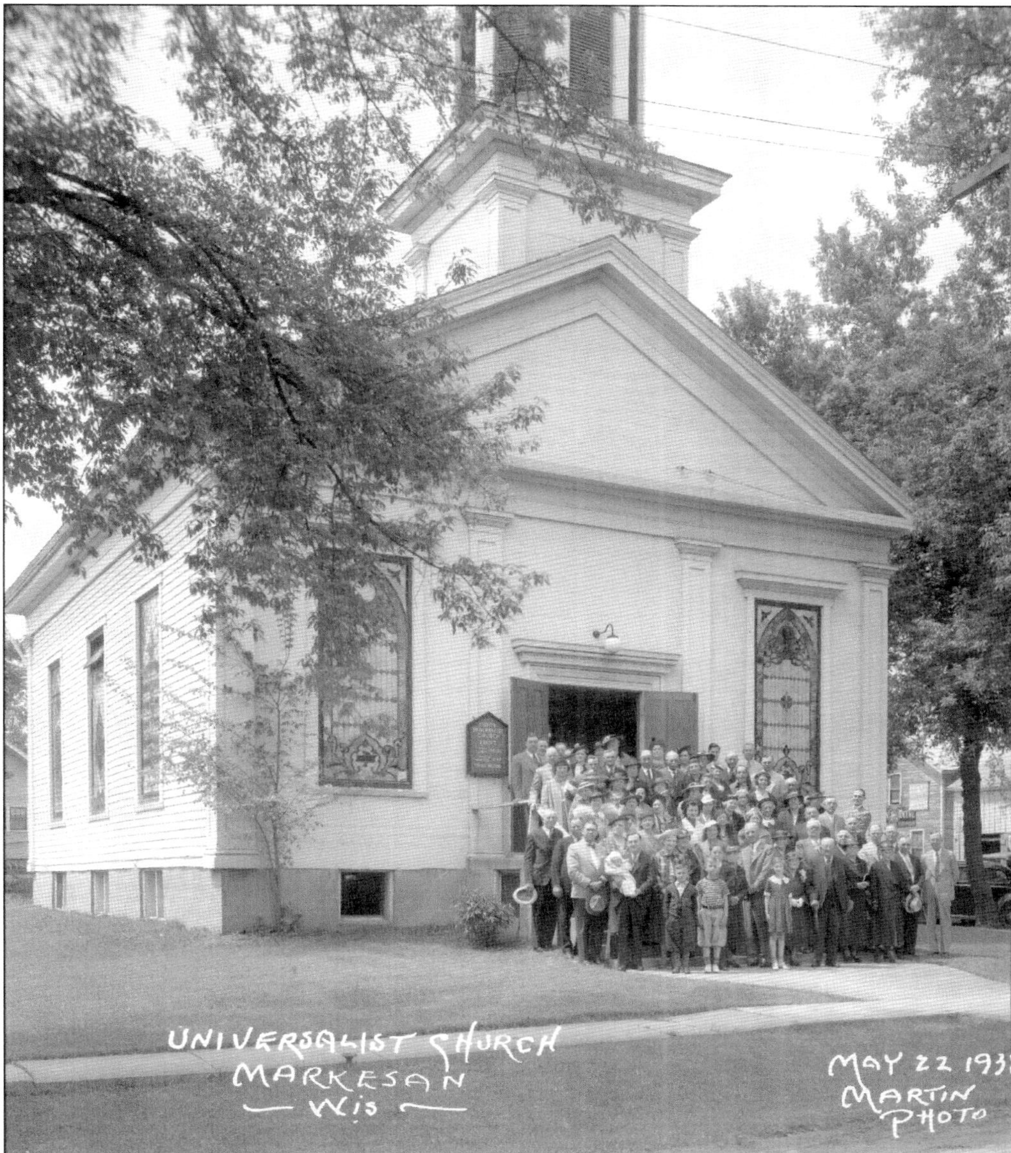

The Universalist Church congregation was organized in 1857, and a wood-frame church was constructed that same year on the southwest corner of Margaret and Caroline Streets. Services were first conducted by Pastor A. Vedder. The church remained a place of worship for the congregation until dissolution in the 1950s; the church was finally demolished July 1954. Here, the congregation poses for a picture on the doorsteps of the church in 1938.

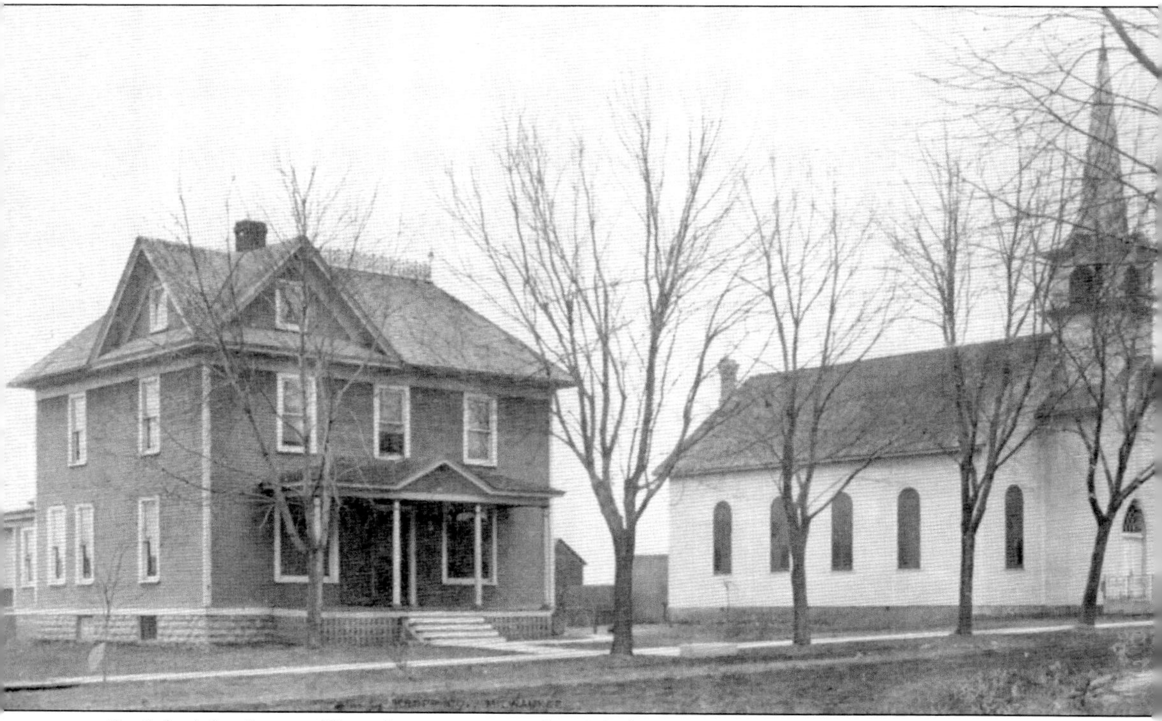

St. John's Lutheran Church was organized in Markesan in 1883 and used the Universalist church for a number of years for religious services. In 1892, the congregation constructed its building on Catherine Street. This photograph shows the wooden church and the parsonage around 1900. The old wooden building was outgrown by the early 1900s, and plans were made to construct a new home for the Lutheran congregation. A large brick structure was built in 1916 and was dedicated in November of that year. That same building remains the place of worship today for the congregation.

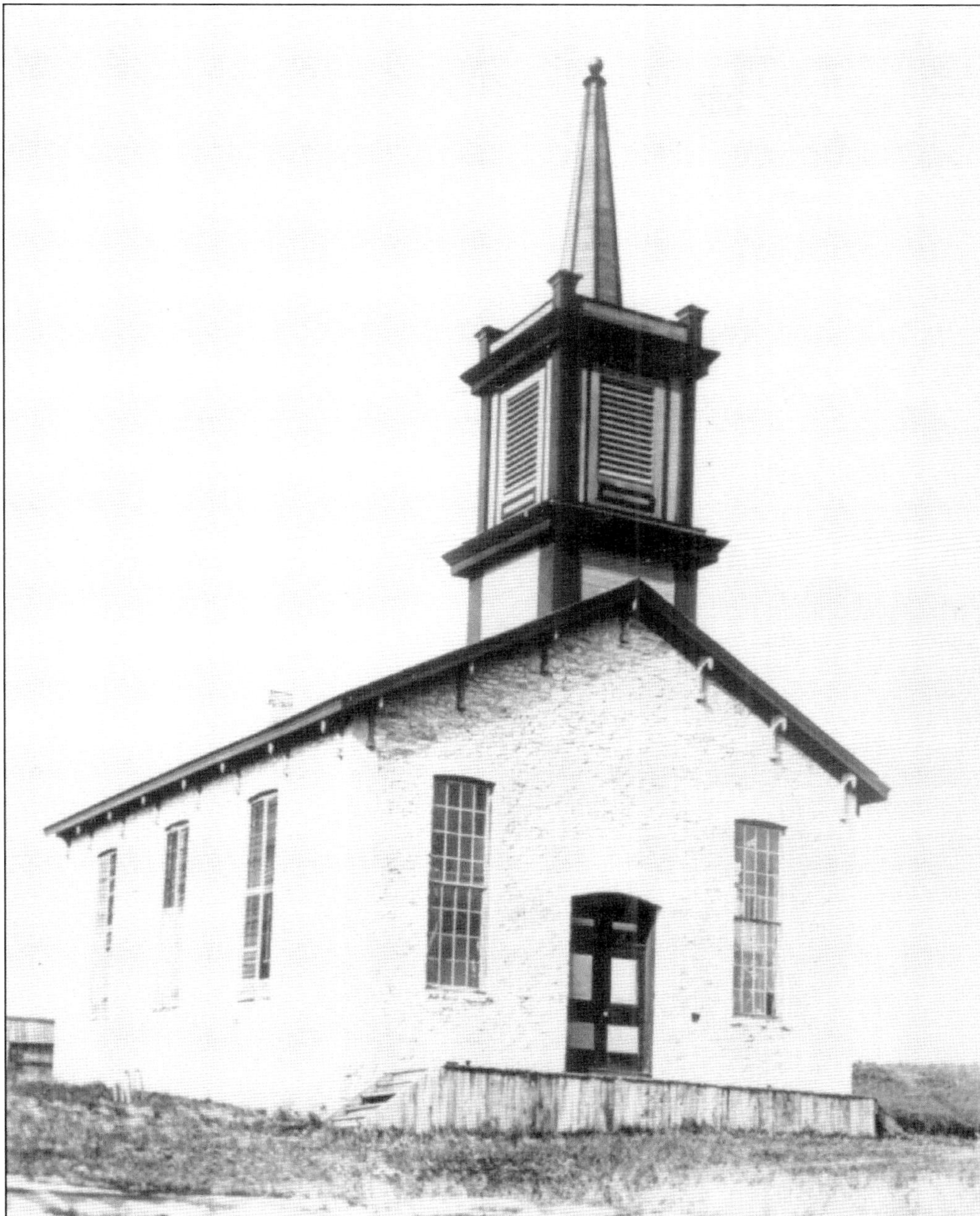

This 1897 picture shows the stone church that was home to the German Methodist Church. This church was built by the Congregational Church Society in 1858. After the congregation disbanded, German Methodists began using it in 1886. It was located on the hill north of the village on Caroline Street. In 1904, the original stone building was demolished and a new building was constructed that same year. The Zion Evangelical Church then occupied the location of the former German Methodist Church. In April 1970, the Zion Evangelical Church and the Methodist Episcopal Church joined to form the United Methodist Church and moved to the church on Catherine Street.

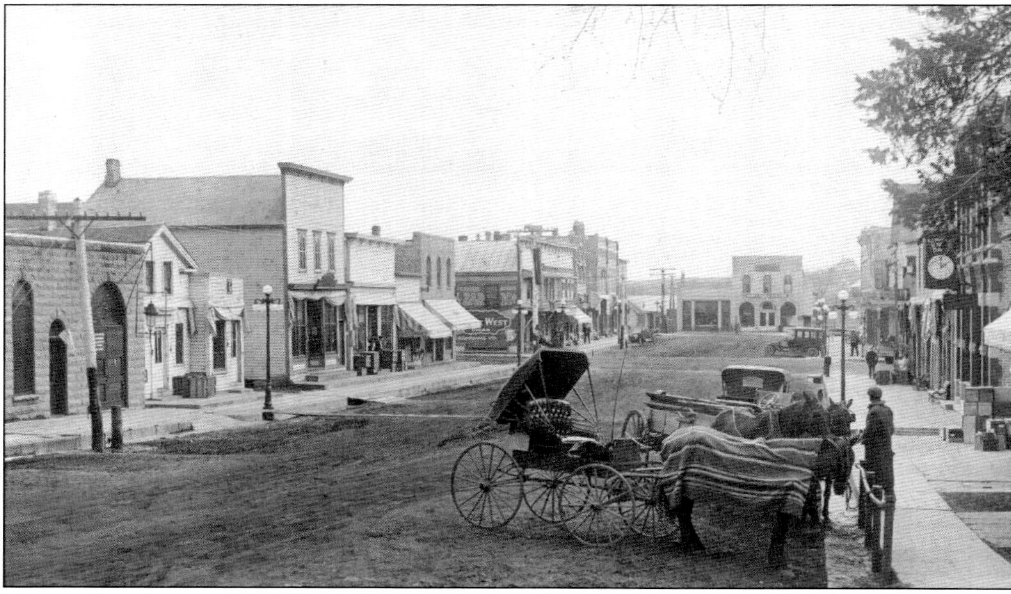

Here is what downtown Markesan looked like around 1916. This was at the dawn of the automobile, as both cars and buggies were modes of transportation; however, roads were still not paved at this time. Electricity was now powering the city, as power lines and electric streetlights are evident. Notice the Markesan State Bank clock hangs outside the offices and reads 2:00 p.m.

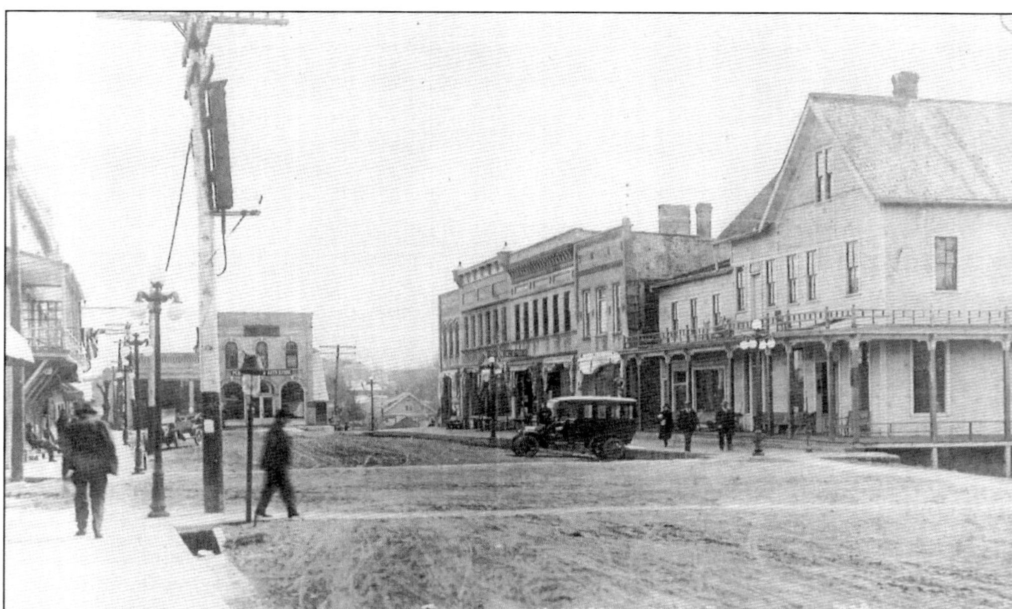

This photograph, taken the same day as the previous image, shows the southern part of Bridge Street. Notice the that the position of the cars here and in the previous shot are the same. The Yosemite Hotel is pictured on the right with the taxi that went to the railroad depot each day. D.D. Williams Big Daylight store is three buildings down from the hotel, and on the end of the street is Perry's Piano & Auto Store.

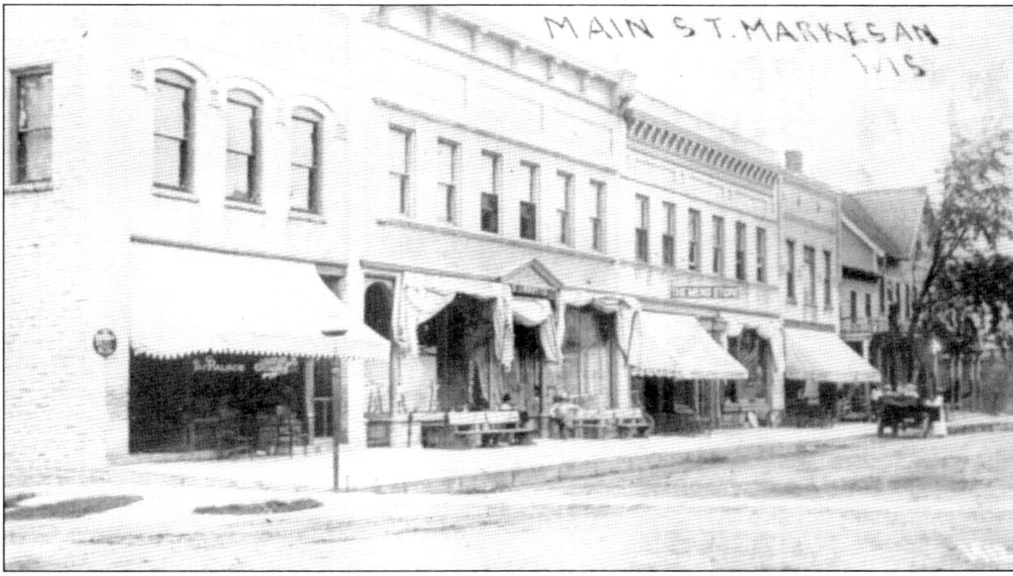

Another picture taken around 1900 shows the south block of Bridge Street. Gus Weber's Tavern is on the left, followed by D.D. Williams Big Daylight Store, Buennings Men's Store, Frederick and Mumbrue Hardware, Rexall Drugstore, and the Yosemite Hotel is the last building on the block. This picture was taken before the electric streetlights were installed, as a kerosene streetlamp can be seen in the foreground.

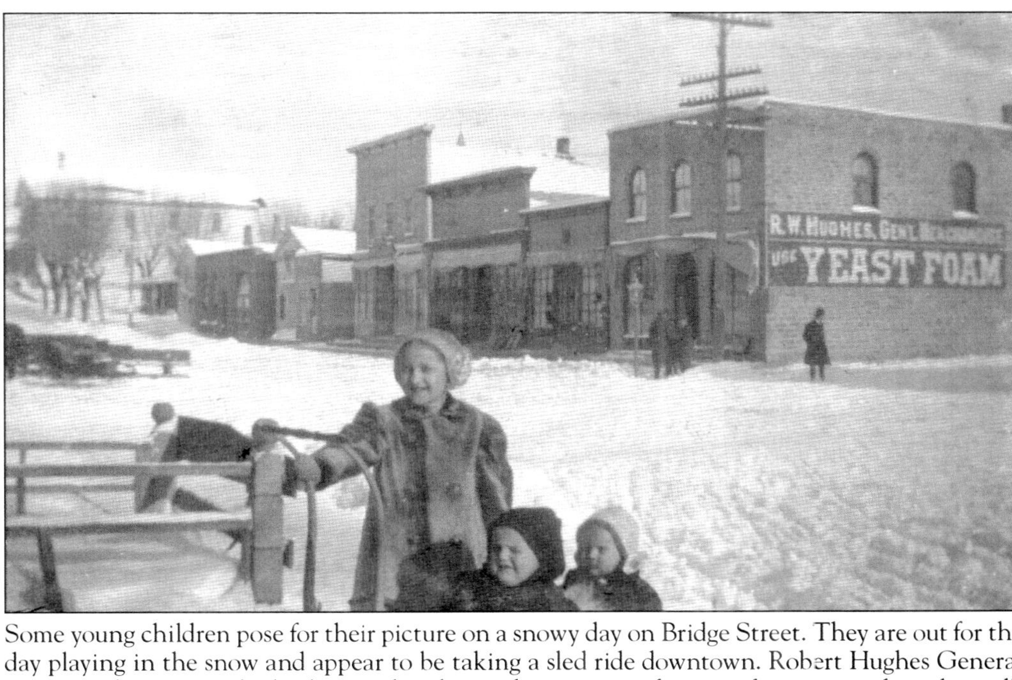

Some young children pose for their picture on a snowy day on Bridge Street. They are out for the day playing in the snow and appear to be taking a sled ride downtown. Robert Hughes General Store can be seen in the background with an advertisement for yeast foam painted on the wall. This same advertisement is faintly visible on the building today.

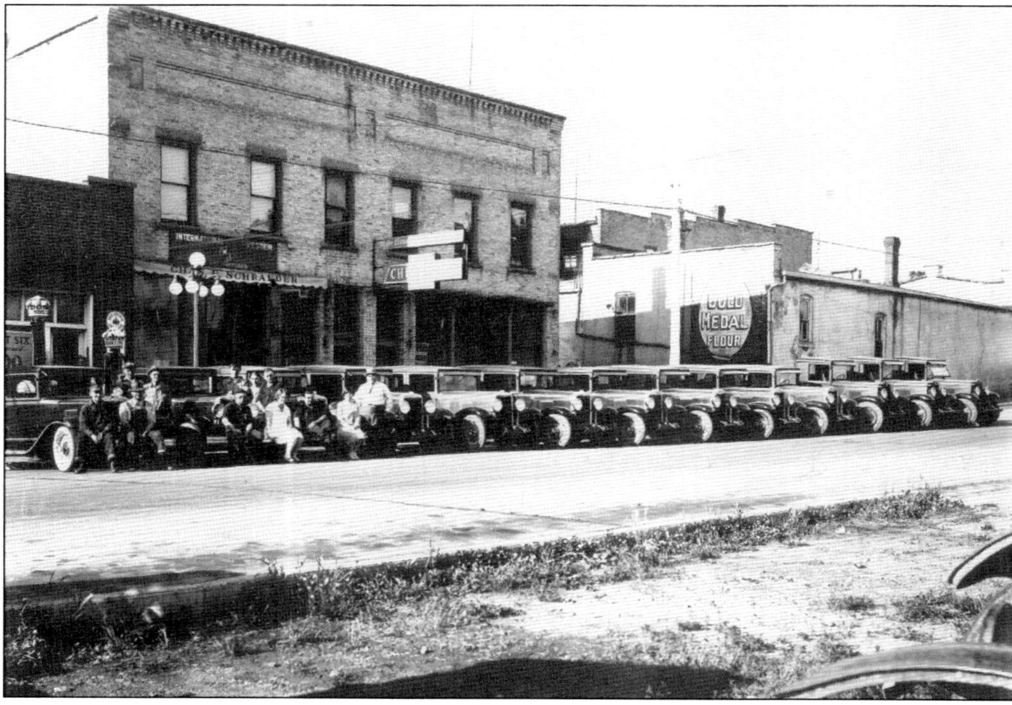

The photograph above shows the front of Schraeder Motor Company in 1929 with a row of new Chevrolet automobiles, and pictured by them are, from left to right, Charles Welk, Fred Klettke, Leo Spievogel, August Lambrecht, Bill Zimmerman, Elmer Kuehn, Art Frieheit, Herb Wastrack, Irma Richards Allen, Milon W. Tonn, Irene Schraeder, and Charles F. Schraeder. Below is a view of the automobile lot in the winter months at Schraeder Motor Company.

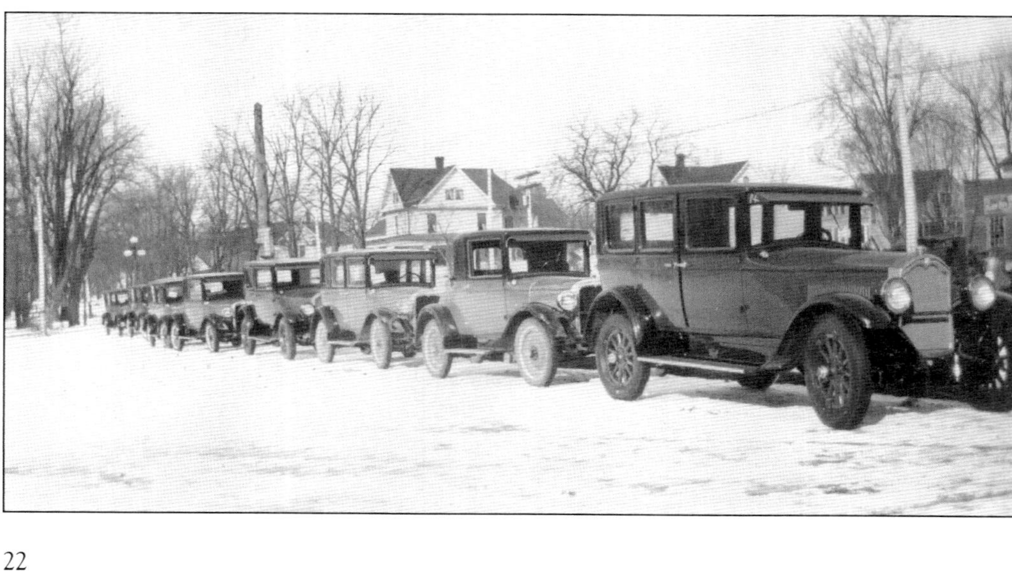

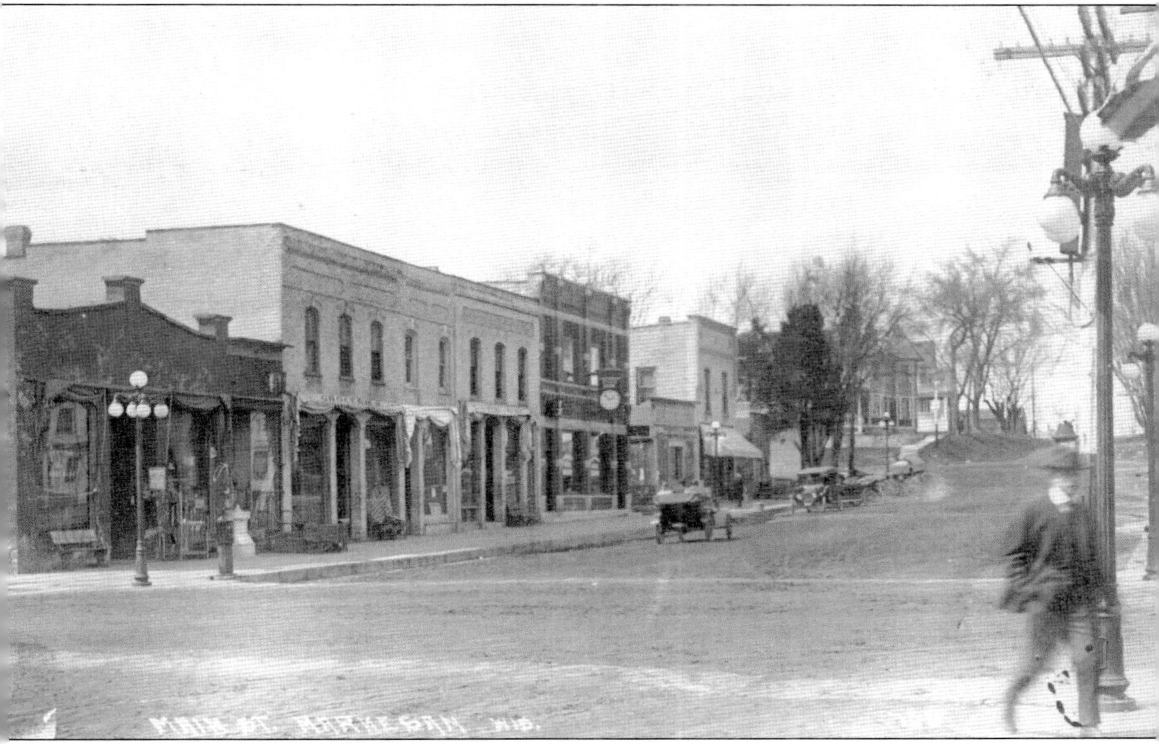

Shown here is the northwest row of businesses on Bridge Street taken around 1916. William F. Dunsmoore Hardware Store is seen at the far left, followed by the grocery store, meat market, and the Markesan State Bank displaying its signature bank clock hanging out to tell the local time. Note the automobile heading up Bridge Street with a full load of passengers.

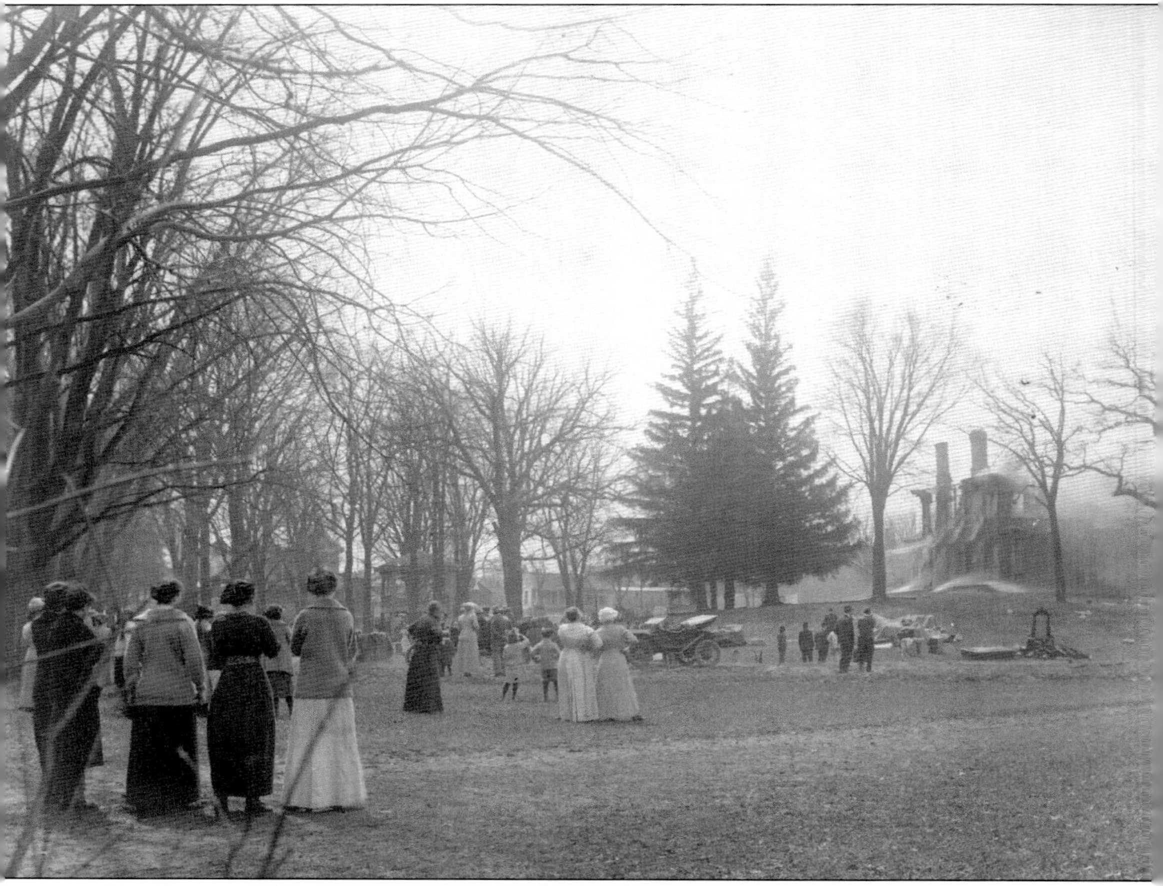

Residents watch in awe as firemen battle the flames that are engulfing the Millard home on Main Street. The house was built by John L. Millard Sr., an early settler in Markesan, who passed it down to his son John L. Millard, who practiced law in Markesan. The fire broke out at the home at 11:00 a.m. on March 28, 1910, and the house was demolished. Remnants of the foundation and stairs can still be seen today in its original location on the corner of Main Street and Millard Avenue.

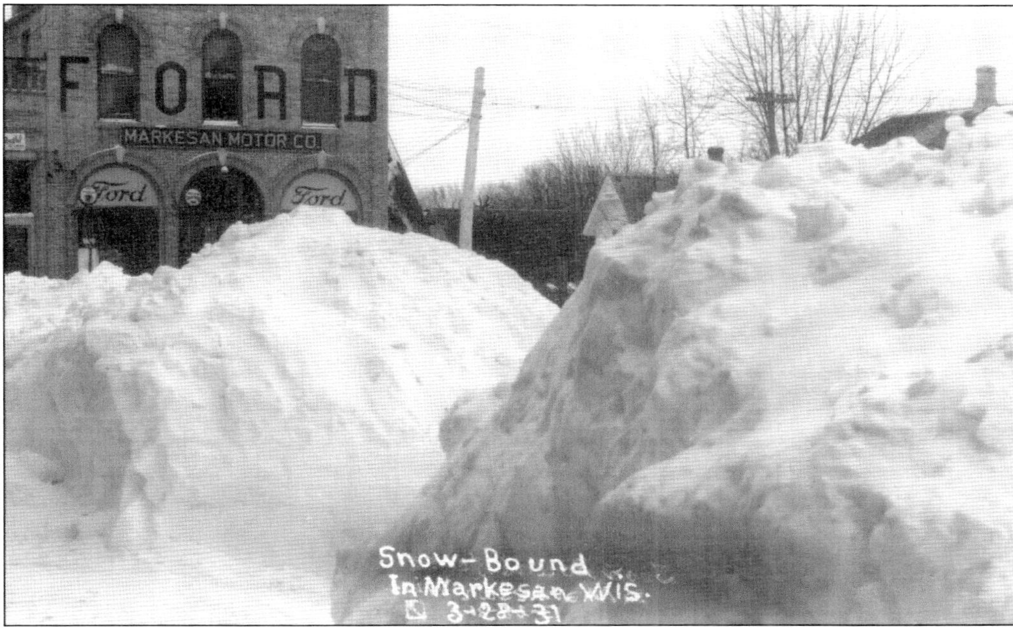

Snow has always posed a danger to automobile travel; the picture above shows downtown Bridge Street following a significant snowfall on Markesan in March 1928. Street crews and local businesses had the daunting task of moving massive amounts of snow to clear streets for travel and allow patrons to come into their stores. Harold Young is pictured below preparing to throw a snowball at the cameraman after this storm hit the area on March 28, 1931.

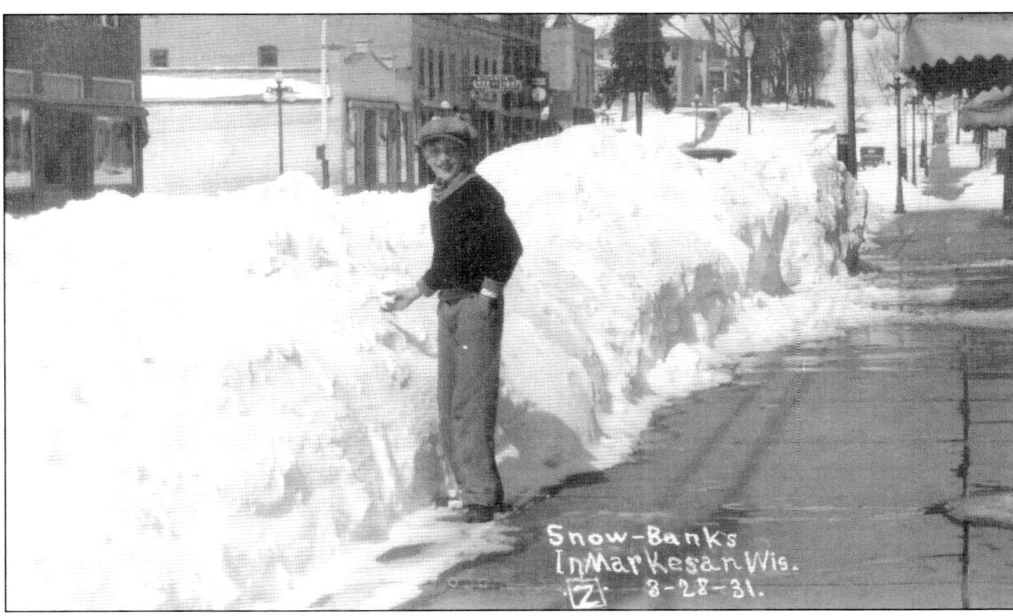

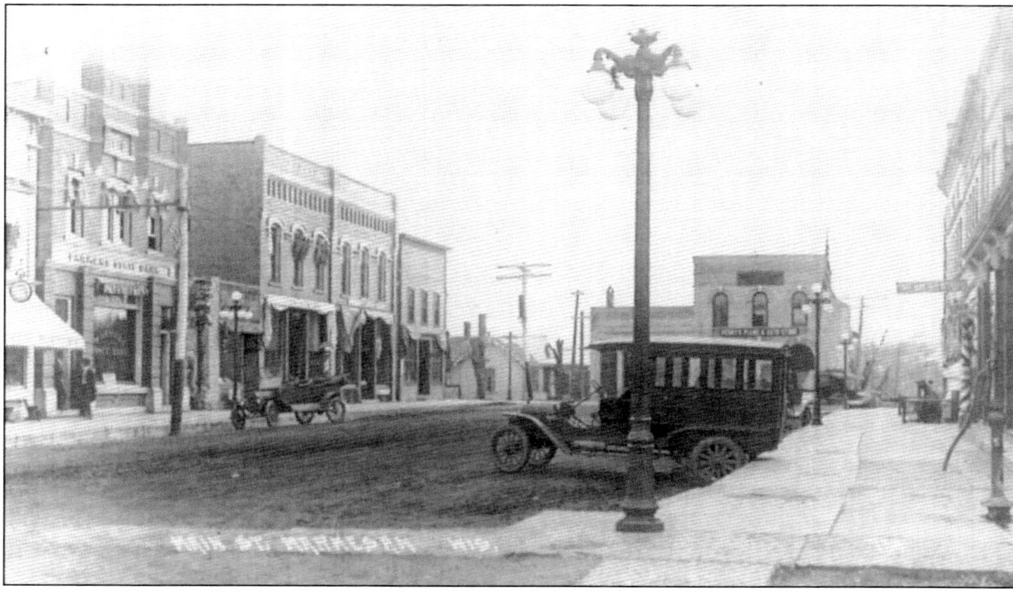

Here is a glimpse of the south end of Bridge Street around 1916. On the left side of the street, the big pocket-watch clock hangs from the storefront of the Henninger Jewelry Store, followed by the Farmers State Bank, The Fair Store (operated by Jacob Davis), Spitzer Millinery (owned by Emma Spitzer), H.R. Kopitzke Undertaker, and William Dehn's Harness and Shoe Hospital. On the end of the street is Perry's Piano & Auto Store. The Yosemite Hotel taxi is pictured in the foreground.

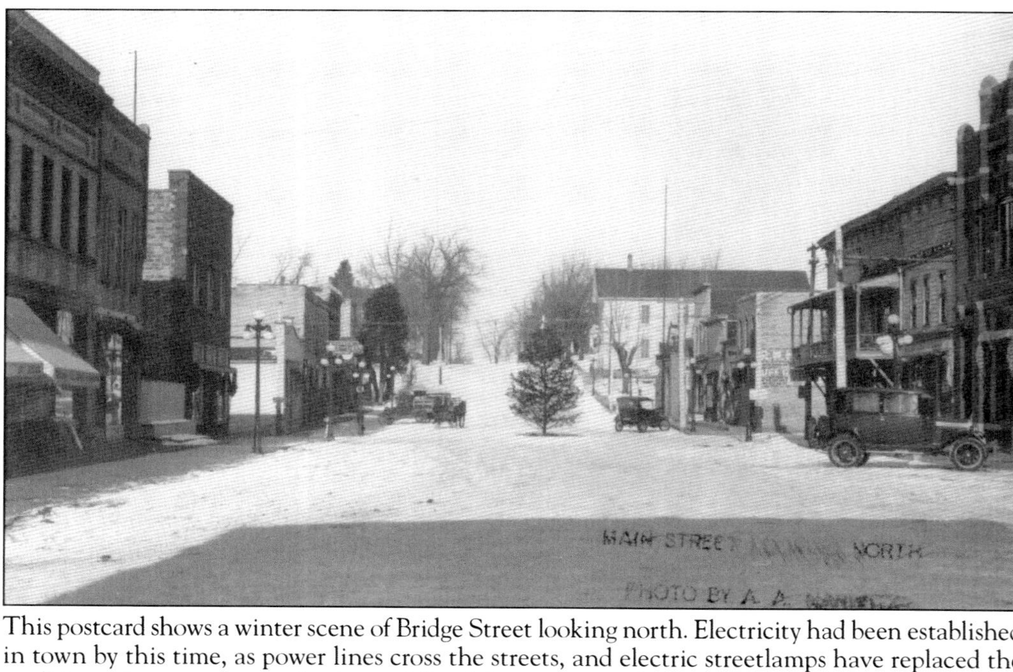

This postcard shows a winter scene of Bridge Street looking north. Electricity had been established in town by this time, as power lines cross the streets, and electric streetlamps have replaced the traditional kerosene lamps. In the middle of the street stands the Christmas tree that decorated the downtown area for the holidays.

These women are out for a stroll on John Street near the railroad tracks. The Markesan train depot can be seen just to the right, and in the background is the Hull Mill. The women are strolling on the many miles of wood plank sidewalks that stretched all around Markesan.

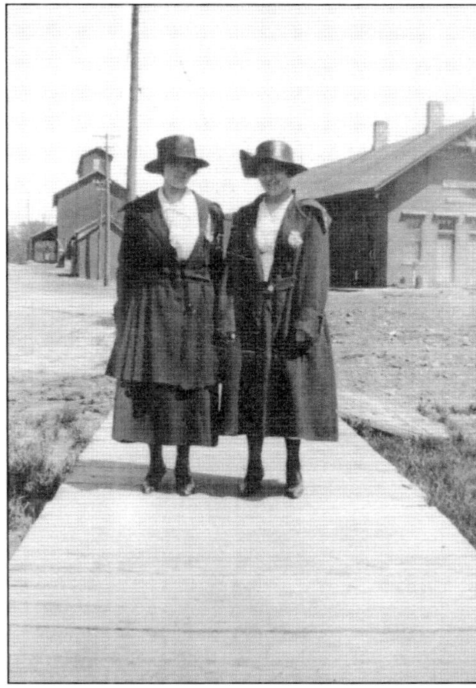

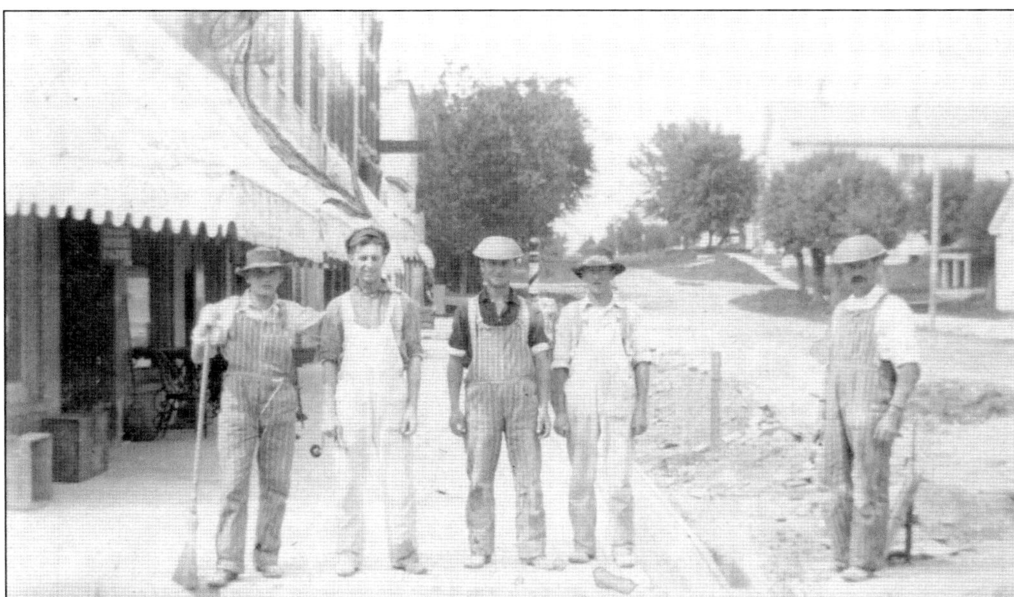

A group of men are doing work on the corner of John Street and Bridge Street in the days before the roads were paved for heavy traffic. It looks as though cement sidewalks are being laid or replaced. Prior to cement or cobblestone sidewalks, wooden planks were laid, lining storefronts to allow a walking area where onlookers could stay out of the muddy streets.

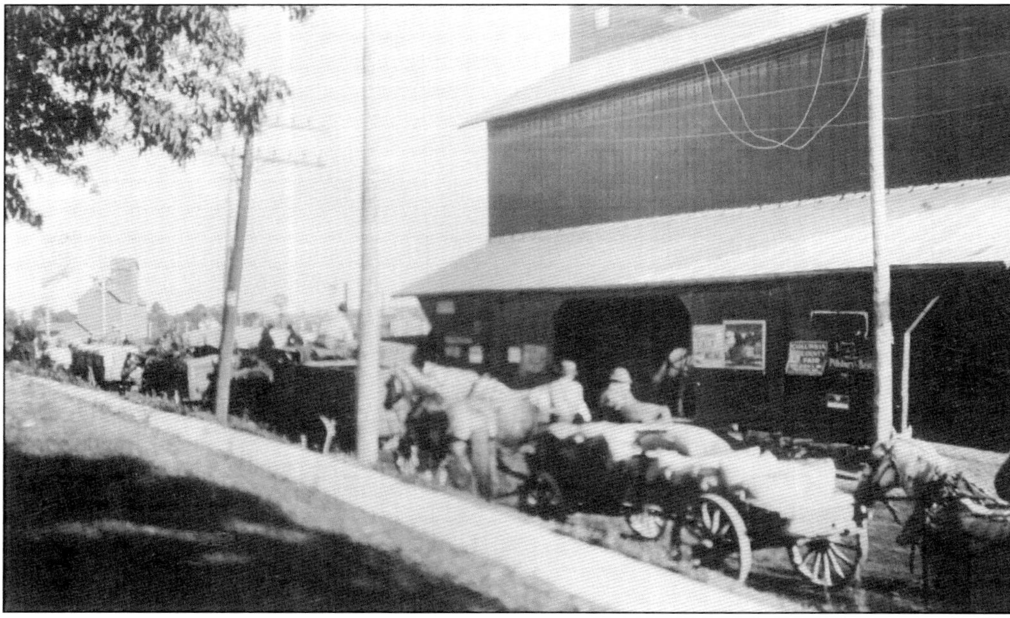

An important aspect of farming was making sure needed supplies were accessible and that there was a place to sell grain. Here, farmers of the surrounding Markesan area line up at John Hulls's mill on John Street around 1920. Wagons can be seen loaded with sacks of grain. His mill provided services for flour, poultry feed, mill feed, dairy feed, and fuel.

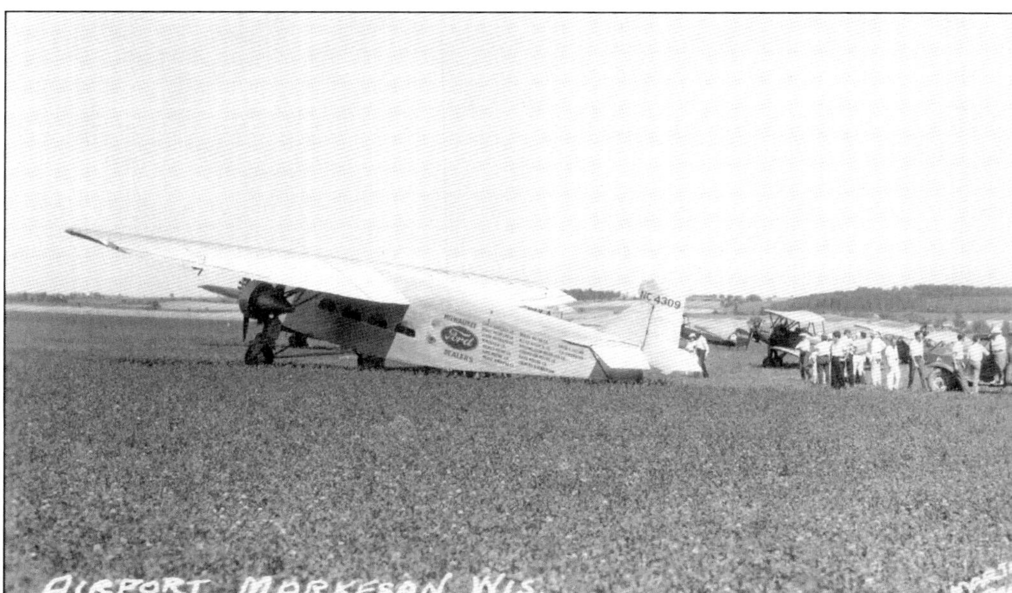

An airport was located just west of Markesan on the farm of George Werth Jr. It was believed that Werth and Kenneth Biesenthal started it in the early 1940s. The airfield was private and had a grass runway; two planes were stored in a steel building nearby, and a small shack was used as an office. Plane rides were given periodically to local residents. The airport is believed to have operated for four years.

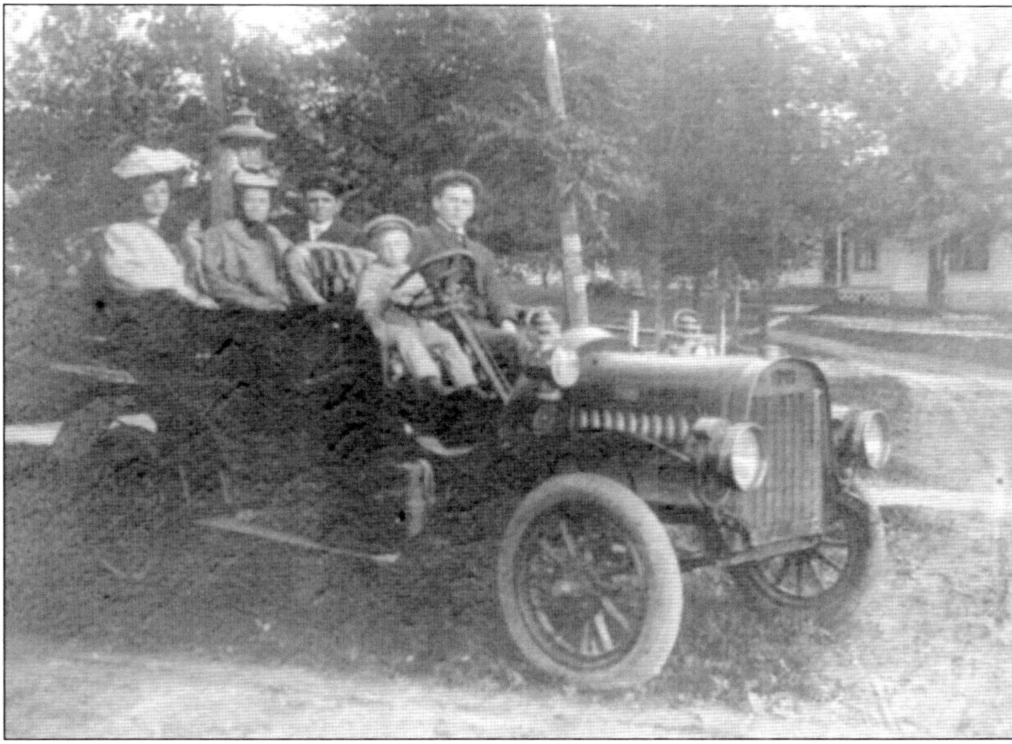

As cars took hold in the early 1900s, Markesan residents did not hold back from progressing with time. Henry Friday and his family are out for a ride in their new Rambler automobile in 1906. The people in the car are, from left to right, (front seat) Floyd Friday and Roy E. Smith; (back seat) Pearl Kaul, Ida Friday, and Henry P. Friday.

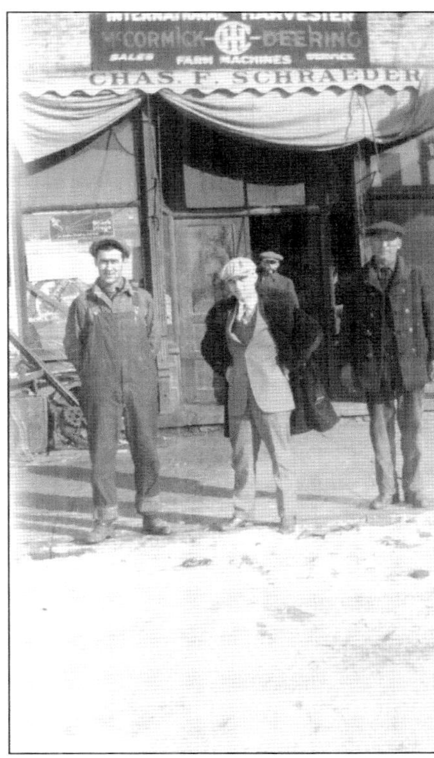

From left to right, Charles Welk, Austin Schraeder, and Christian Yerk pose for a picture outside Charles F. Schraeder Motor Company on John Street. Austin was the son of Charles Schraeder and would take over the business in 1939 and sell Buick and Chevrolet automobiles until the 1970s.

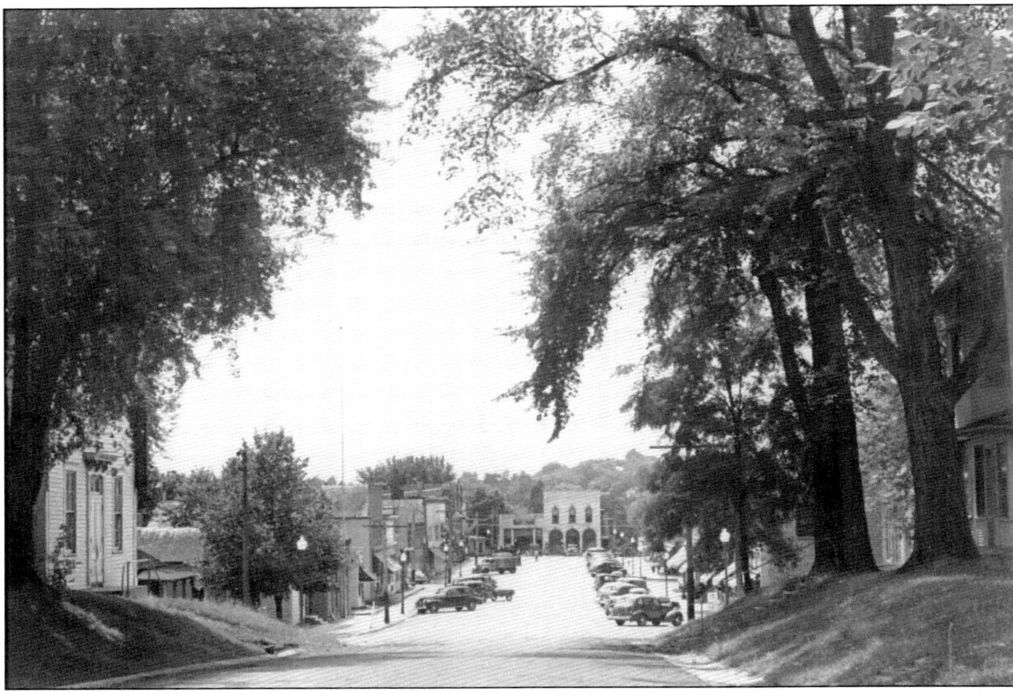

Above, the entire downtown block of Bridge Street can be seen. Following the war years and the return of local soldiers, Markesan was a beehive of activity. Every store downtown was occupied, and there were all sorts of merchandise to be bought and sold. Street dances were held on summer nights, and the local movie theater provided entertainment for people of all ages. The photograph below shows John Street looking east, which cuts through downtown. This stretch of road led down to the busy activity near the railroad. It was there that the Markesan Canning Company, Grand River Co-op, Markesan Hemp Company, and many other industries manufactured and put out goods that would be shipped out on the rails or by truck. Notice the taverns located on each corner; one displays a Miller beer sign and the other Pabst.

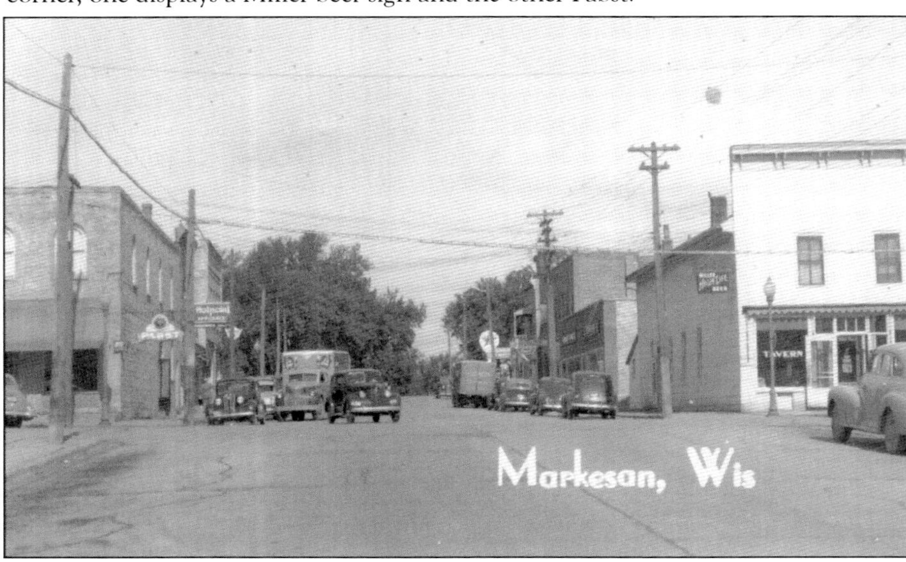

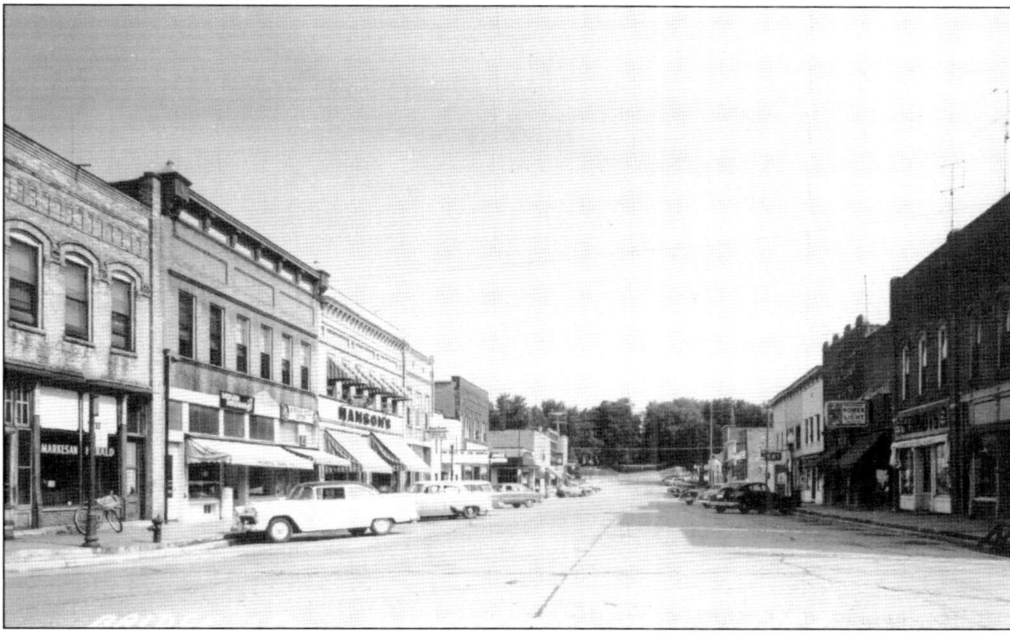

This picture is looking north on Bridge Street in 1956. Markesan once had a movie theatre, which is seen on the left with the motion picture *One Night in the Tropics* showing. Nehring Hardware and Birkies Food Center, also on the left, were steady businesses in the downtown area until a fire destroyed the buildings on May 19, 1957.

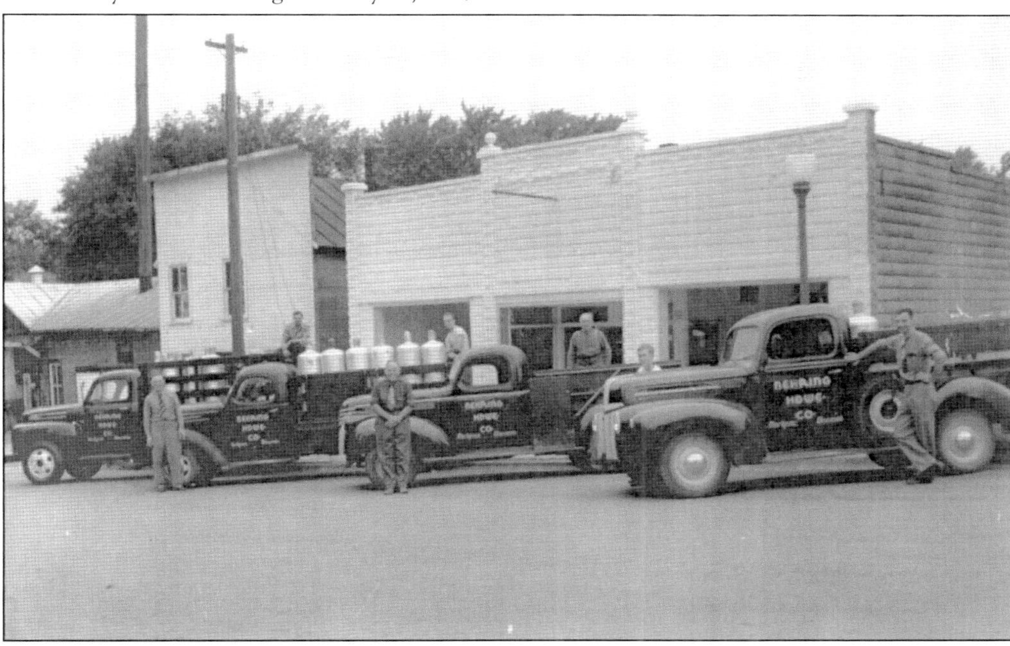

The employees of Nehring Hardware Company pose for a picture by the company trucks. The hardware store was started in 1927 with a partnership of Clarence Mielke and Earl Nehring. The store was known as Nehring-Mielke Hardware. Eventually, full ownership of the store was held by Nerhing, and he continued to operate the business until he sold it in 1978.

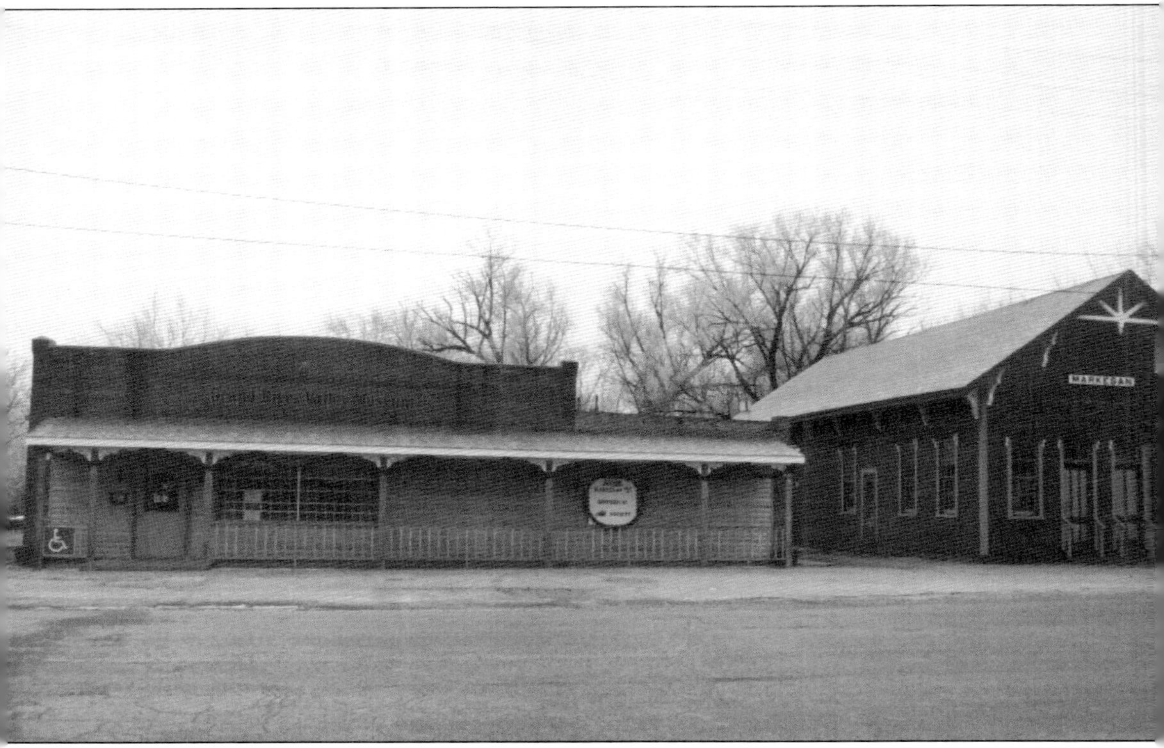

The Markesan Historical Society was incorporated September 1, 1981, at the request of William Slate, Joan Slate, and Samuel E. Smith of Markesan; however, the organization lacked funds, a building, and any historical artifacts. In 1983, a considerable amount of items were left to the historical society by longtime area resident Anna Olsen. In 1990, a building was acquired on East John Street from a donation made by Mildred Draeger. The building was cleaned and remodeled for use as a museum. In 1995, the Markesan Train Depot was moved to the museum, and restoration was completed in 1998. In 2005, the Arthur Jahns Memorial Agricultural Museum was dedicated; it stores antique farm machinery and tools from around the area. The Markesan Historical Society proudly displays thousands of pictures and pieces of historical items from Markesan's past.

Two

School and Academic Activities

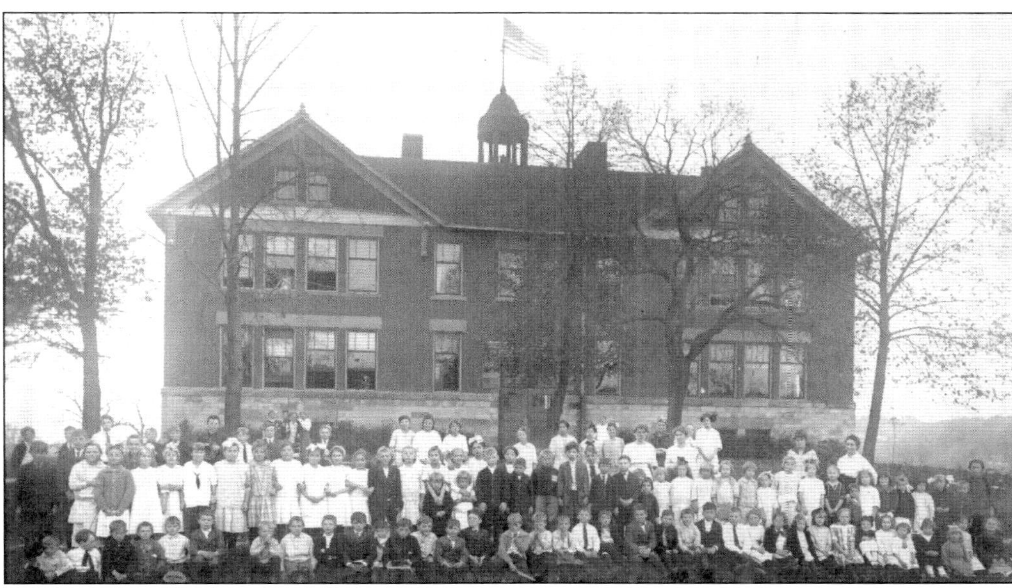

Education was important to the citizens of Markesan. The first classes started in 1850, as community members saw the need for an education system. This 1915 picture shows students in front of the school built in 1906. This school was located on Margaret Street on the high ground next to the Grand River.

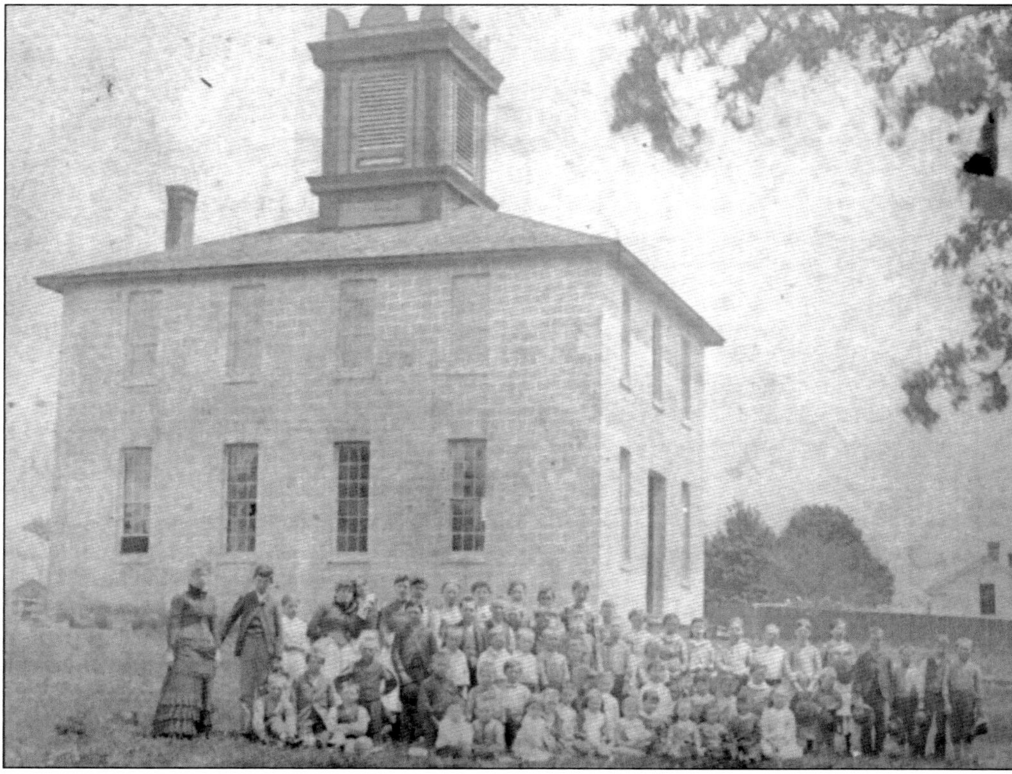

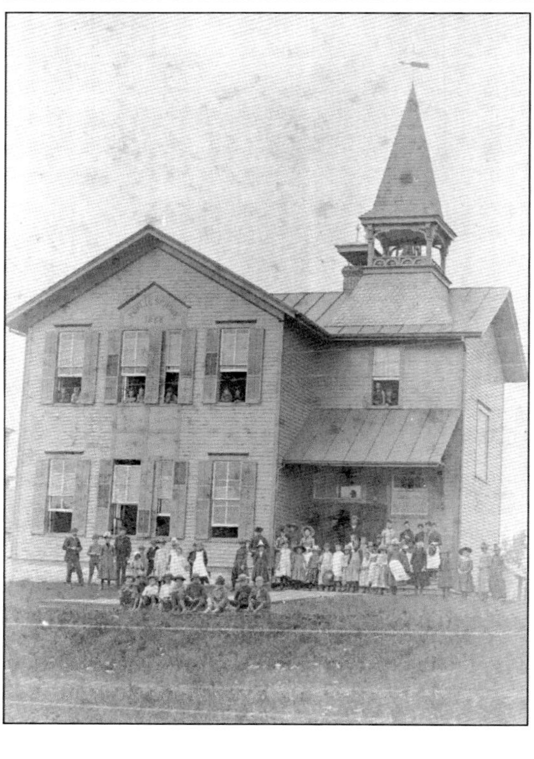

Pictured here is the original school, built in 1856. This two-story schoolhouse served the village of Markesan for 32 years until the student population outgrew it. It was demolished, and a new two-story schoolhouse was constructed nearby in 1888.

Following the demolition of the old stone school, this two-story schoolhouse was built in 1888 to replace the old one. This picture was taken around 1895 before an annex was added on the right in 1898 to accommodate more students. The old school was located on the northeast corner of John and Margaret Streets. This school was then replaced in 1906 by a much larger brick structure.

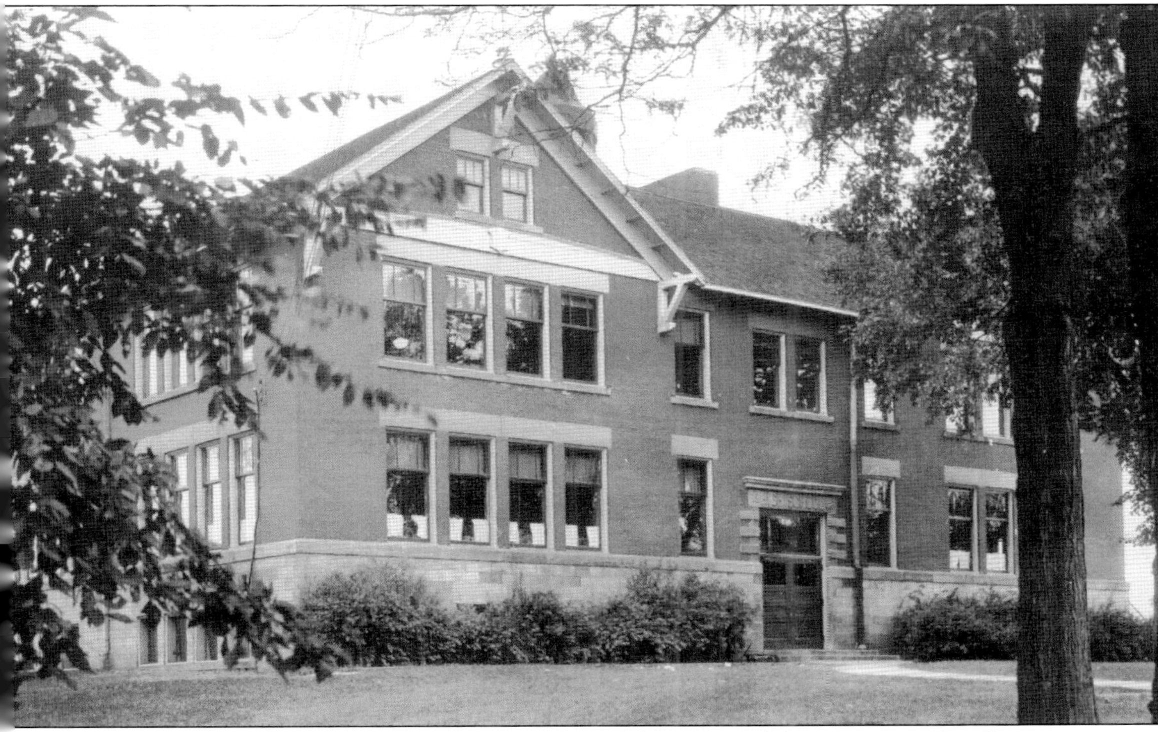

A new school was built in 1906 near the Grand River, and classes started that same year. Enrollment was growing, and the old school was not large enough to handle the new influx of students, even after an addition was added on. High school courses were only three years long, but with the advent of the new school building, a fourth year was added to the curriculum. The building held all grades from kindergarten through 12th grade. A gymnasium and auditorium was added on in the 1930s and an elementary wing in the 1950s. The high school was eventually relocated north of Markesan in the 1960s. The original 1906 structure was demolished and rebuilt to serve as the current Markesan Elementary School.

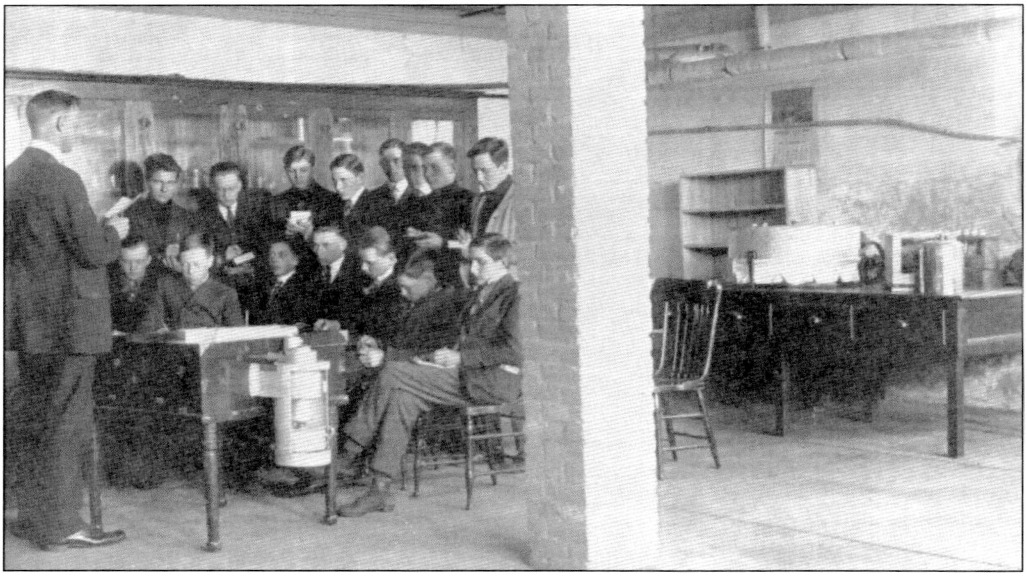

Farming was important to the Markesan area, so agriculture was an important class offering for students who would become farmers. The course was added in 1912 and taught by E.M. Cox. A 1917 Markesan High School yearbook states, "The course aims to make better farmers and give the people, who expect to take up farming, a general knowledge of their chosen work."

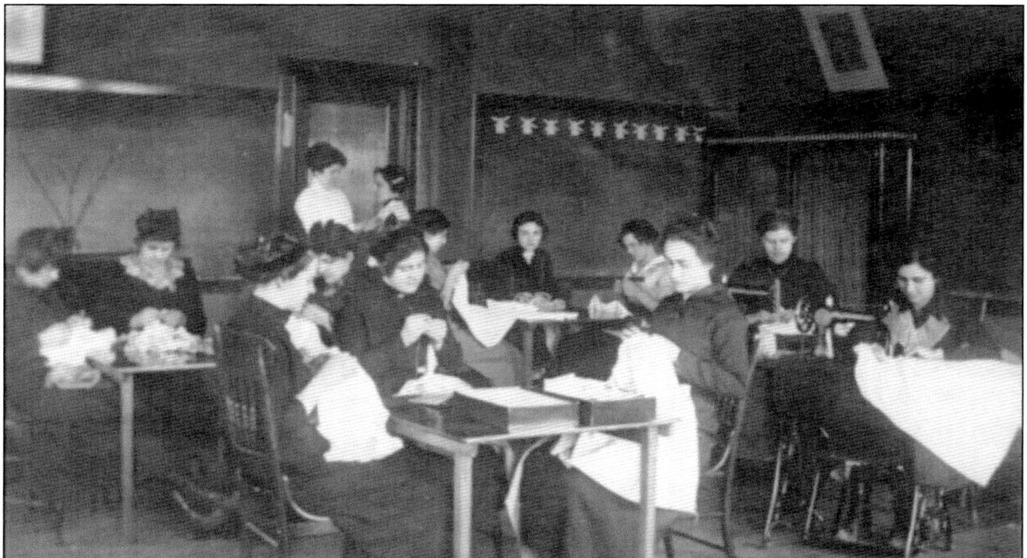

Domestic science, a course added in 1912, was aimed at teaching young women household skills. Pictured is a class of young women being taught how to sew. A 1917 Markesan High School yearbook states, "Food values, sanitation, home care of the sick, and personal neatness comprise the most important of its topics."

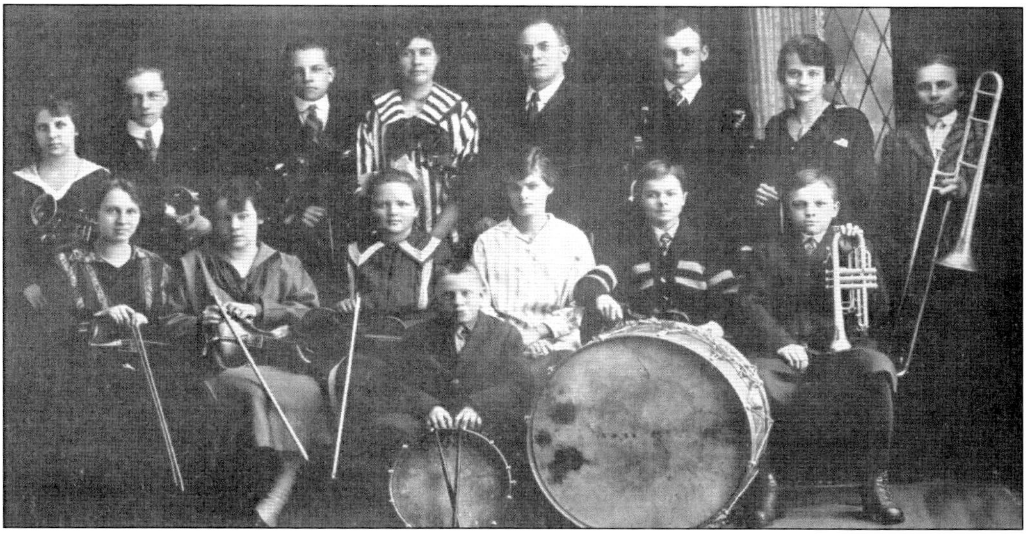

The school orchestra was assembled in 1909 by Mrs. Gustav Saecker. The group originally only had four members, but membership grew as more pupils became interested. The orchestra was the first music organization in the Markesan school system. It was created to help musically gifted students enhance their playing abilities and serve as entertainment for classmates and the community.

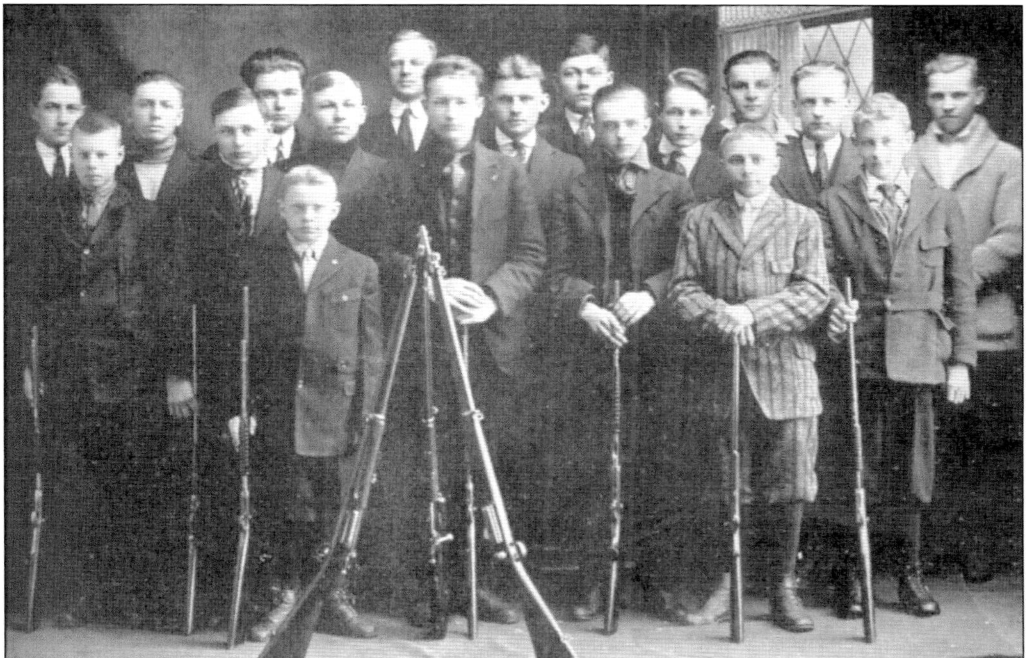

Pictured here is the 1916–1917 Markesan Rifle Club, which had been established that year at the school. The club was affiliated with the National Rifle Association and received Krag rifles and ammunition. In its first year, the club consisted of 17 members, and as the 1917 Markesan yearbook explains, "Rifle shooting trains the eye, the muscles, the nerves, develops character, and self reliance."

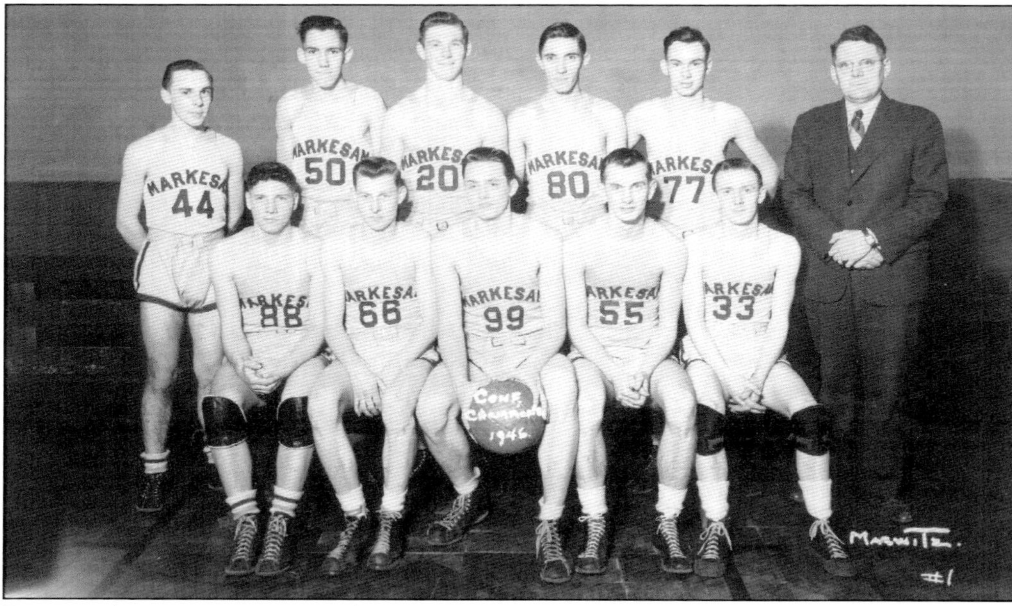

By 1920, the young men at Markesan High School had a basketball team. The team was not all that good; however, the team practiced and played its hardest. The men's team eventually disbanded and was nonexistent for few years due to "the enormous financial demands required for a season," as a 1921 Markesan yearbook states. Pictured is the 1946 conference-championship basketball team.

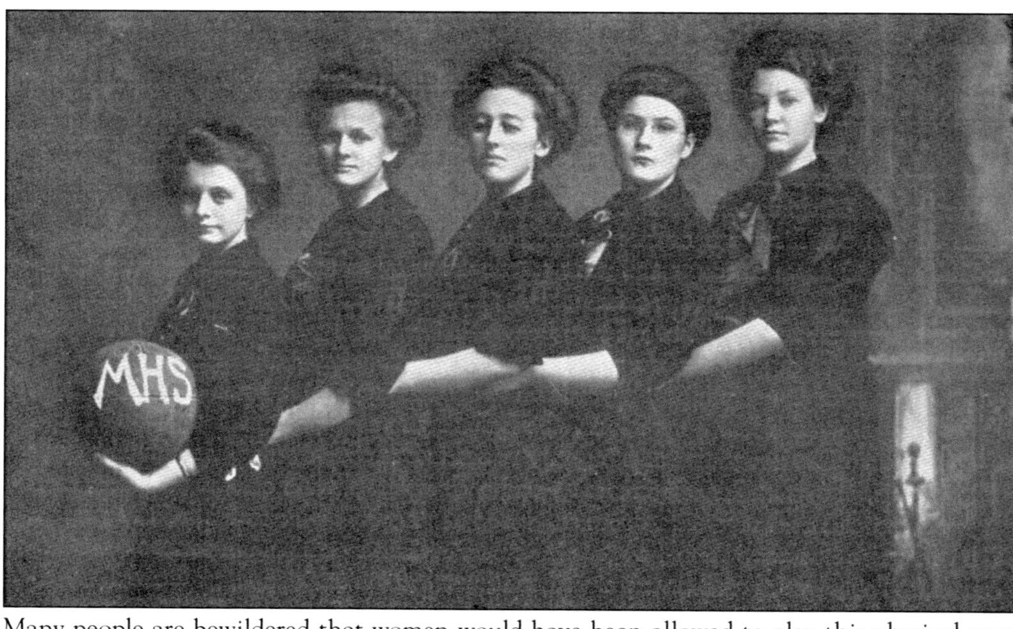

Many people are bewildered that women would have been allowed to play this physical sport in the early 20th century. The high school girls came together and formed a school team that was coached by a Mrs. Stam. It was not an all-star team by any means, but the 1921 Markesan yearbook suggests there were high hopes that Markesan girls would "climb toward the top of the high schools in basketball."

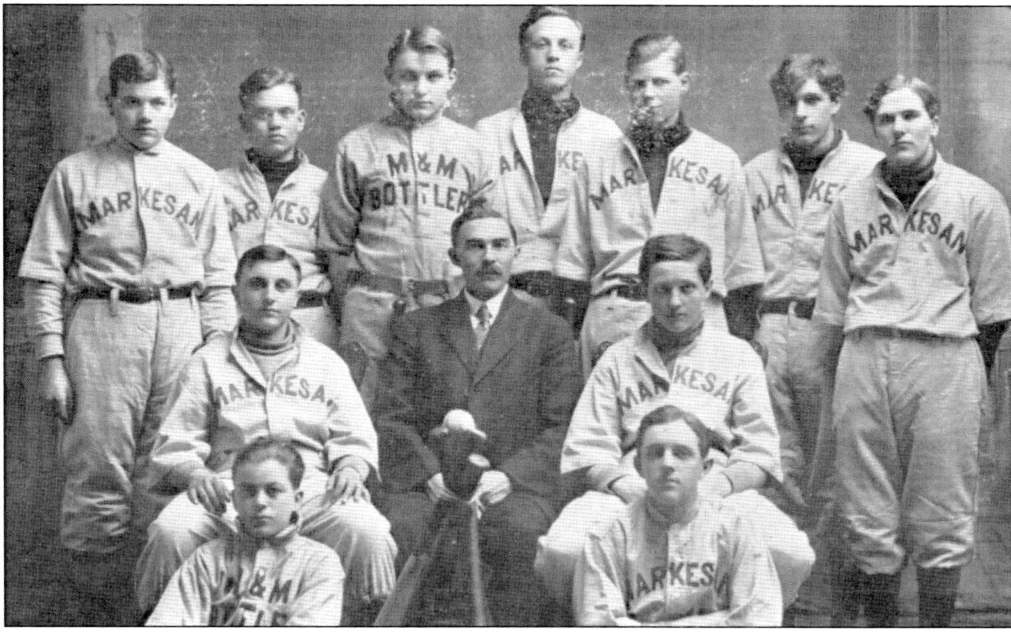

In the early 1900s, baseball was perhaps the most popular sport at Markesan High School. It was hard for other sports to get started because of limitations. A 1913 Markesan High School yearbook states, "There are hardly enough boys for the organization of a good football team, and no place is available for practice so that a basketball team might be organized."

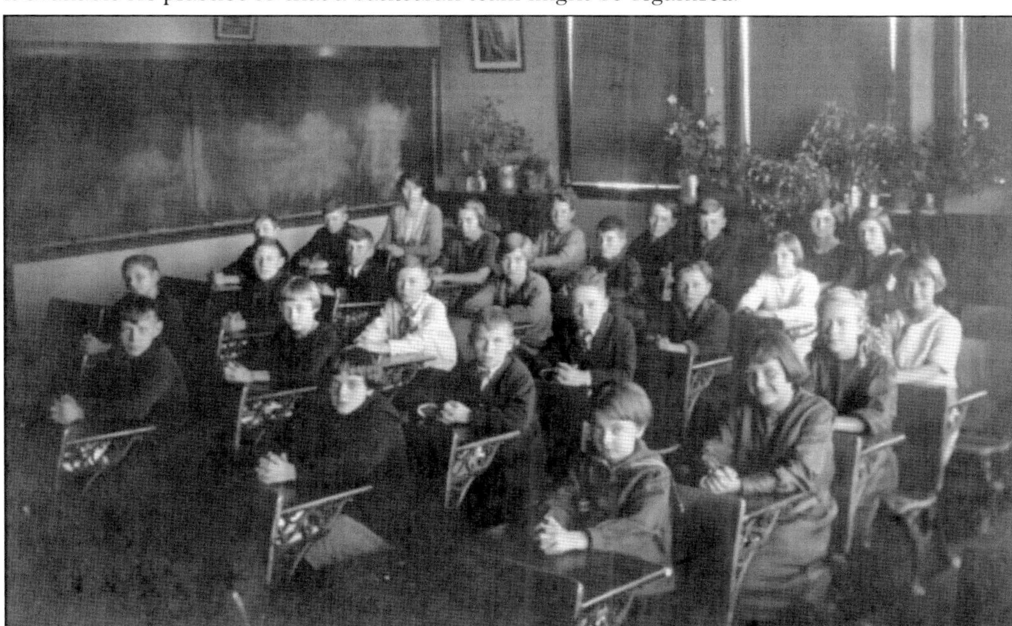

Pictured here is the fifth-grade class of Markesan Elementary School in 1923. The teacher, Edna Lotz, can be seen sitting in the back of the fifth row of students. Elementary students were in the same building as the high school students until the high school students were moved to a new building in 1961.

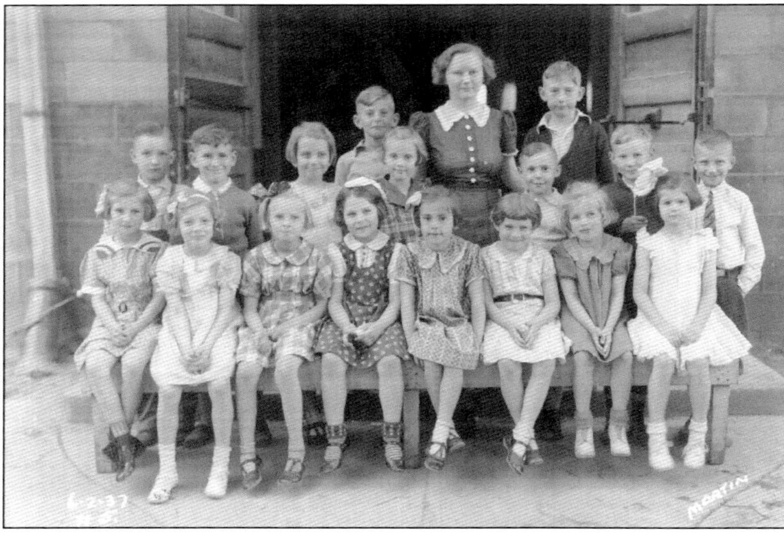

This June 2, 1937, photograph shows an unknown Markesan grade school class; the children were taught by Laura Posvic (third row, center). This image was taken at the end of the school year and could possibly be a grade school promotion picture.

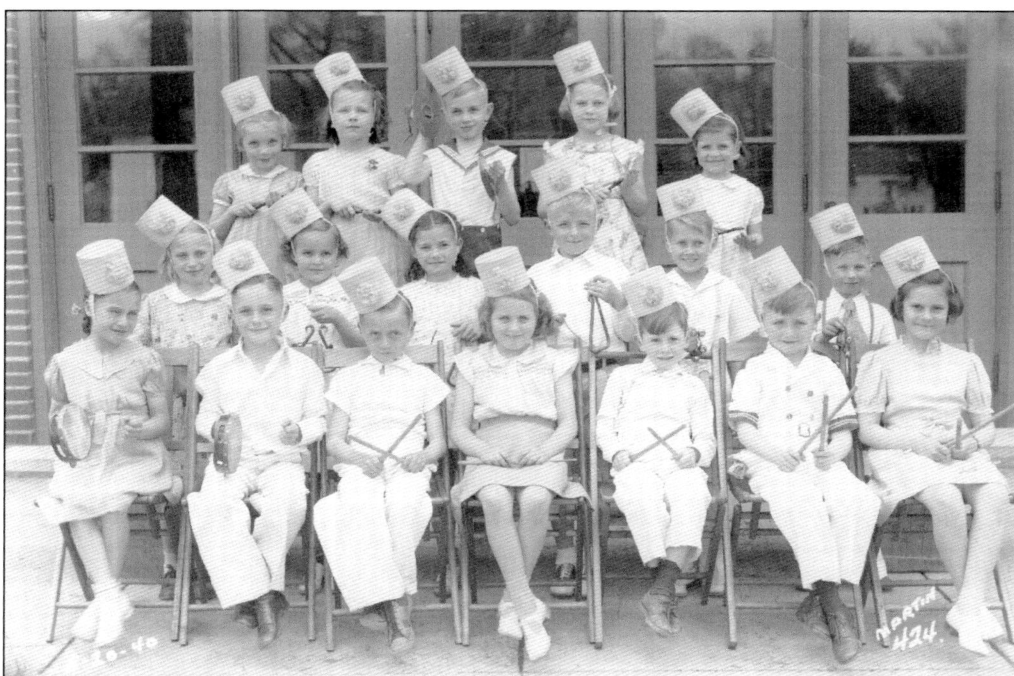

The 1939–1940 first-and-second-grade rhythm band poses for a picture with their instruments. The picture is dated May 20, 1940. The students pictured are, from left to right, (first row) Lorriane Lohry, Dickie Martin, Bobby Hanneman, Marilyn Mielke, Leroy Lowry, Russel Kobs, and Marilyn Sell; (second row) Rosemarie Niklaus, Ardyce Zanto, Nola Kearley, Verlin Wandrey, Verle Sellmacher, and Michael McNabb; (third row) Darlene Zanto, Joanne Krause, Robert Nehrin, Sally Cotterill, and Ardelle Freiheit.

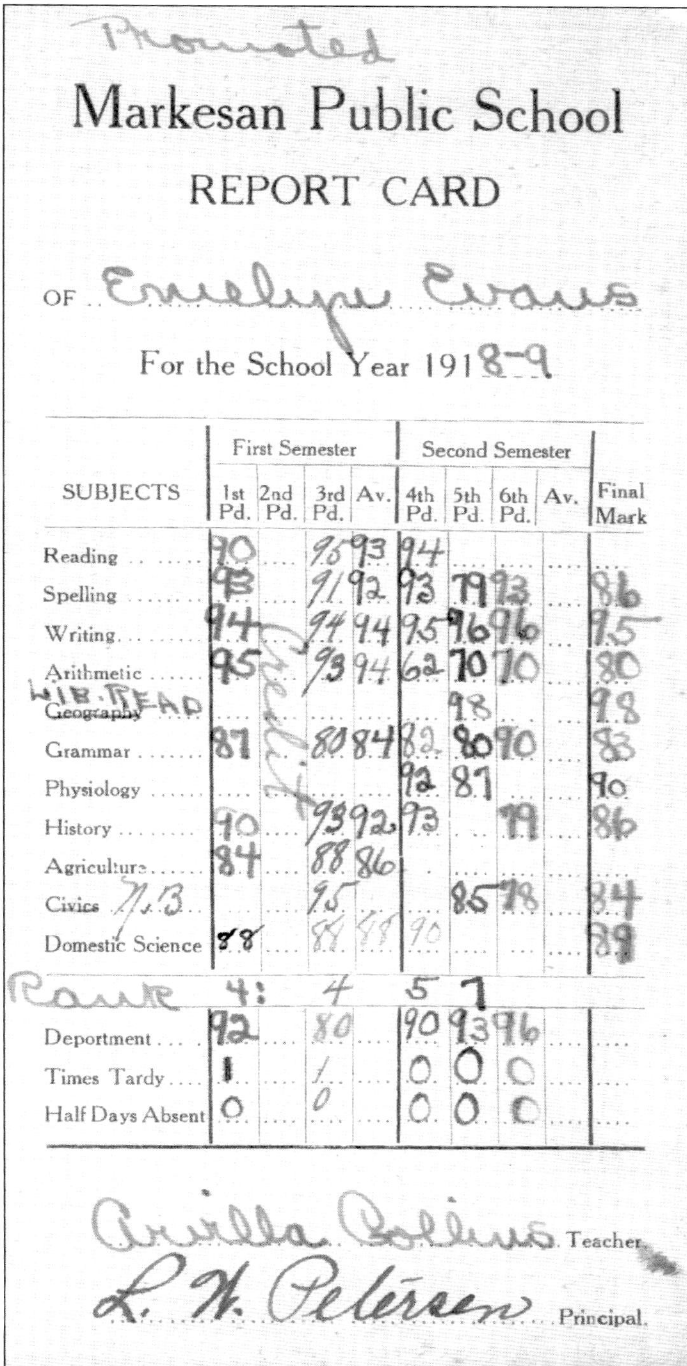

Promoted

Markesan Public School

REPORT CARD

OF Emelyn Evans

For the School Year 1918-9

SUBJECTS	First Semester 1st Pd.	2nd Pd.	3rd Pd.	Av.	Second Semester 4th Pd.	5th Pd.	6th Pd.	Av.	Final Mark
Reading	90		95	93	94				
Spelling	93		91	92	93	79	93		86
Writing	94		94	94	95	96	96		95
Arithmetic	95		93	94	62	70	70		80
WIB. READ Geography						98			98
Grammar	87		80	84	82	80	90		83
Physiology					92	87			90
History	90		93	92	93		79		86
Agriculture	84		88	86					
Civics N.B.			95			85	78		84
Domestic Science	88		88	88	90				89
Rank	4:		4		5	7			
Deportment	92		80		90	93	96		
Times Tardy	1		1		0	0	0		
Half Days Absent	0		0		0	0	0		

Arvilla Collins Teacher

L. W. Petersen Principal.

This is the eighth-grade report card of Emelyn Evans, and it indicates that she was promoted to the ninth grade. Emelyn was born in 1905 in Markesan and graduated from Markesan High School in 1923. She then moved to Milwaukee, where she found work as a nurse.

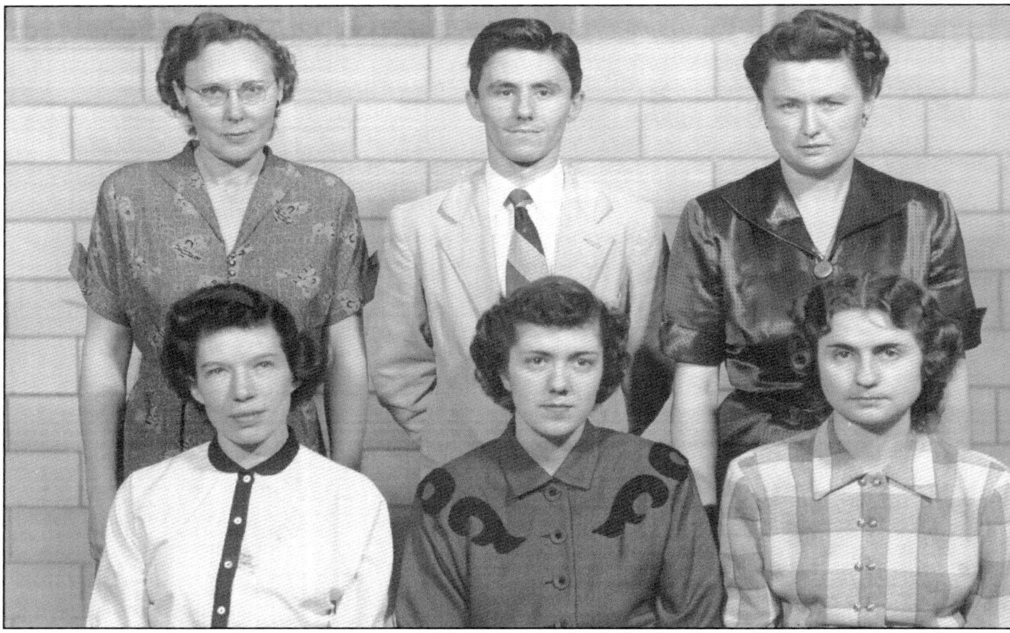

Pictured here is the 1952–1953 Markesan Elementary School faculty. The date of the picture is unknown, but the teachers pictured are, from left to right, (first row) Ada West, Elaine Constance, and Corinne Wickmann; (second row) Inez Henslin, James Marks, and Vyonne Backhaus.

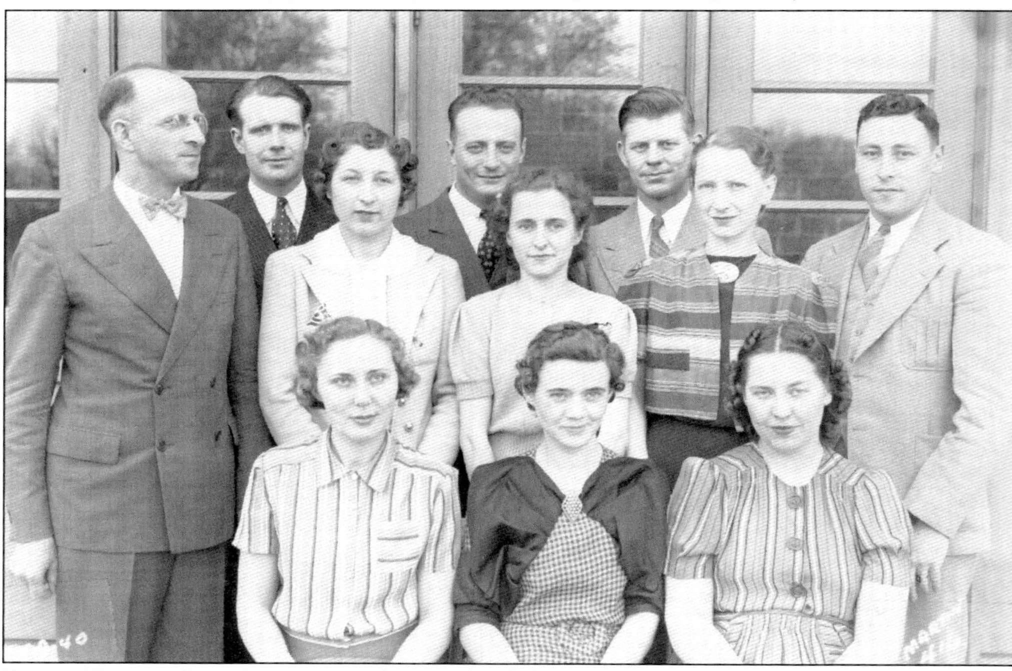

Pictured here is the 1939–1940 Markesan school faculty, which includes, from left to right, (first row) Inez Kotz, Lois Luck, and Miriam Ohmsted; (second row) Arno A. Wipperman, Evelyn Schroeder, Zona Mae Schwandt, and Dorothy Coward; (third row) A.R. Kuecherer, John Kimball, William Welti, and Don Morrissey.

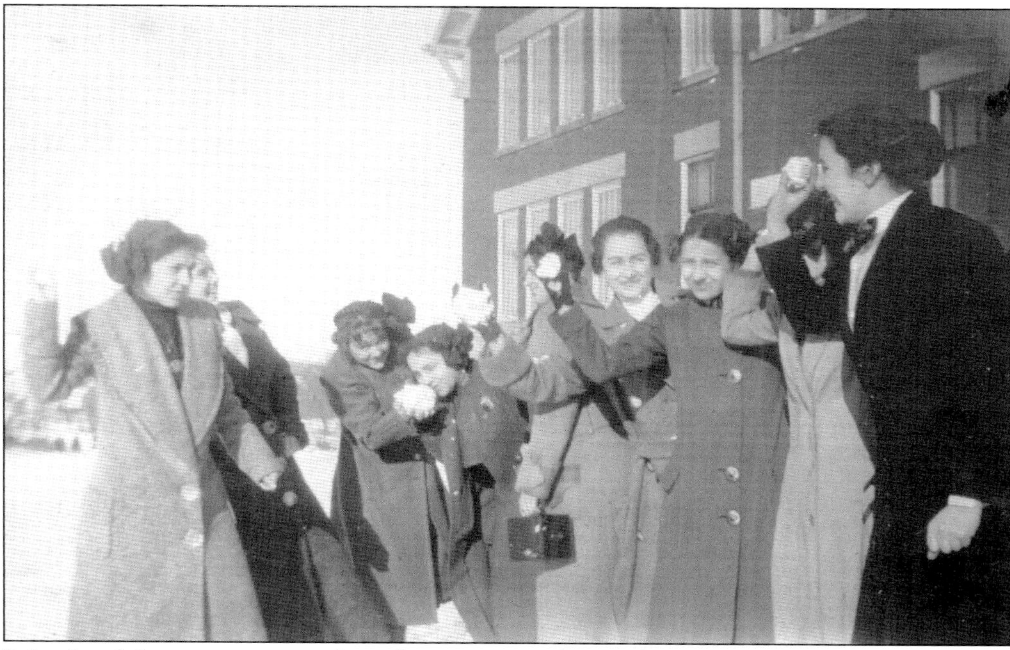

Schoolyard shenanigans were always happening on the Markesan campus. This undated picture shows some students having some fun in the winter months, as they pause during a snowball fight on the school grounds. The Markesan schoolhouse can be seen in the background.

This picture, dated 1914, shows some more playful activity underway on campus. The Markesan schoolhouse is pictured in the background here as well, and in the windows of the school people can be seen peering out while a group poses in front for this quick snapshot.

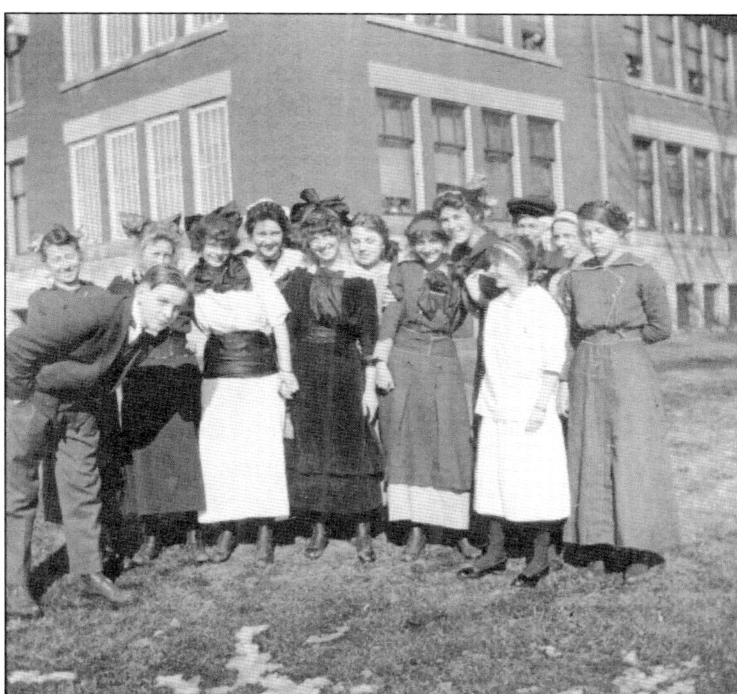

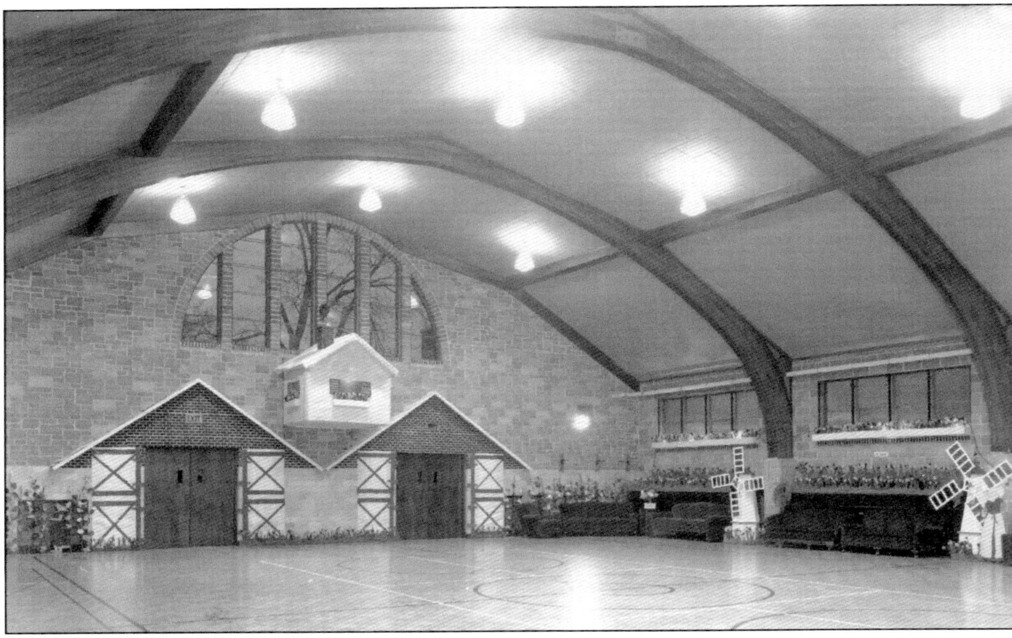

With the addition of an auditorium, seen above in 1935, events could be held at the school. Previously, the Masonic Hall on Charles Street had been the location for many sporting, recreation, and social gatherings. The auditorium had a wood floor and lines painted on for basketball games, and a stage was built for performances. Pictured below is the junior prom on May 1, 1946. The gym was decorated to resemble a rose garden blanketed by a canopy of stars. The performer at the 1946 prom was Tom Temple and his accompanying orchestra.

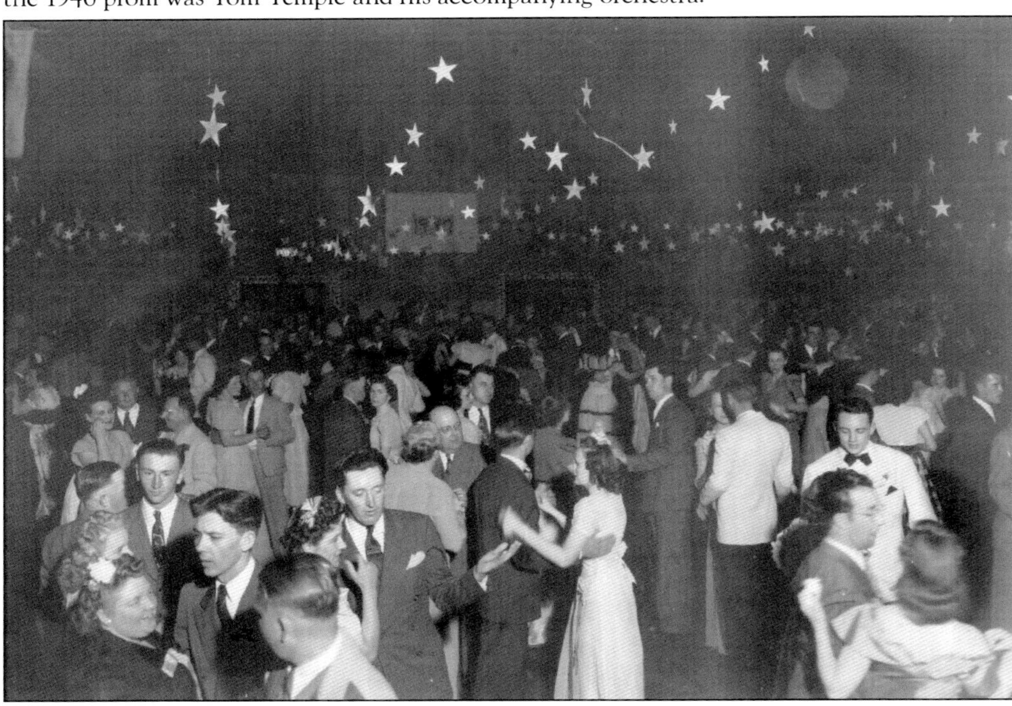

An archery club was introduced at the high school in 1941 and was under the direction of Principal Arno A. Wipperman. The sport was open to both young men and women. The club was self-supporting and raised its own funds by various means; one way was by collecting the profits from a Coca-Cola machine. Pictured here is the 1950–1951 archery team.

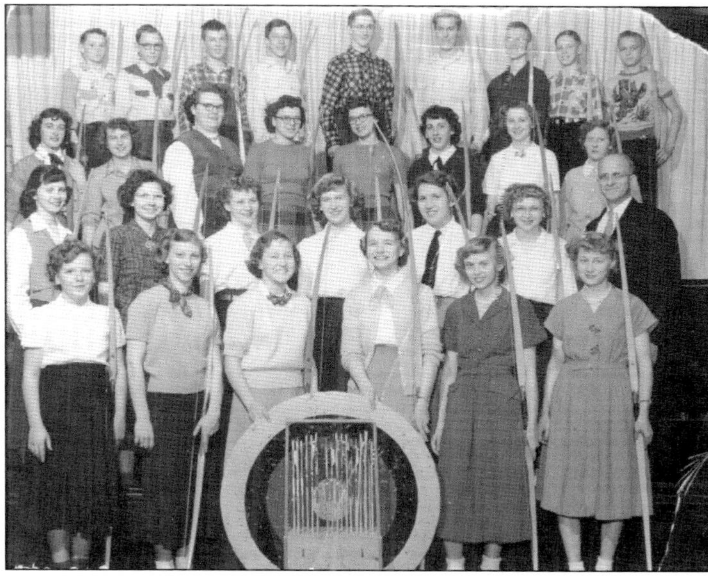

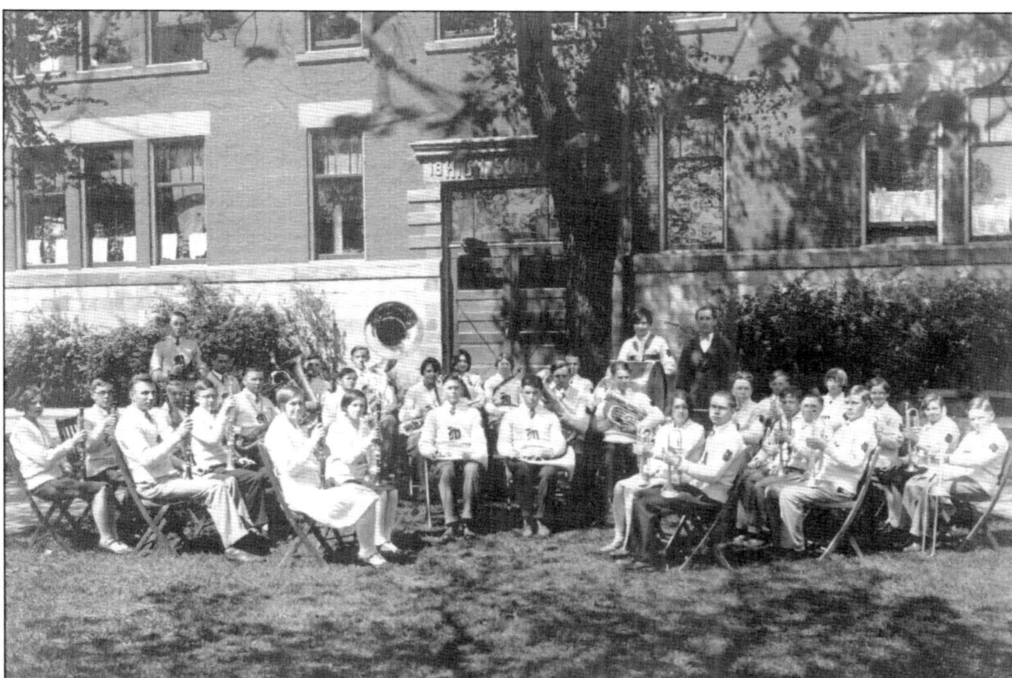

This undated picture shows the students of the Markesan High School band practicing in front of the school. The band was just one of the ways students could get involved in extracurricular activities. The school originally offered orchestra and glee club, but those groups gave way as band and chorus took hold. Musical productions were another way musically gifted students were able to get involved.

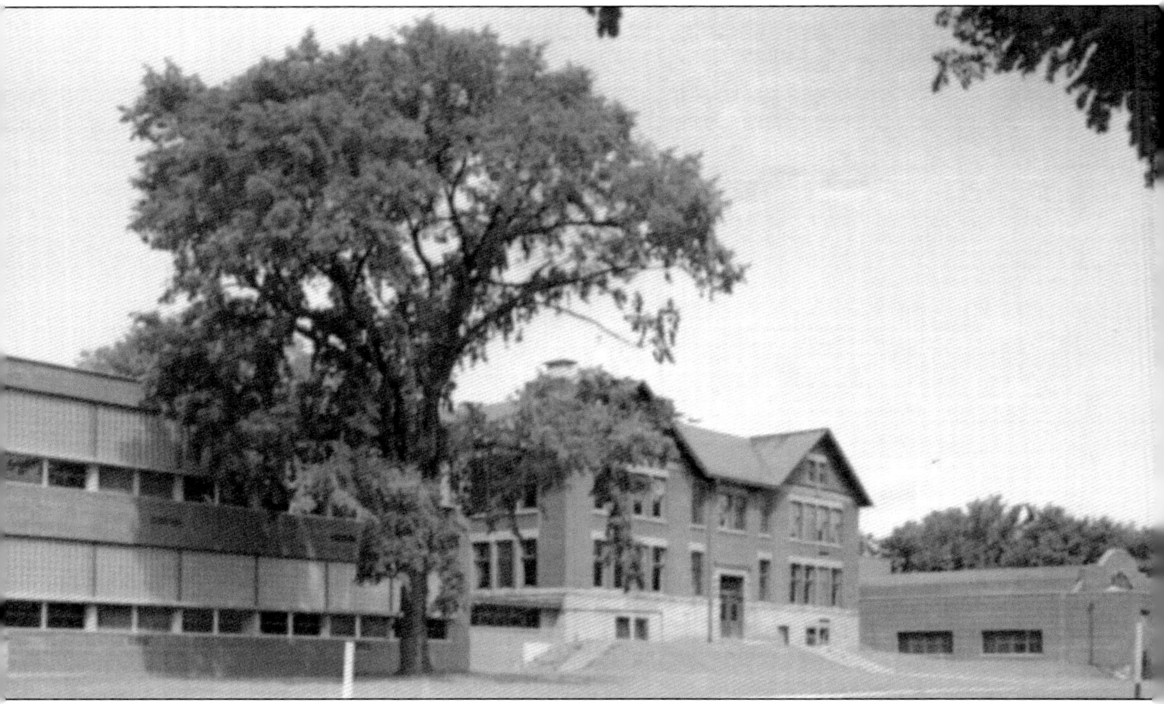

This 1954 photograph shows the 1906 school (center) with all of the additions added onto the building over the years. The auditorium (right) was added on in 1935 to allow for sports and other indoor activities. As enrollment increased, there was a need for more rooms to hold the growing student body. The south wing (left) was added to the school in 1950, and a cafeteria followed in 1952. By 1959, the high school population was around 238 students and 14 teachers. The school district voted to build a new high school in order to house the increasing enrollment. A location at the north end of town was set as the new home for the Markesan High School. The class of 1960 was the last graduating class housed in this school building.

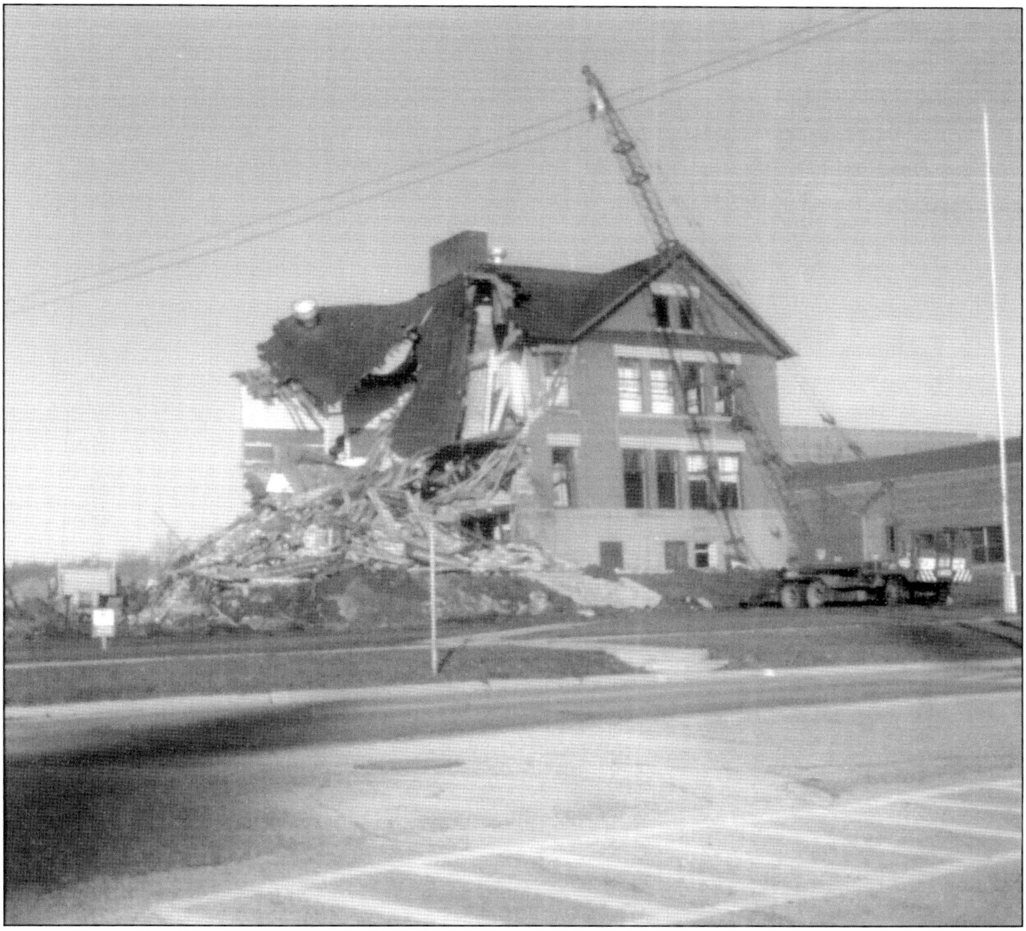

A new Markesan High School building was constructed four blocks north in 1960. The former high school building was used as the Markesan Elementary School. In 1973, the Markesan Board of Education presented a proposal to demolish the old two-story school building and replace it with a more modern one-story complex. The proposal was approved in July 1973, and the school building was demolished in October of that year. The south wing and auditorium were saved from the wrecking ball and became part of the new elementary school complex.

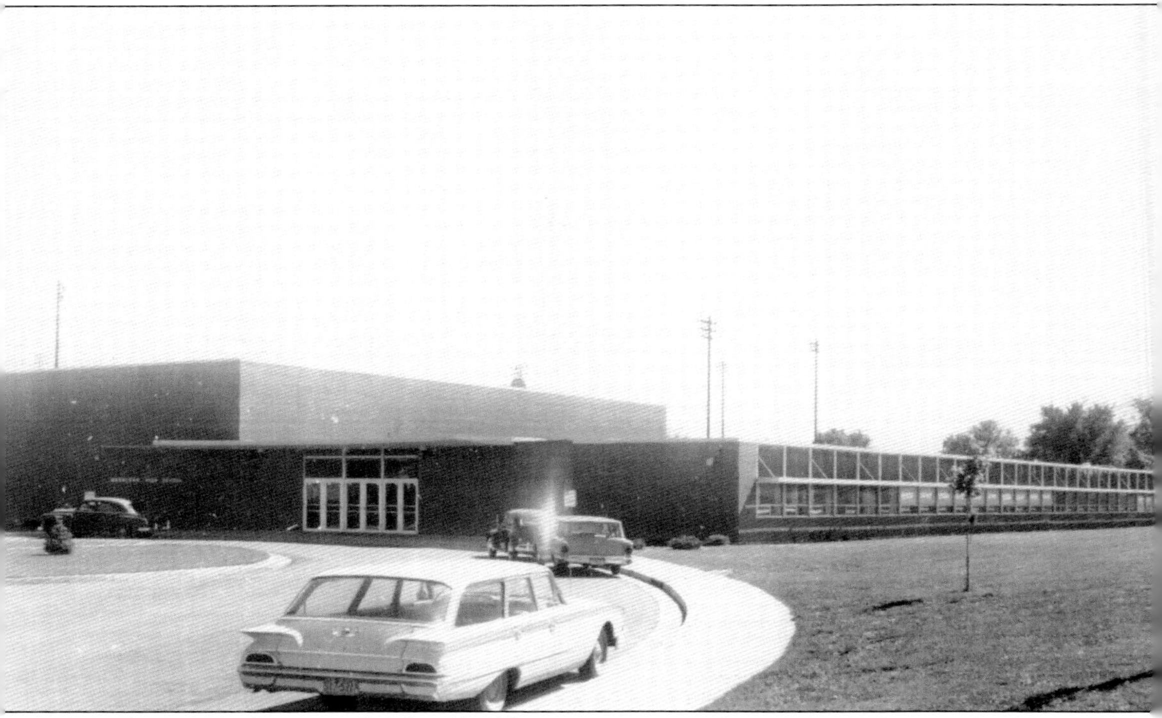

The new Markesan High School building was constructed in 1960 to make room for the growing student population. Its location is on Vista Boulevard just off of Margaret Street on the north end of town. This building would serve as the high school until 2001, when a new high school building was added to the former building. It now serves as the Markesan Middle School and is connected to the current high school.

Three

Residents and Their Residences

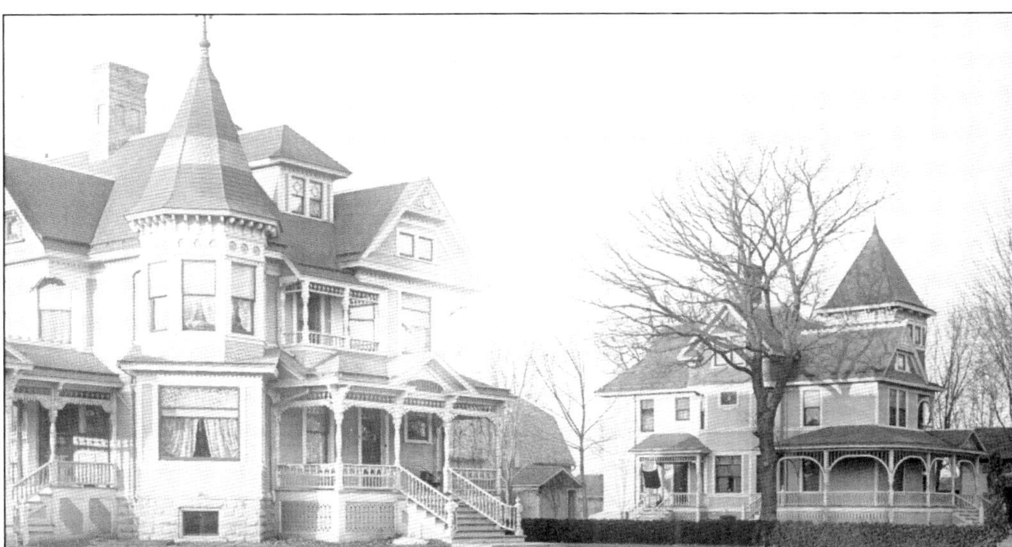

Markesan is a town of many homes of all different shapes and sizes. Some of them were home to very wealthy residents who essentially helped build Markesan, and others were the homes of common hard-working citizens. A majority of these homes still stand today to signify the glory days of the Victorian era of Markesan. This undated picture shows the home of Silas W. Phelps (left) and the home Edgar C. Smith.

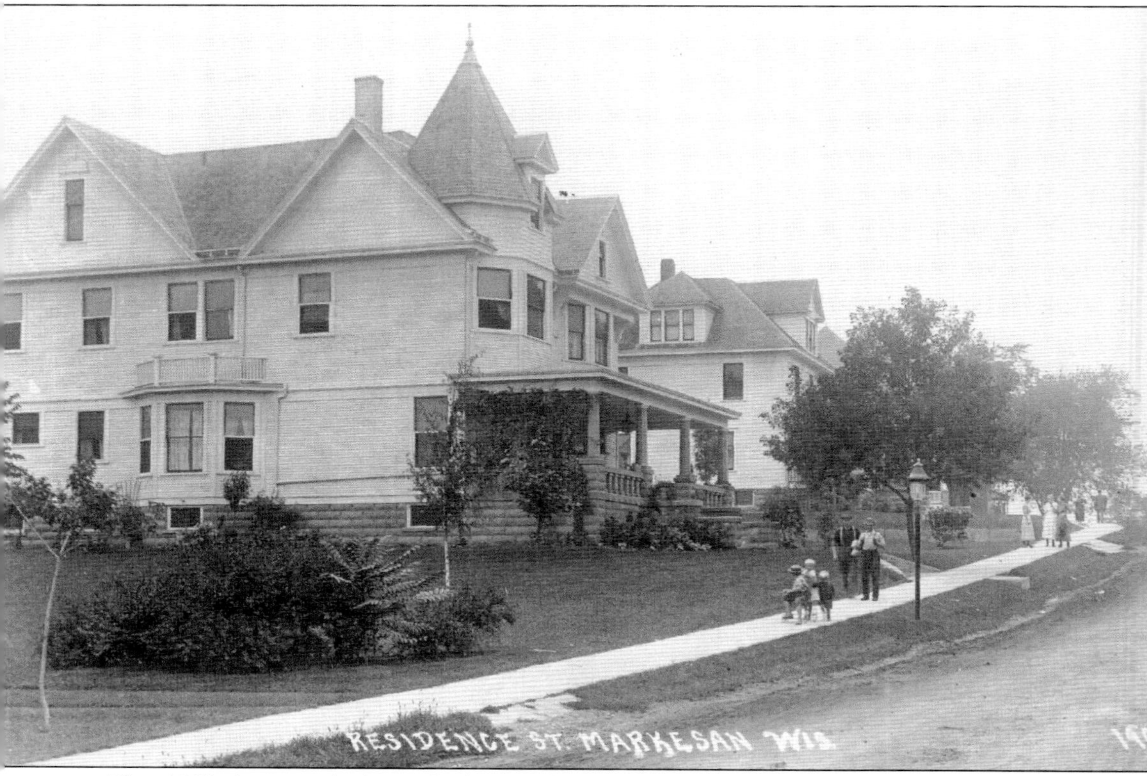

This 1901 photograph shows the home of William Sink (left), located on John Street. Sink was born in Michigan in 1859 and sought a career in the grain industry. He spent his early years of employment at the grain mills in Winnebago, Minnesota, and later in Eau Claire, Wisconsin, before finding his way to Markesan in 1884. When he settled in town, he served as the manager of the M.B.M. Peacock Mill. Sometime later, he purchased the mill and operated it for a number years. Sink was also responsible for establishing the Markesan Hemp Company. He served on the school board in Markesan for four years and also played a part in the establishment of the Markesan Public Library. Sink resided in Markesan until his death in 1945.

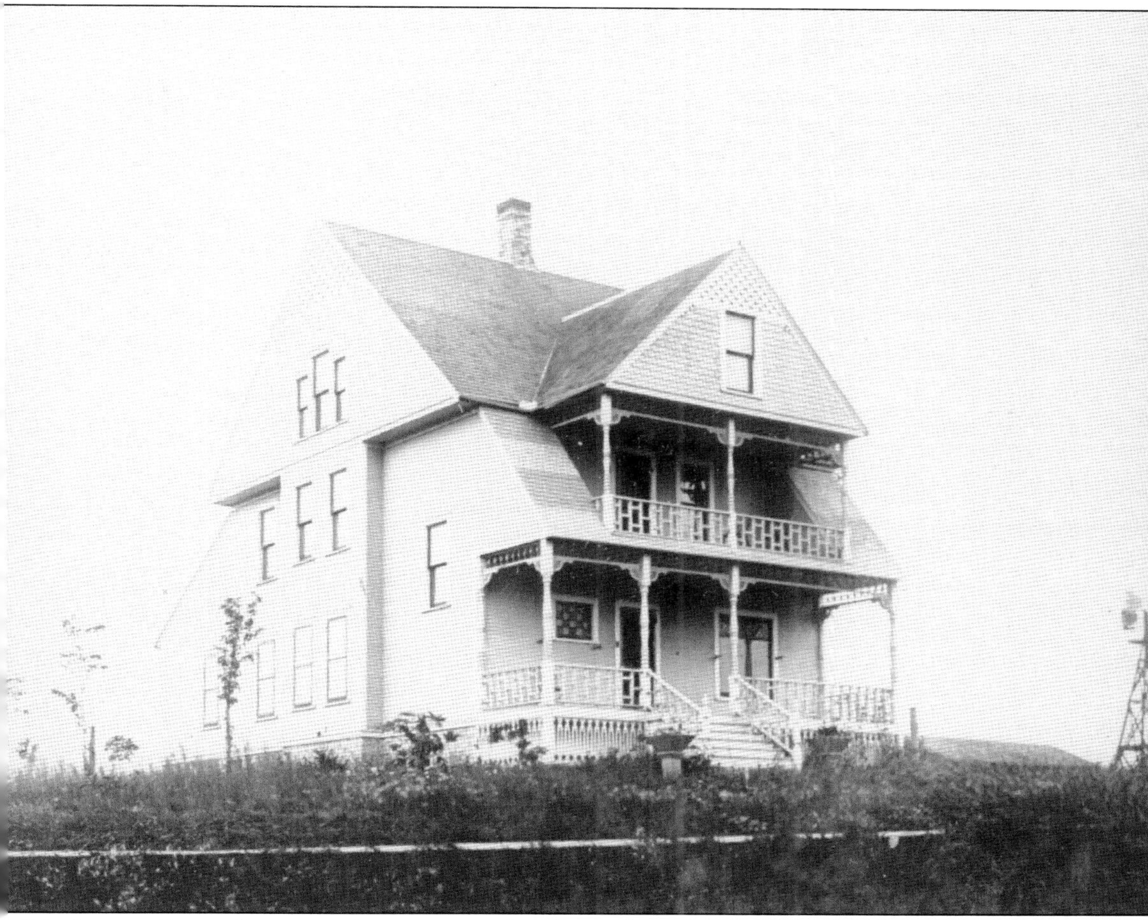

The home of James Densmoor Sr. was situated on East John Street near the railroad tracks. This picture, dated 1897, shows the first wood-frame home that was constructed as the Densmoor home. He was born in Chester, Vermont, in 1829. He came to Wisconsin when he was 18 years old and began his career in business. He operated a mill near the Markesan area for some time and headed a project on Lake Puckaway to build a ditch for moving cargo to steam ships that operated on the Fox River. He was also responsible for getting a railroad line stretching to Markesan and was the president of the Markesan and Brandon Railroad Company before its merger with the Chicago, Milwaukee, and St. Paul Railroad. Densmoor was a well-respected man in the community of Markesan at the time of his death in 1905.

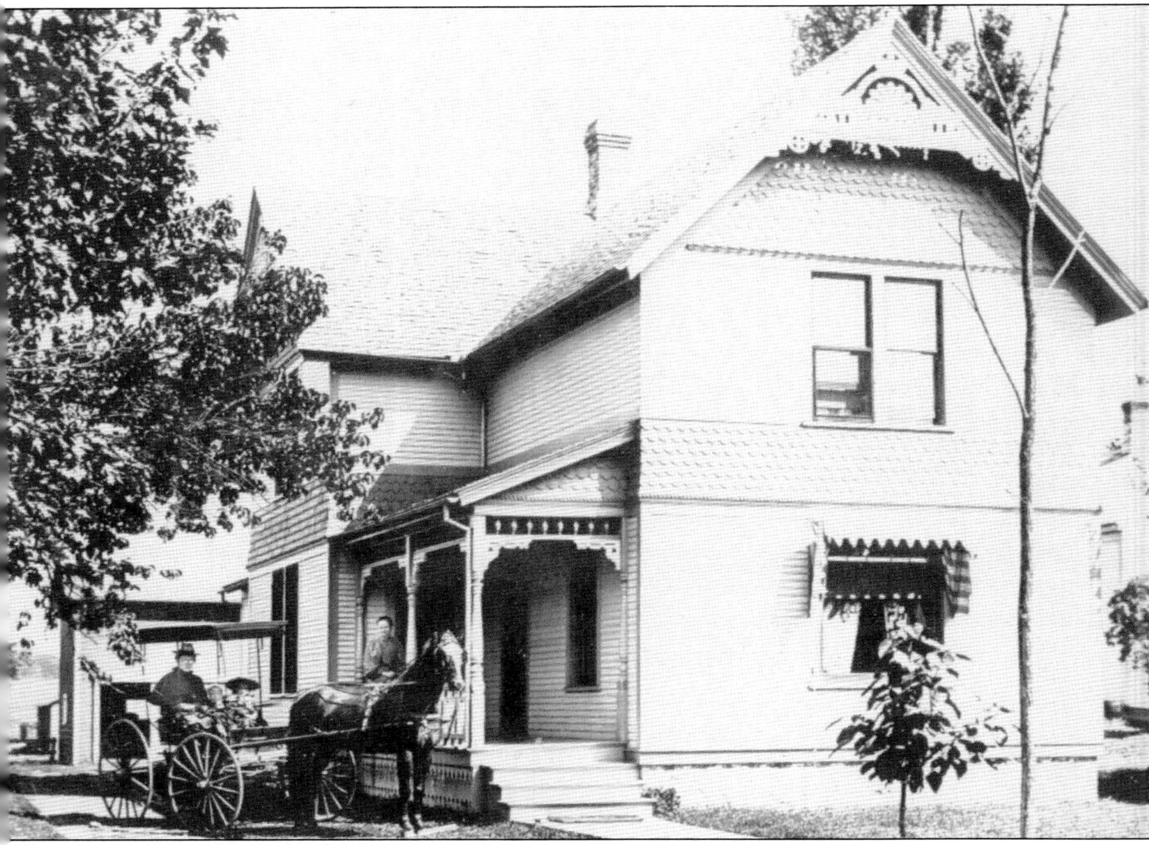

Pictured here is the Henry P. Friday family in 1897 by their home on South High Street. Born in 1866 in nearby Manchester, Wisconsin, he grew to be a successful man in the area. He founded the Markesan Creamery in 1892, which he sold in 1912. He helped found the Farmers State Bank of Markesan in 1910 and served as its president until 1921. He also served as a director of the Markesan Canning Company for 25 years and served as president of the company from 1907 to 1921. In addition to all of that, Friday was also the president for the Markesan Village Board for a number of years and was one of the first people to own a car in Markesan. Friday passed away in 1935.

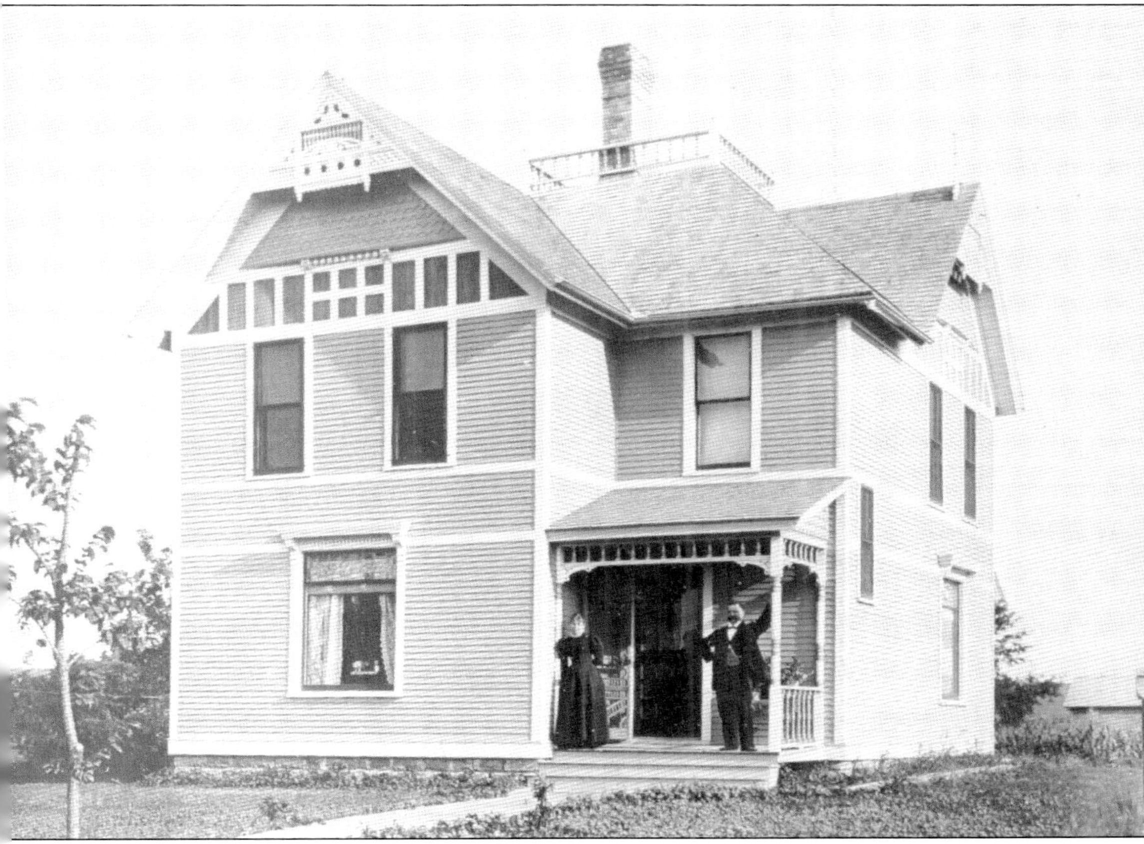

This picture shows the home of Charles H. Lambert on West Catharine Street in 1897. Lambert was born in Markesan on March 23, 1853, and attended public school in the community. He found work at the McMillan & Davis Lumber Company in Oshoksh, Wisconsin. Later, he worked at the Oconto Box Factory in Oconto, Wisconsin, before returning to Markesan in 1883. Upon his return, he was the postmaster for Markesan and also an insurance agent. He was involved in politics, serving on the Markesan Village Board and Green Lake County Board for a few years. Lambert passed away in 1934.

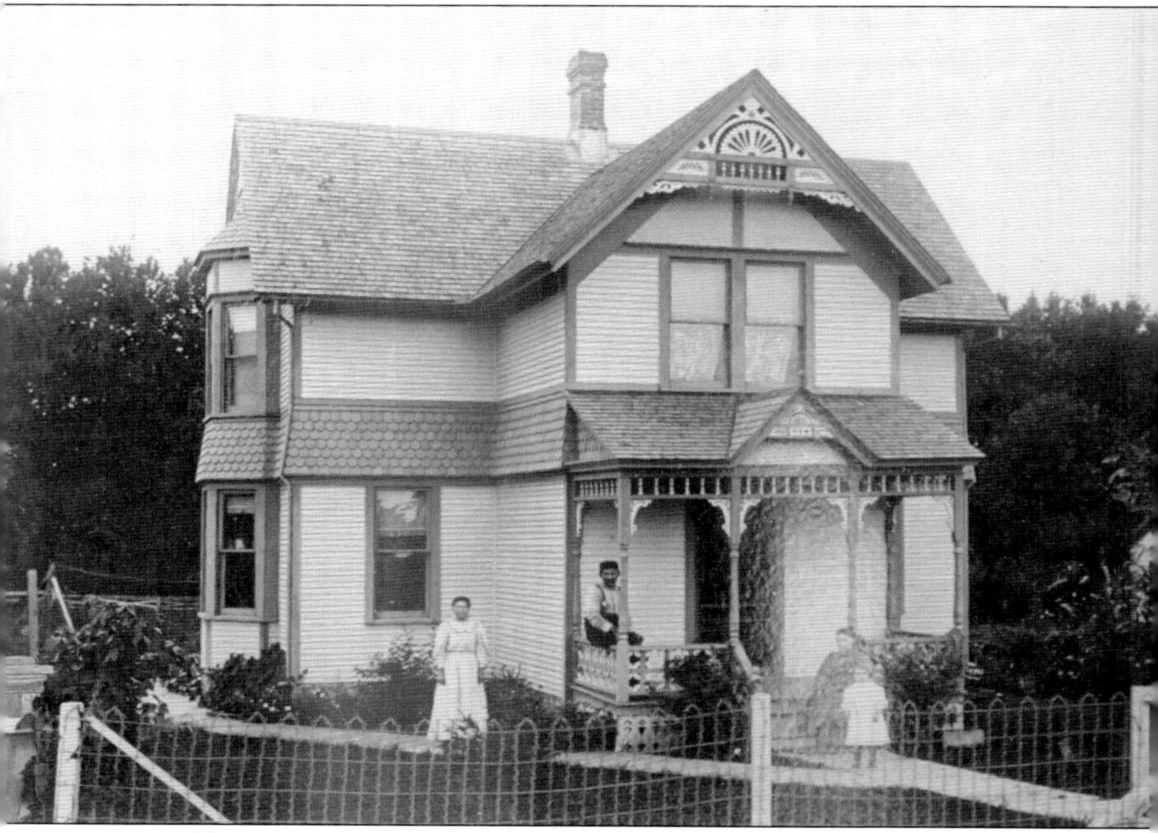

Pictured here is the home of William Salzwedel on South Bridge Street in 1897. Salzwedel was an area farmer for most of his life until 1890, when he retired and moved to this home with his wife. When his wife died in 1913, his daughter moved in to care for him. He resided in his home in Markesan until his death in 1917.

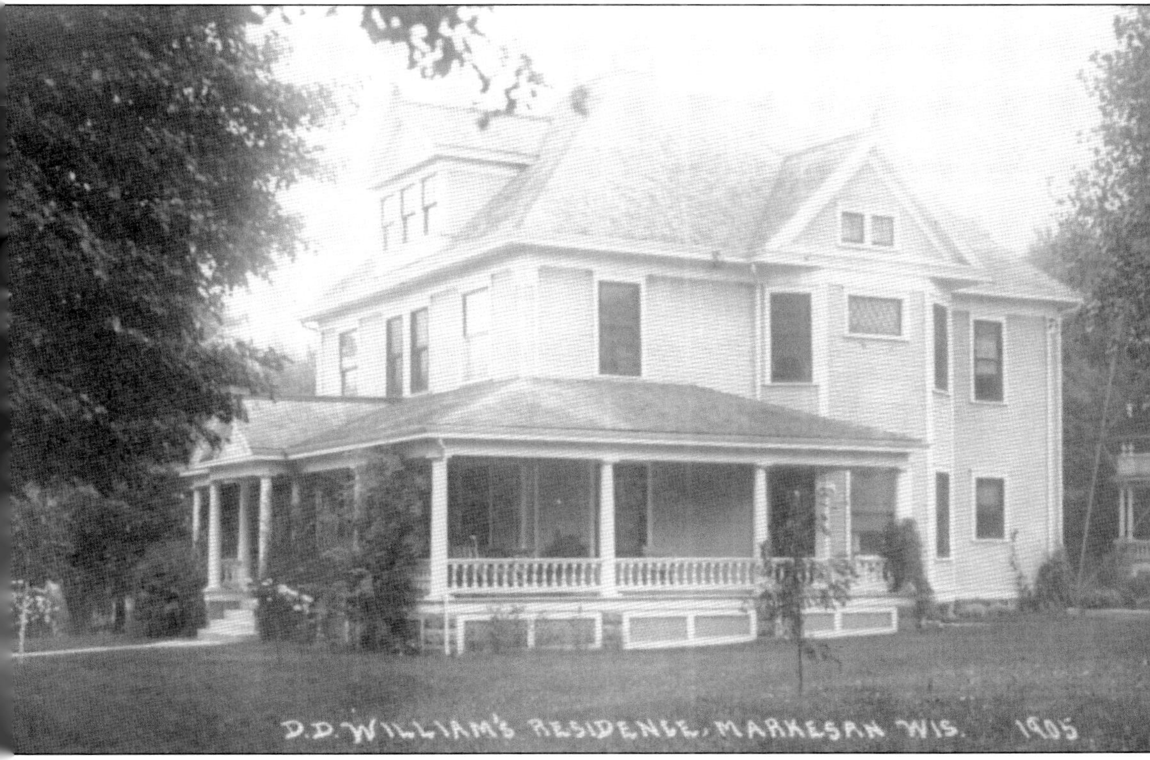

The home of David D. Williams is located on the corner of Main and Caroline Streets. He was a prominent businessman and is said to have been one of the leading merchants of Markesan in his day. He was born in Wales in 1847 and moved to America with his family at the age of nine. The family settled near Cambria, Wisconsin. At age 17, he moved to Fox Lake, Wisconsin, where he worked at a general store. In 1881, he moved to Markesan and established the D.D. William Big Daylight Store. He played a significant role in the establishment of the Markesan State Bank in 1891 and served as a director. In 1903, he was elected vice president of the bank. Williams retained both positions at the bank until his death on January 23, 1921.

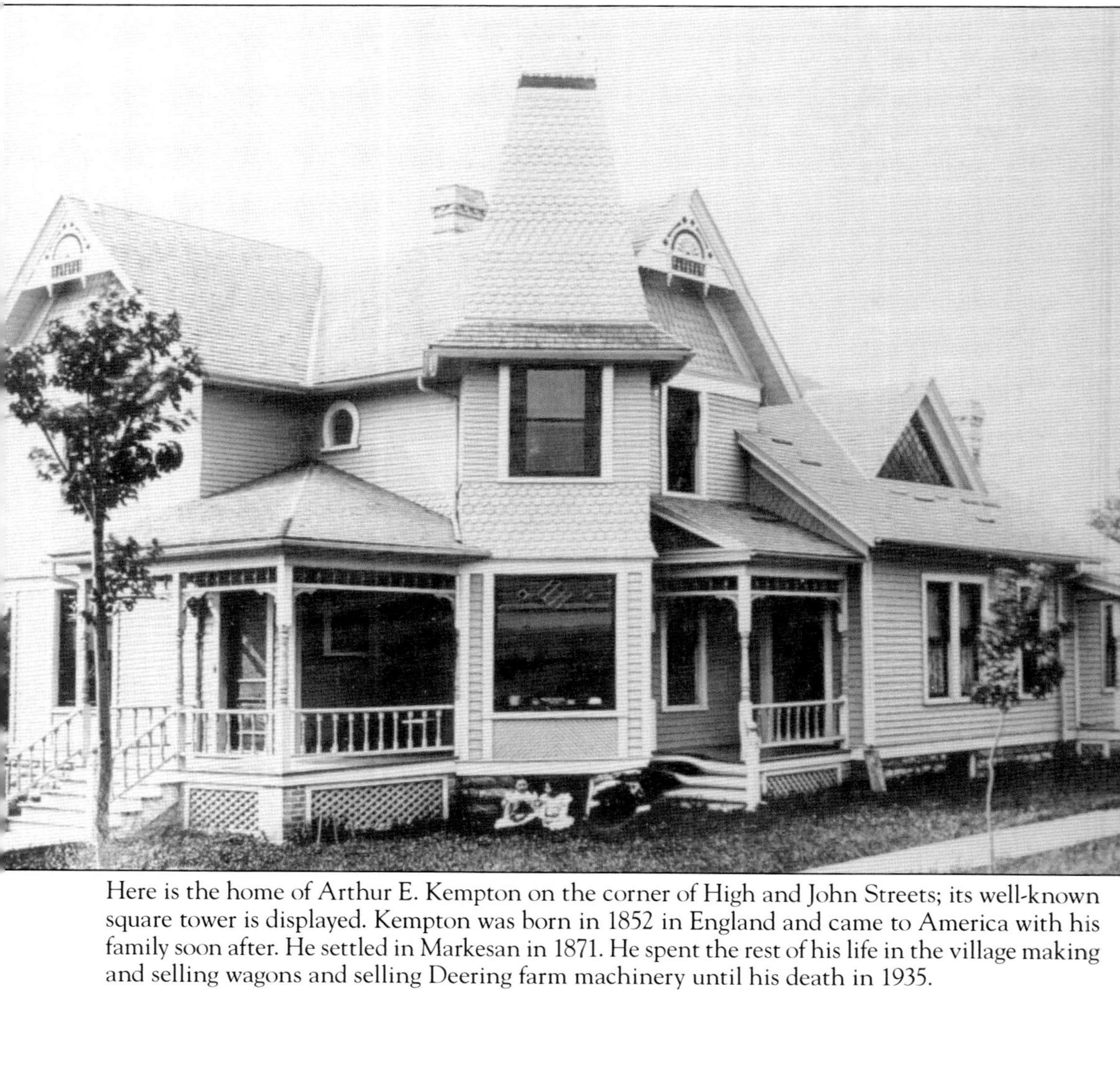

Here is the home of Arthur E. Kempton on the corner of High and John Streets; its well-known square tower is displayed. Kempton was born in 1852 in England and came to America with his family soon after. He settled in Markesan in 1871. He spent the rest of his life in the village making and selling wagons and selling Deering farm machinery until his death in 1935.

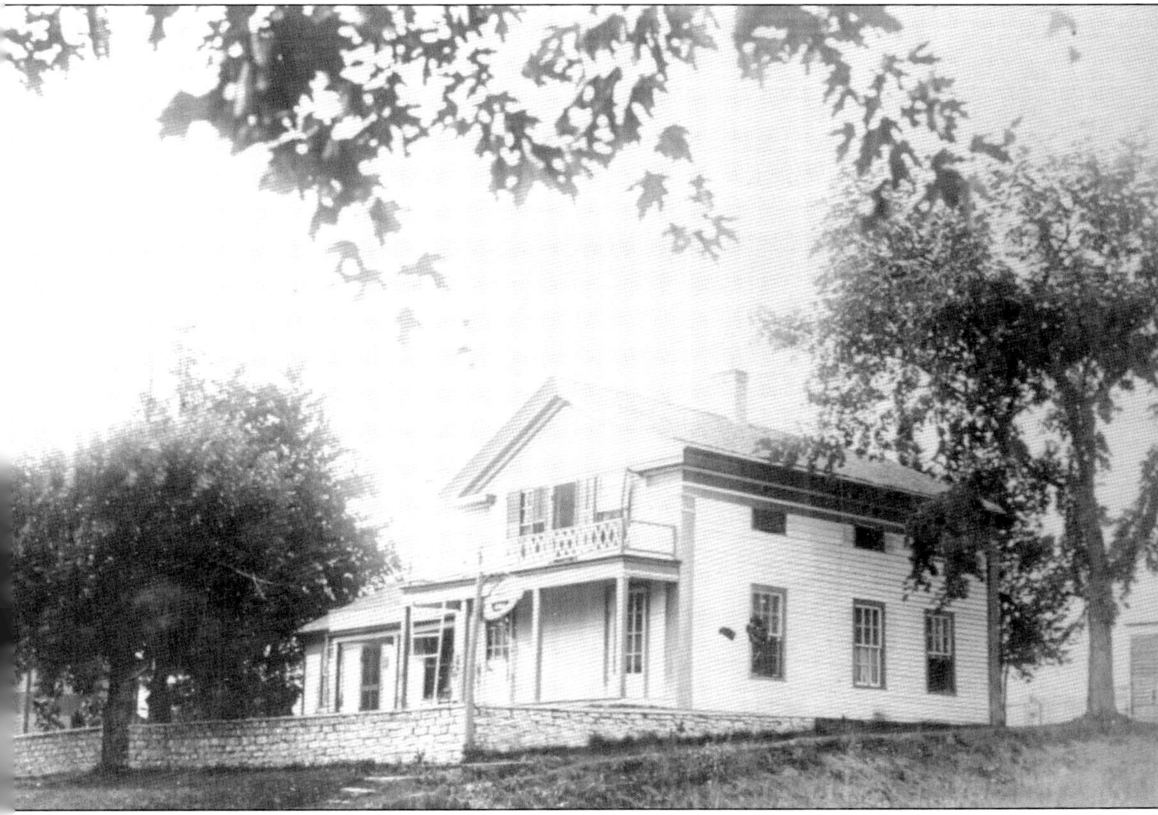

This photograph, dated 1897, shows the home and office of physician Dr. Ira Manley Jr., who was born in Willsboro, New York, in 1822. He and his father, Ira Manley Sr., were among the first settlers of Markesan. Dr. Manley became the first president of the Markesan Village Board. He also served the Union during the Civil War as a surgeon in the 1st Regiment of the Wisconsin Heavy Artillery. Following the end of the war, Manley returned and opened his practice in Markesan. He lived in this home until his death in 1892; it then became the residence and office of physician Dr. Jame Monroe for a few years. Around 1900, August Laper sold his farm north of the village and made his home here until his death in 1910.

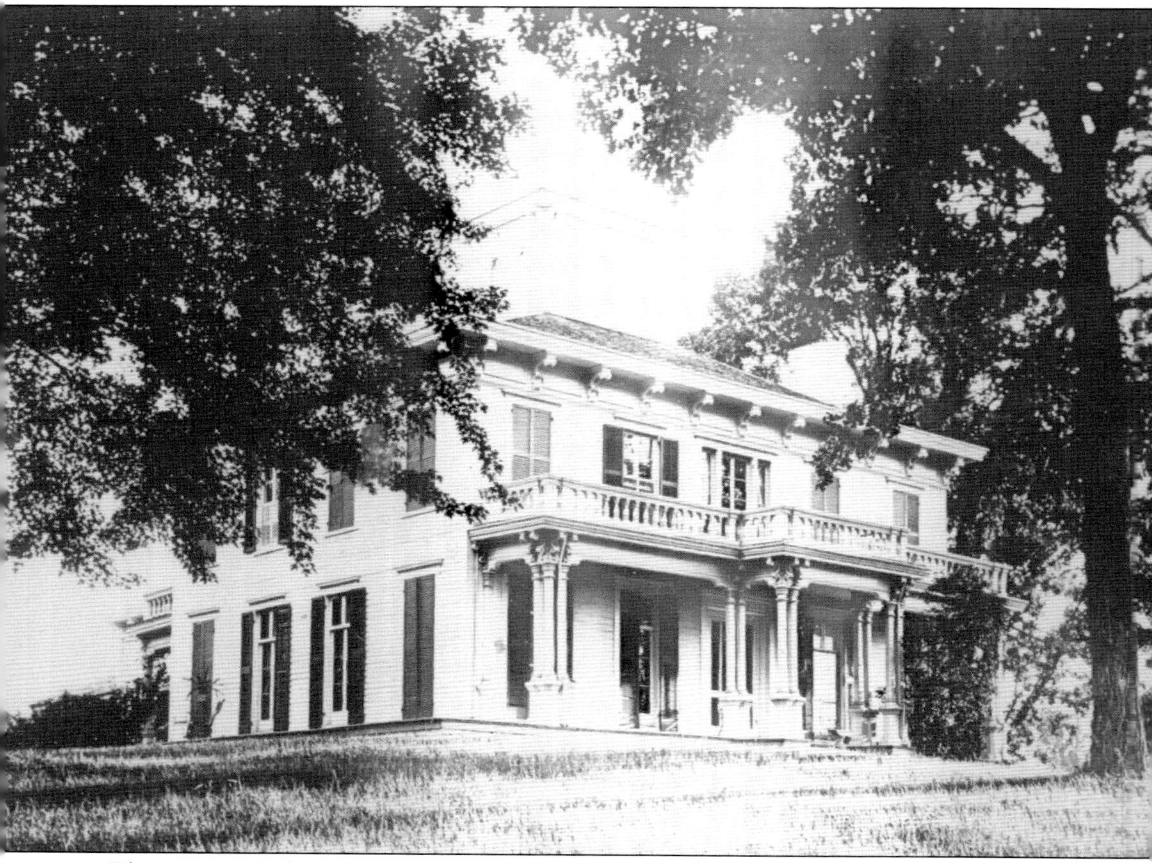

This is an 1897 photograph of the John L. Millard Sr. home, once located on Main Street. Millard Sr. moved from New York to the area of what would become Markesan in 1846 and constructed this house. He was involved in different businesses in the area for many years before his death in 1896. The house was left to his son, John L. Millard Jr., who was born in Markesan in 1866. Millard Jr. received his law degree and opened his own law practice in Markesan in 1890. Tragedy struck on the morning of March 28, 1910, when a fire broke out, and the Millard home was lost. Later, John Millard Jr. moved to Florida and resided there until his death in 1943.

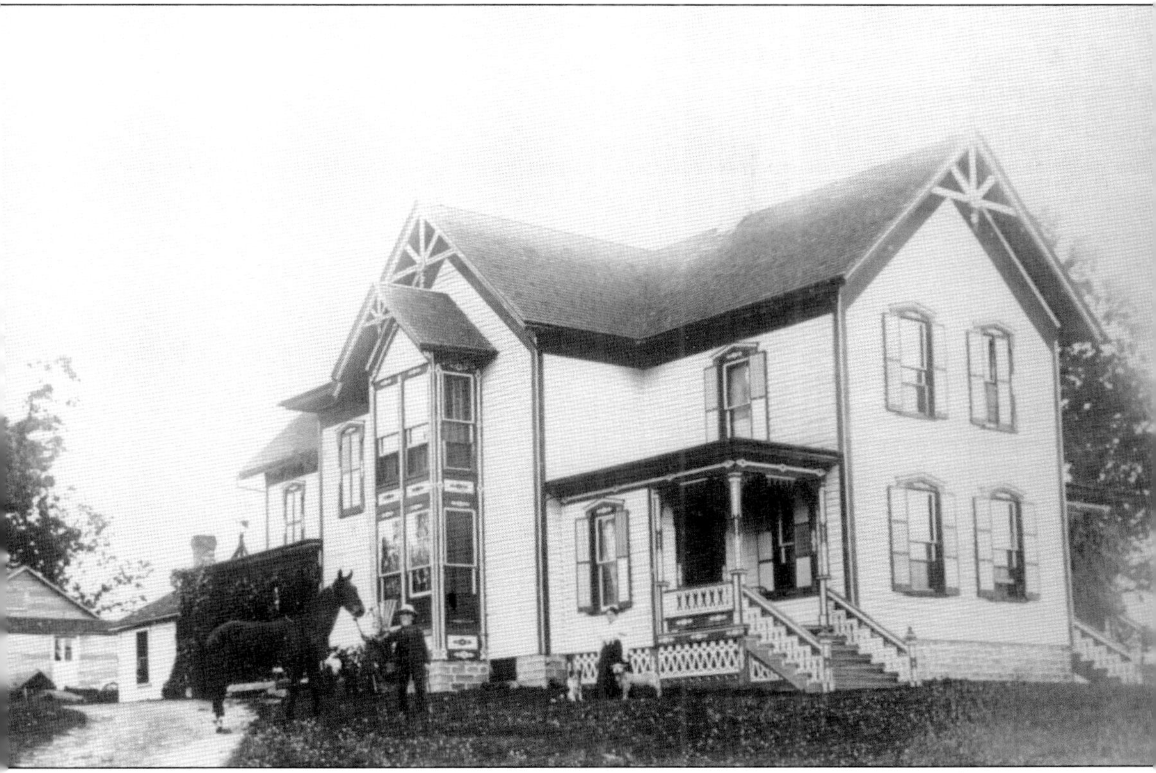

The Samuel Perry farm is located on the west side of Markesan on State Road 44. The house is believed to have been built in 1879 and was on 295 acres of land. The original homestead had four farm buildings accompanied by two houses. One of the houses burned down around 1900. The other house was then occupied by Nettie (Perry) Duffies and later by her daughter Gladys (Markham) Freudenburg. Gladys's husband, Dr. J. A. Fruendenburg, was accused of murdering his mother-in-law, Nettie Duffies, in 1920; it was said that he poisoned her in order to collect the Perry estate and other inheritance. An inquest held at that time vindicated Dr. Freudenburg of any foul play. Old newspaper articles on the matter suggest that the family was one of the wealthiest in the area.

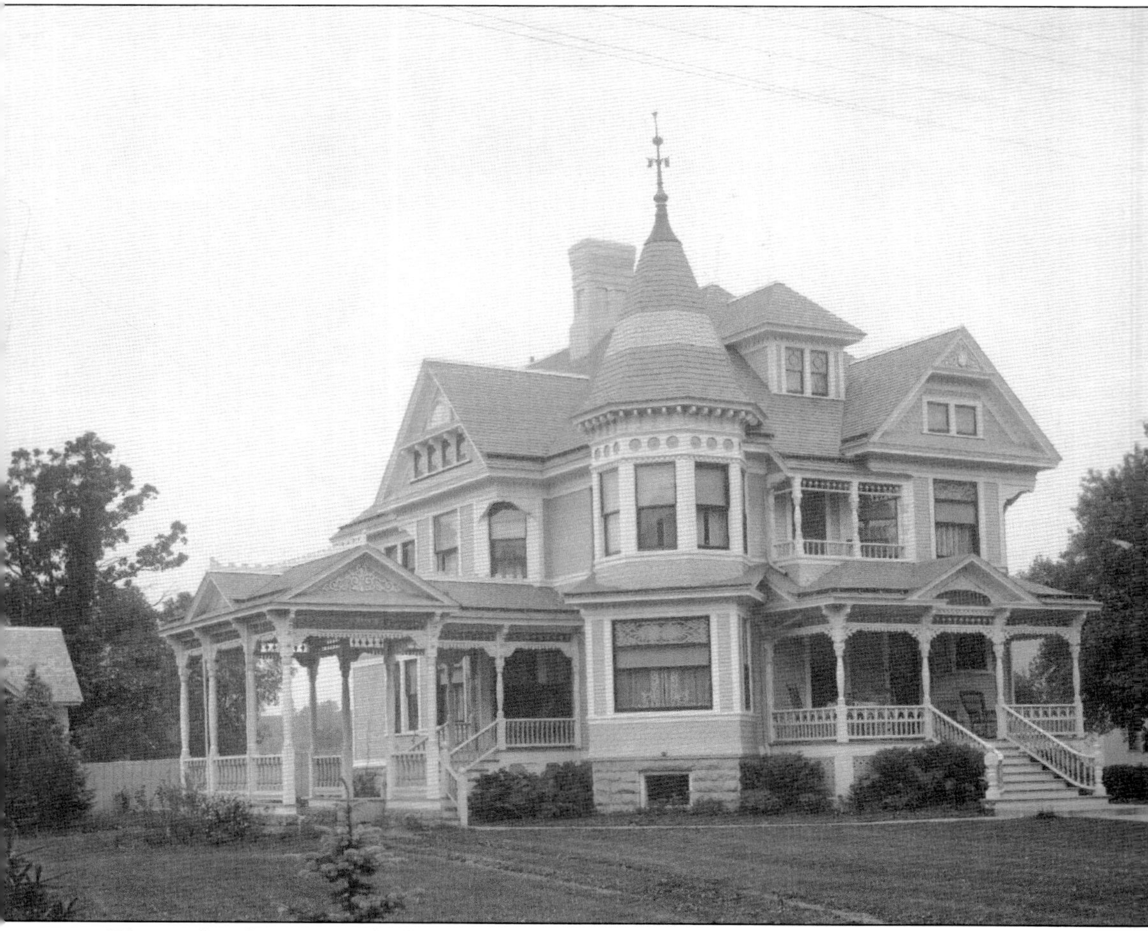

This undated picture is the home of Silas W. Phelps that once stood on the southwest corner of John and Margaret Streets. Phelps was born in 1848 in Washington County, Wisconsin. In 1853, the family moved to Green Lake County, Wisconsin, where they lived and worked on a farm. Silas moved to Markesan in 1896; he resided in this home until his death in 1924. Upon his death, the house was willed to his son Stanley Silas Phelps, born in 1906. He attended the University of Wisconsin and graduated in 1939. He was the manager of the Riverview Canning Company in Markesan for two years; however, tragedy struck in 1942 when he became ill and died at the age of 35. The house was demolished in 1962 following the death of his half-sister Edna Straight.

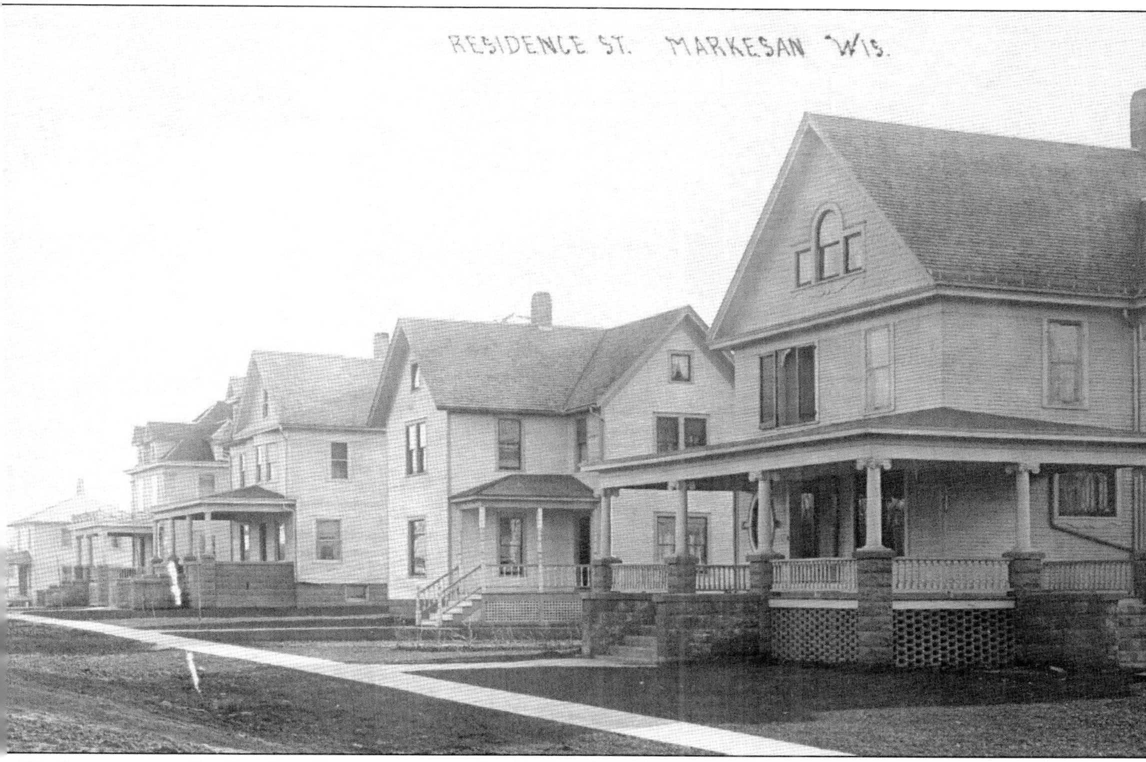

Big homes were built when business started taking off in the area. Upon the advent of railroad service to town, many residents of the community saw the potential for profit. Businesses were started, and they flourished to create a surplus of money for citizens. They used their money to build the Victorian homes that are still seen in Markesan today. This photograph shows the south end of High Street. The street meanders around until it is cut short at the banks of the Grand River. Because of this street's curvy features, it was nicknamed "Pig Tail Alley." Many of these homes still stand today, displaying their unique architectural features.

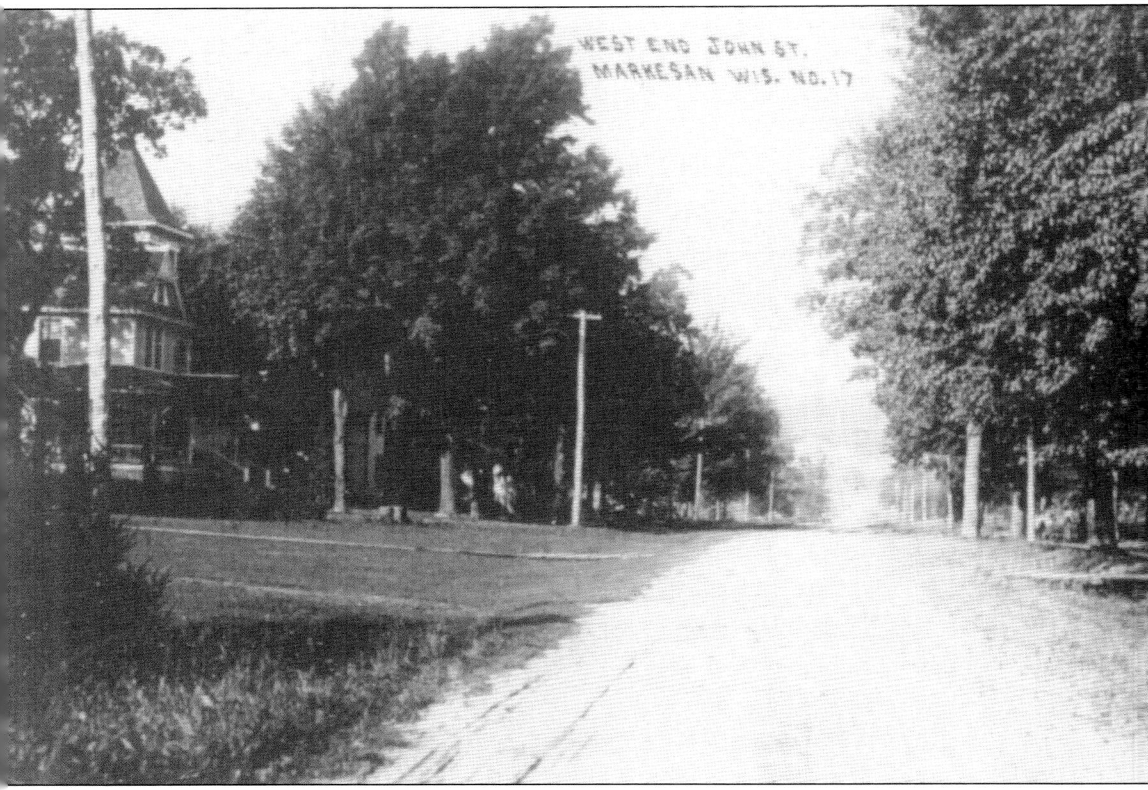

The streets in town are uniquely named after people or features of Markesan. John Street and Charles Street are named after John Chapel and Charles Russell, the men who platted and established Granville, which eventually became Markesan. Their wives, Margaret and Catherine, also had streets named after them. Millard Avenue was named after resident John Millard Sr., who resided there. Bridge Street was the location of the first bridge in Markesan. High Street ran to the top of the highest point in Markesan. St. Joseph's Street was named so because of the little Catholic church built there. Over time, more streets were added and named for people or significant landmarks.

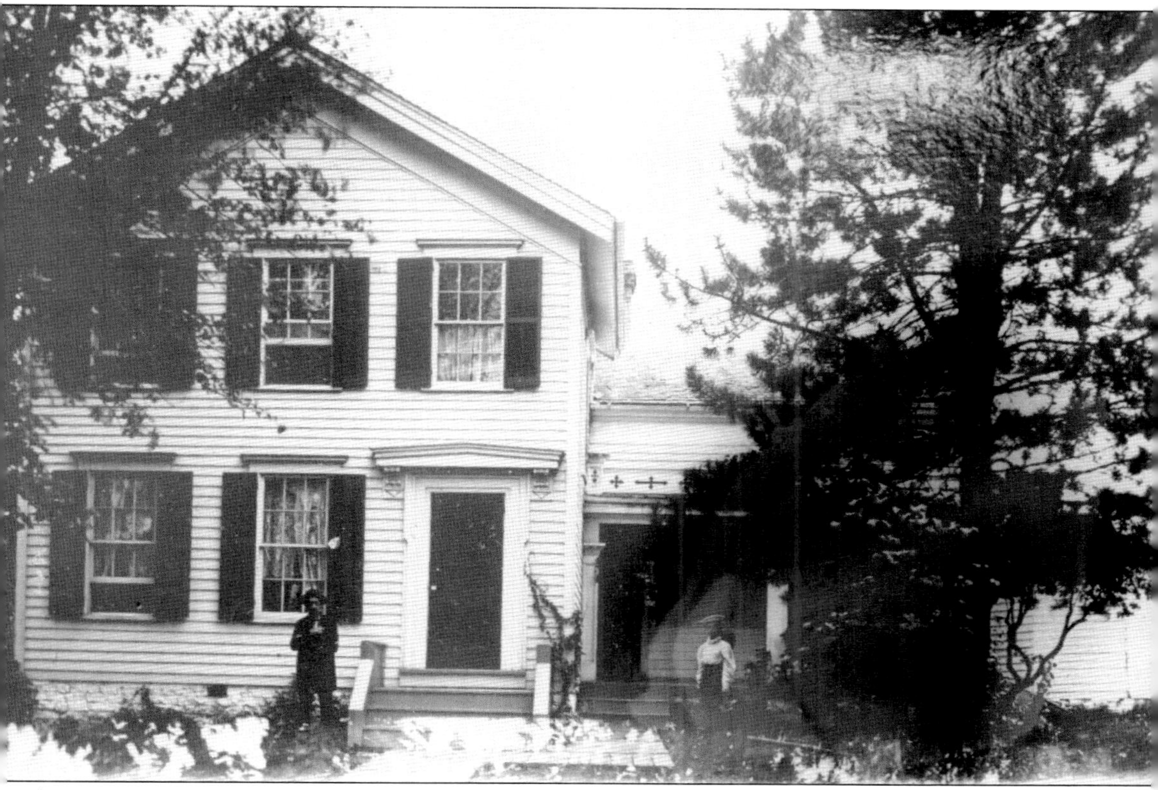

This 1897 picture shows the home of John B. Seward. Built in 1844, it was the first frame house in the area of what would become the village of Markesan. The house stands today in its original location on Manchester Street. John and his son William Seward came to the area in 1844 after his other son, Miller Seward, made a long trip by mule from Illinois to the area. John purchased 300 acres of land from the US Land Office in Green Bay and constructed this home. John lived out his days operating a business in Markesan until his death in 1900.

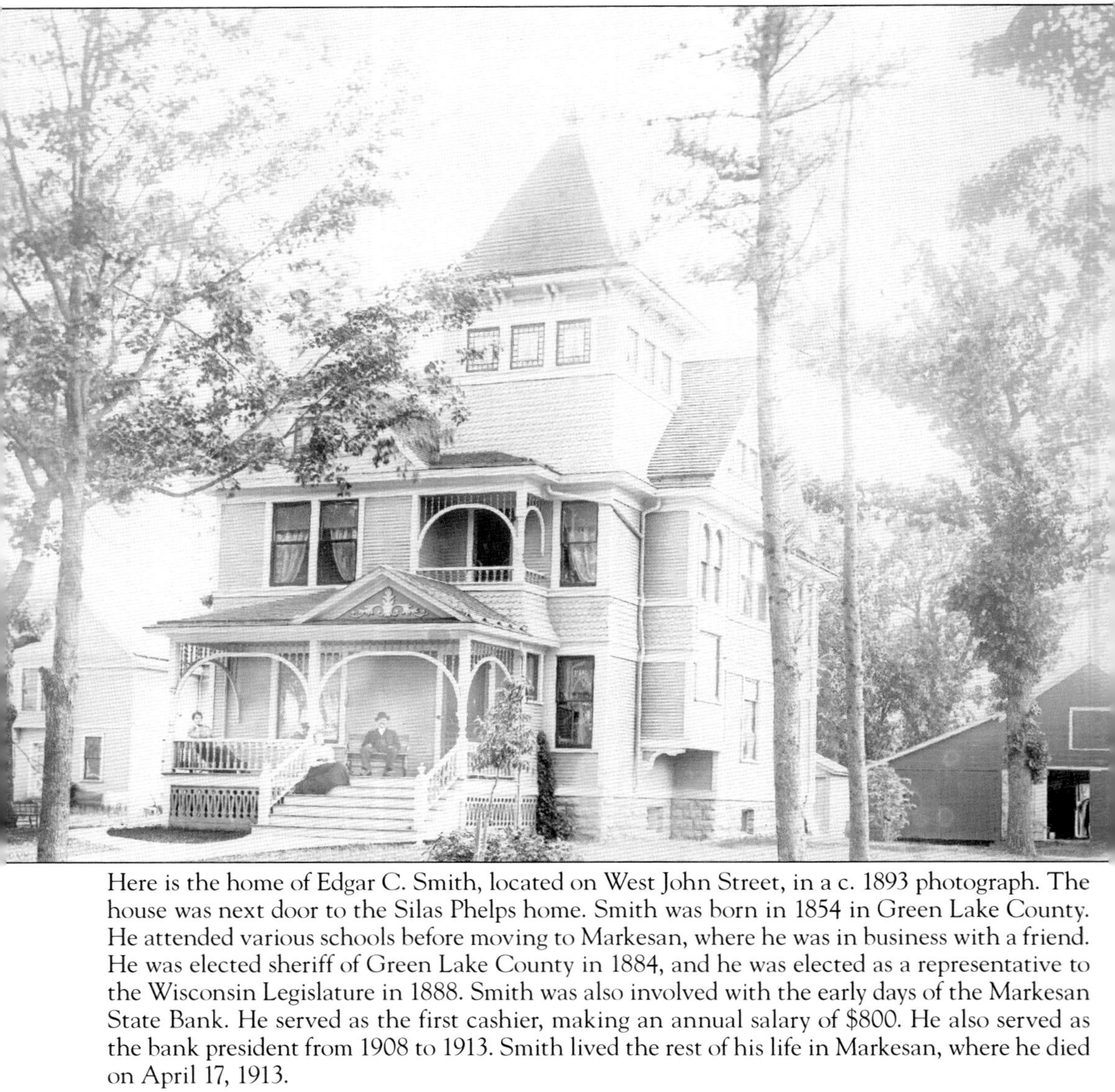

Here is the home of Edgar C. Smith, located on West John Street, in a c. 1893 photograph. The house was next door to the Silas Phelps home. Smith was born in 1854 in Green Lake County. He attended various schools before moving to Markesan, where he was in business with a friend. He was elected sheriff of Green Lake County in 1884, and he was elected as a representative to the Wisconsin Legislature in 1888. Smith was also involved with the early days of the Markesan State Bank. He served as the first cashier, making an annual salary of $800. He also served as the bank president from 1908 to 1913. Smith lived the rest of his life in Markesan, where he died on April 17, 1913.

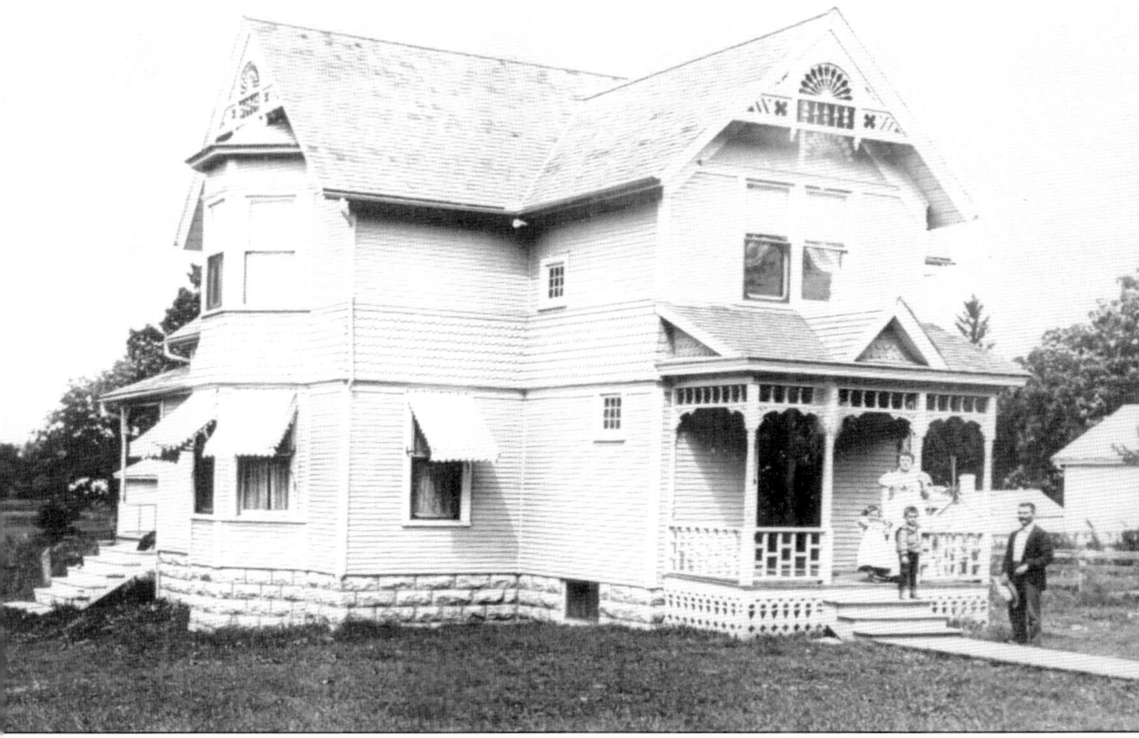

This 1897 picture shows the home of John A. Walker, located on Manchester Street. Walker was born in Manchester, Wisconsin, in 1859. In 1893, he moved his family to this home in Markesan. He was involved with cigar manufacturing in town. He served on the Markesan School Board for 15 years and also served as president of the Markesan Village Board. Walker lived in Markesan until his death in 1944.

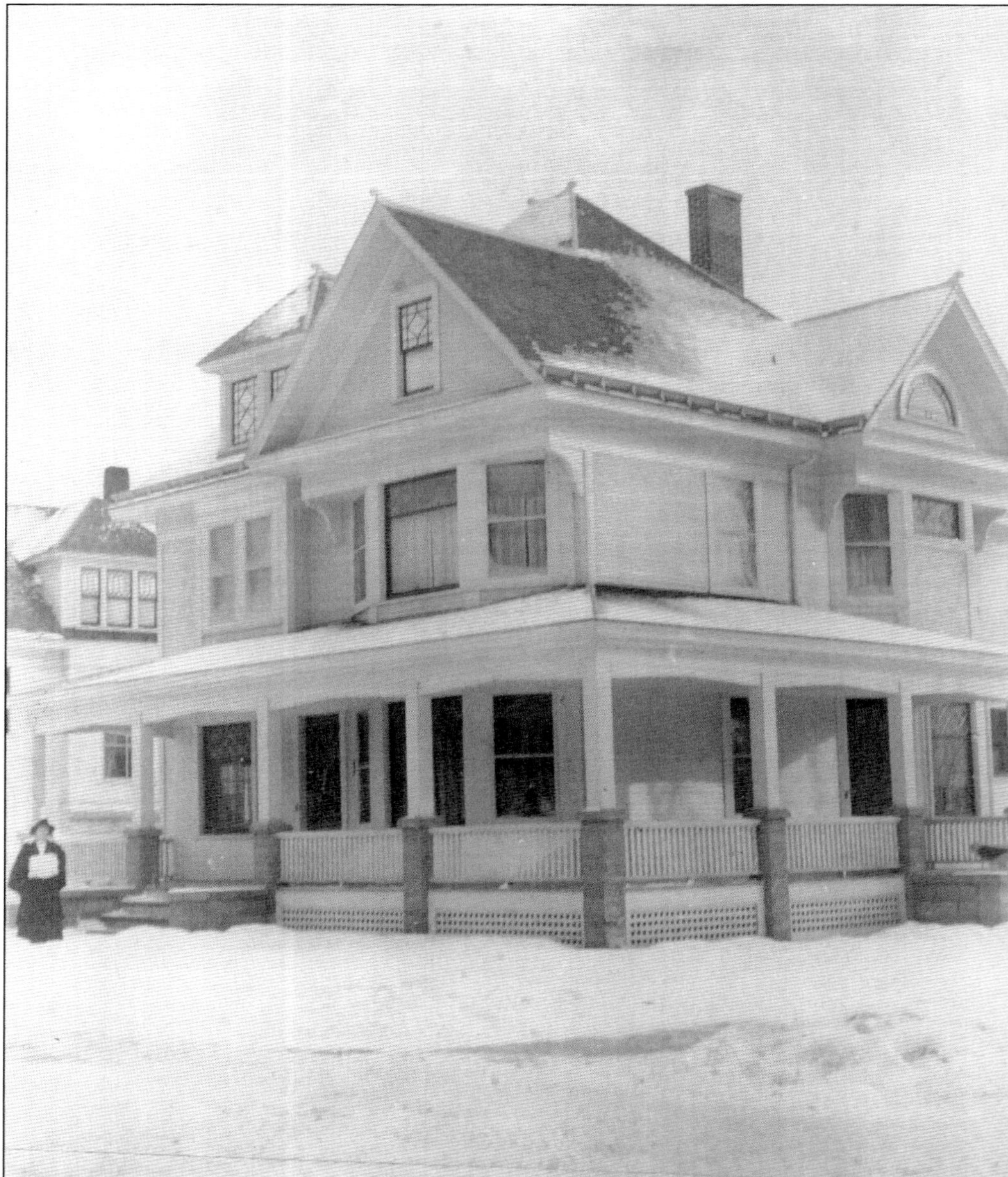

This undated photograph shows the home of Charles A. Yunker on the corner of High and John Streets. Yunker was born in 1873 in Fox Lake, Wisconsin. He spent a great deal of his life working on his father's farm until he became the manager of the Markesan Canning Company in 1902. He served as the president of the Markesan Village Board from 1924 to 1927. He was labeled as a pioneer in the canning industry in the state of Wisconsin. He served as president of the Wisconsin Canner's Association and was the director of the National Canners Association. He was also part of the library association, which helped found and build the Markesan Public Library. Yunker passed away at his home in 1954.

Four

BUSTLING BUSINESSES

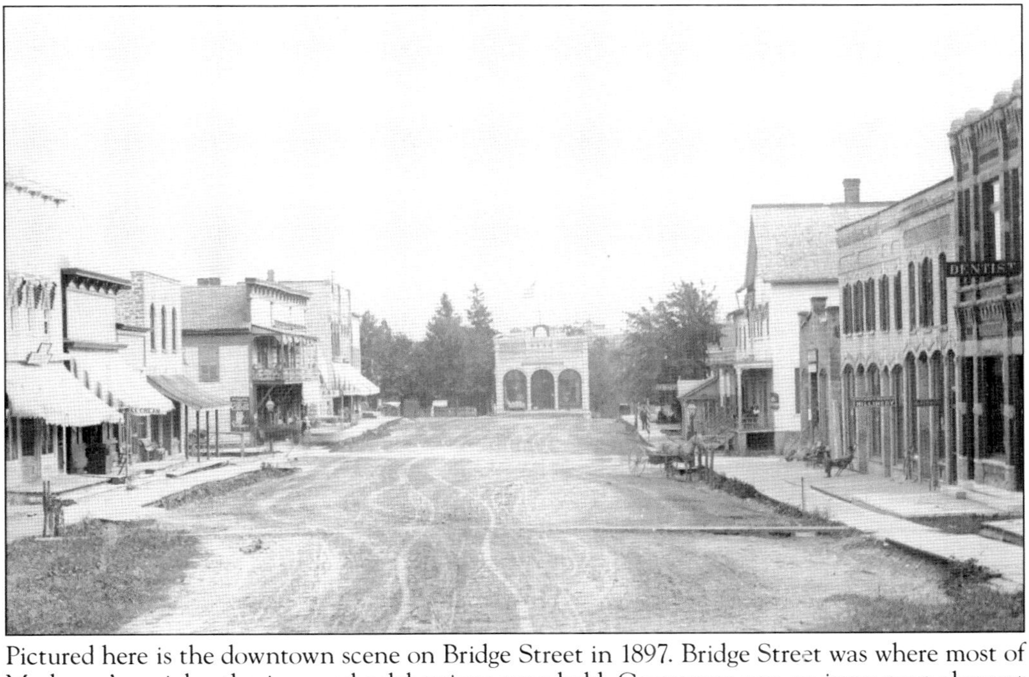

Pictured here is the downtown scene on Bridge Street in 1897. Bridge Street was where most of Markesan's social gatherings and celebrations were held. Commerce was an important element downtown, and it is where many business owners of Markesan set up stores. This picture was taken as part of a series documenting various structures around Markesan.

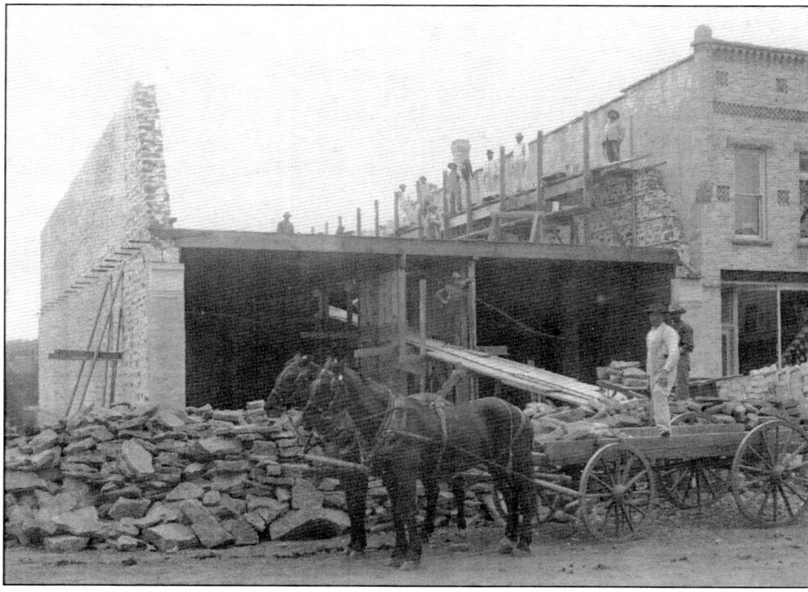

As Markesan grew, so did its downtown business district. This building was constructed on the corner of Bridge and Water Streets. The stones used to construct this building came from a quarry north of Markesan on Highway 44 near Little Green Lake.

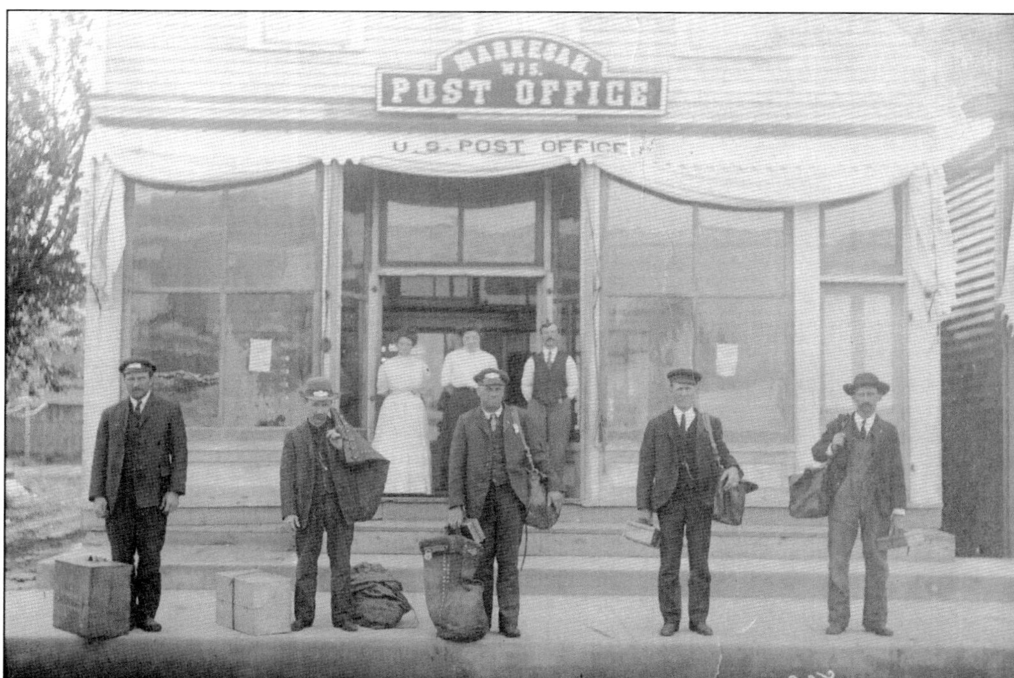

This undated photograph shows the Markesan Post Office and its staff. Over time, the post office moved around to several different structures. The building pictured here is currently occupied by the *Markesan Regional Reporter.* The people are identified as, from left to right, (first row) Herman Lachelt, Albert Roeske, Charlie Baker, Bob Williams, and George Davids; (second row) Mary Mottram, Barbara Henninger Miller, and postmaster Ernest Mottram.

The Bender Meat Market was started by William Bender, who moved to Markesan in 1893. His store advertised, "All kinds of fresh and salted meats, poultry, game, farm produce, etc, can be had at reasonable prices and the purchaser is always are sure of the best in the market."

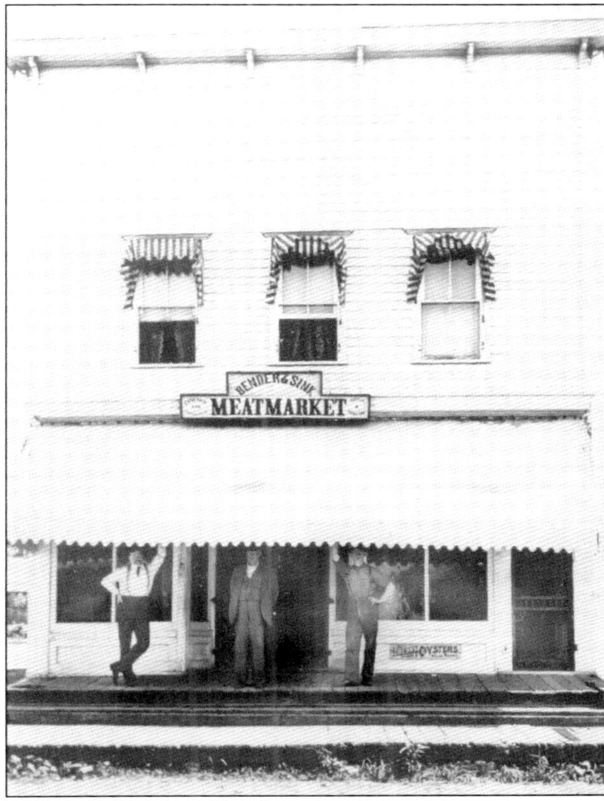

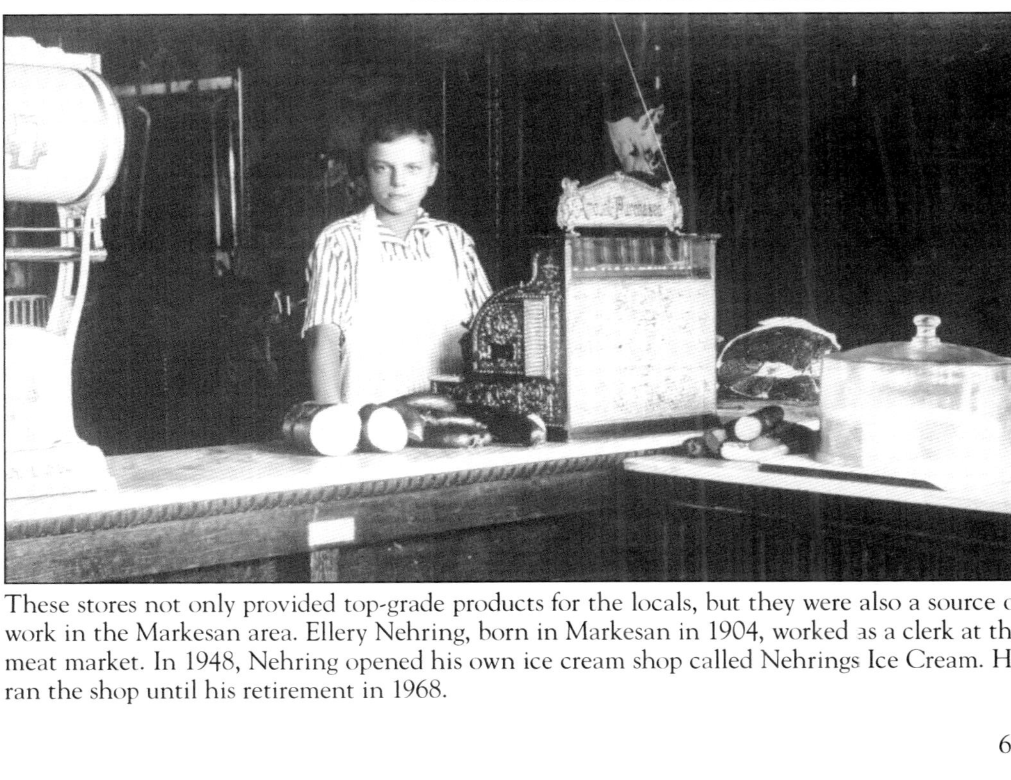

These stores not only provided top-grade products for the locals, but they were also a source of work in the Markesan area. Ellery Nehring, born in Markesan in 1904, worked as a clerk at the meat market. In 1948, Nehring opened his own ice cream shop called Nehrings Ice Cream. He ran the shop until his retirement in 1968.

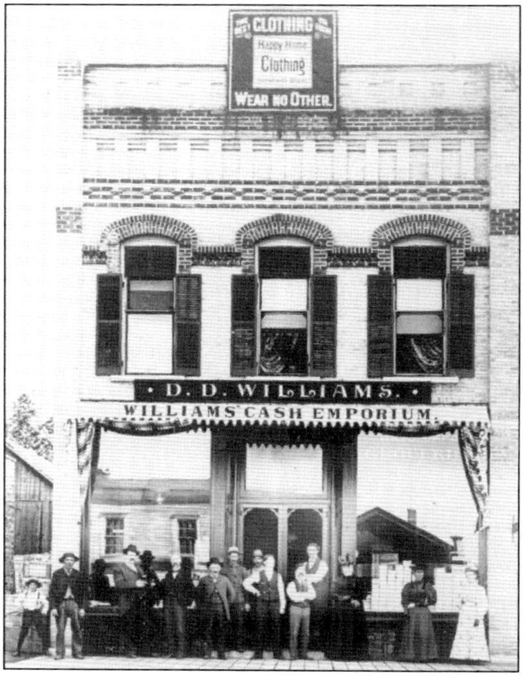

Pictured here in 1897 is D.D. Williams Big Daylight Store, one of the biggest stores in the area at the time. The store offered everything from clothing and shoes to groceries and household decor. Williams moved to Markesan, set up his store on Bridge Street in 1881, and operated it until his death in 1921.

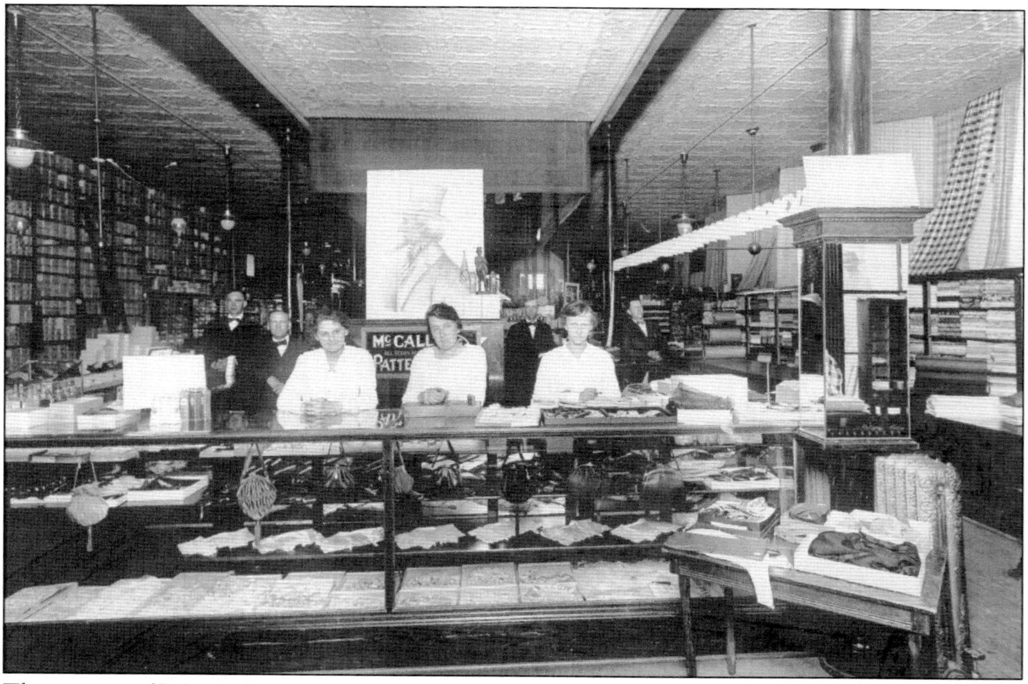

The interior of D.D. Williams Daylight Store was just as spectacular as the exterior. The vast amount of merchandise he had on his store's shelves provided everything a family of that era needed. The staff is seen here sometime in the early 1900s. An old slogan explains that the store's ambition was "to sell good merchandise at the very lowest prices consistent with dependable quality and to serve you so pleasantly that our every transaction will be mutually pleasurable."

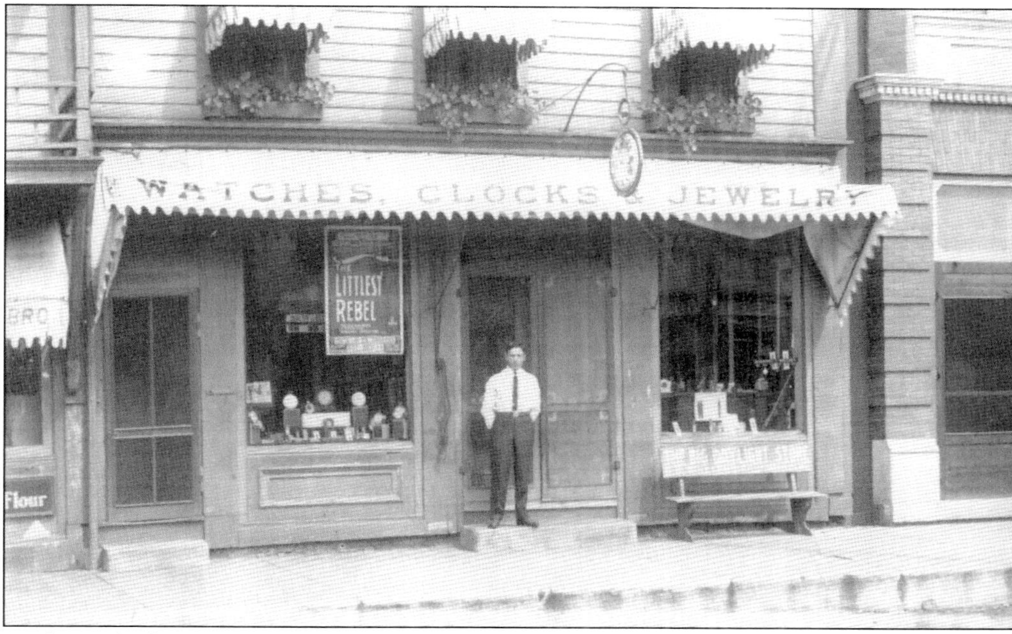

Markesan had its very own fine jewelry, watch, and clock store. It was located on Bridge Street next to the Farmers State Bank. The Henninger Jewelry Store was started by John Henninger Sr. in 1878. He was only 18 years old when he opened his shop, and he continued to operate the business in partnership with his son until his death in 1931. Following his death, his son Barnett Henninger took control of the business and continued the trade.

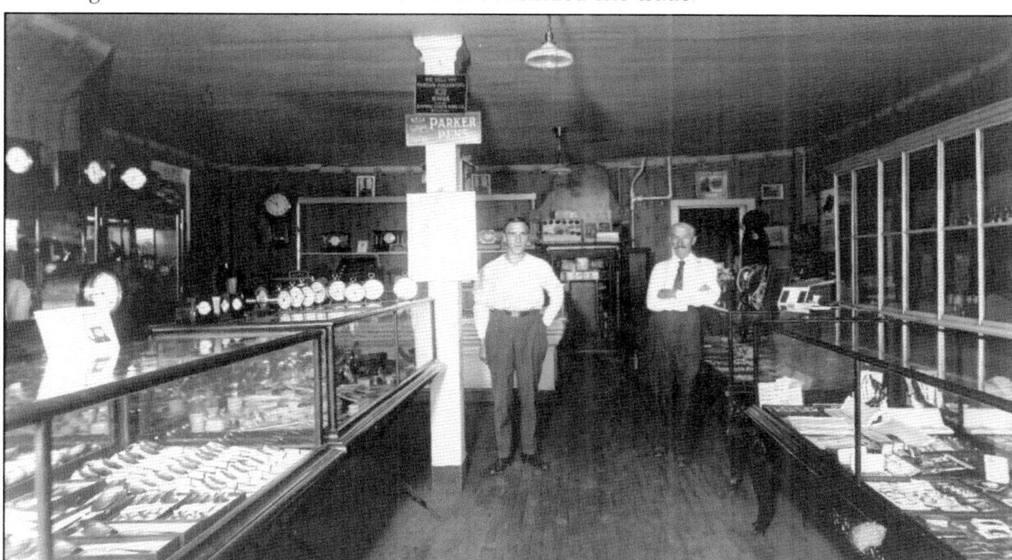

Pictured here is the interior of the Henninger Jewelry Store; posing for the shot are Barnett Henninger (left) and his father, John Henninger Sr. Barnett joined his father's business in 1921 as his partner, and the duo operated the store until Barnett took complete control when his father passed away in 1931. The Henninger Jewelry Store remained in business until 1955 when Barnett Henninger retired.

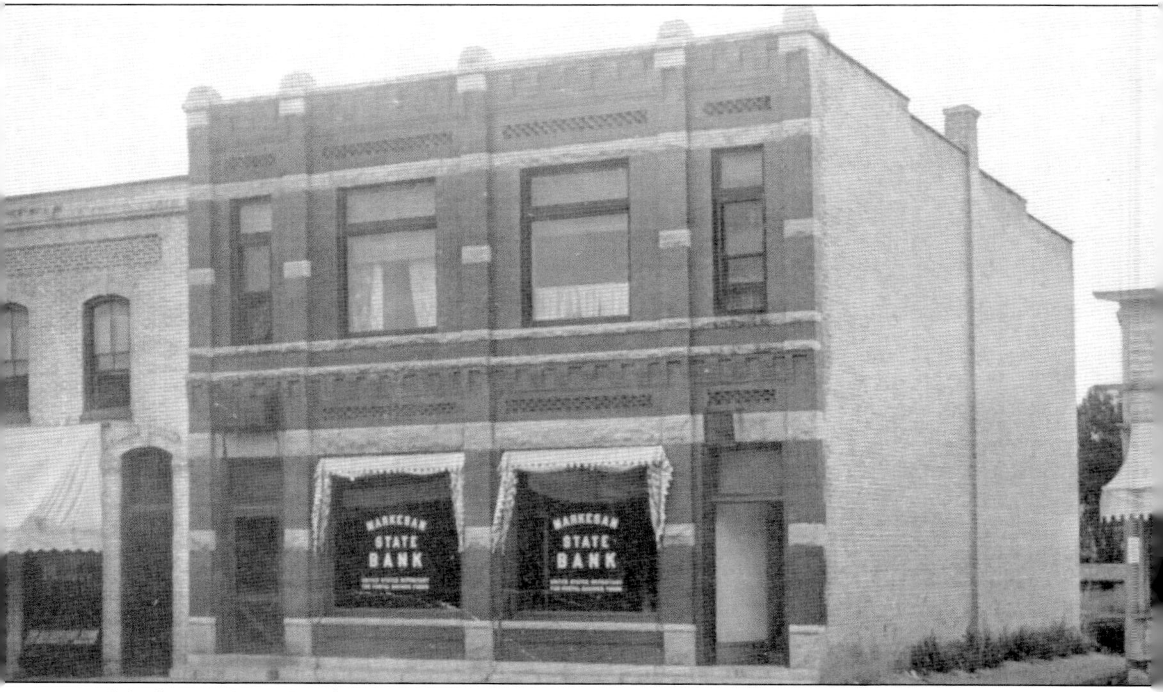

Markesan State Bank was organized on October 7, 1891, with an initial investment capital of $30,000. It was the first successful bank to be established in Markesan, and the first meeting was held in the McCracken Hotel parlor room. Organizers of the bank were Mel Folsom, David D. Williams, and Samuel Barter. Barter became the first president of the bank, and Edgar Smith was hired as the sole cashier of the bank. This June 23, 1915, postcard shows the front view of the bank located on Bridge Street. The bank was located in this building until 1977, when a new building was constructed across the street. The old bank building is currently used by Slate Law Office.

This 1905 booklet was a souvenir customers could obtain from the bank. It gave information about banking hours, services, capital, and staff. Inside it contained a set of complementary sewing needles for different types of material, as well as a pocket calendar for the year 1905. This souvenir would be the equivalent of receiving a book of matches or candy from the bank today.

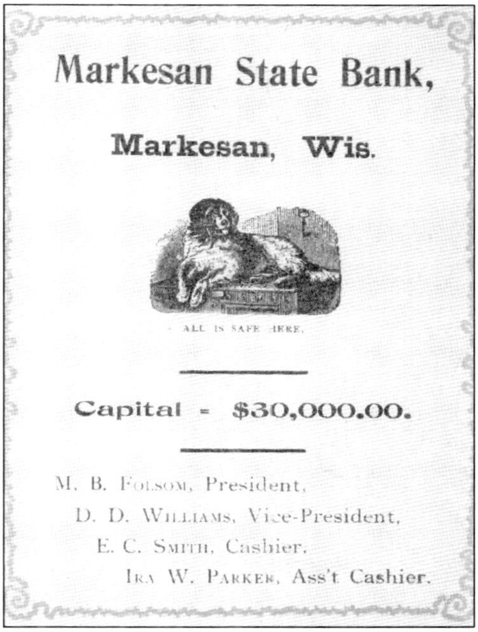

This picture, dated 1926, shows the massive undertaking of installing a new bank vault. The vault door can be seen being slid across timbers and moved to the vault deep inside the bank. There is no doubt that this must have been a massive undertaking, as the door itself weighed thousands of pounds.

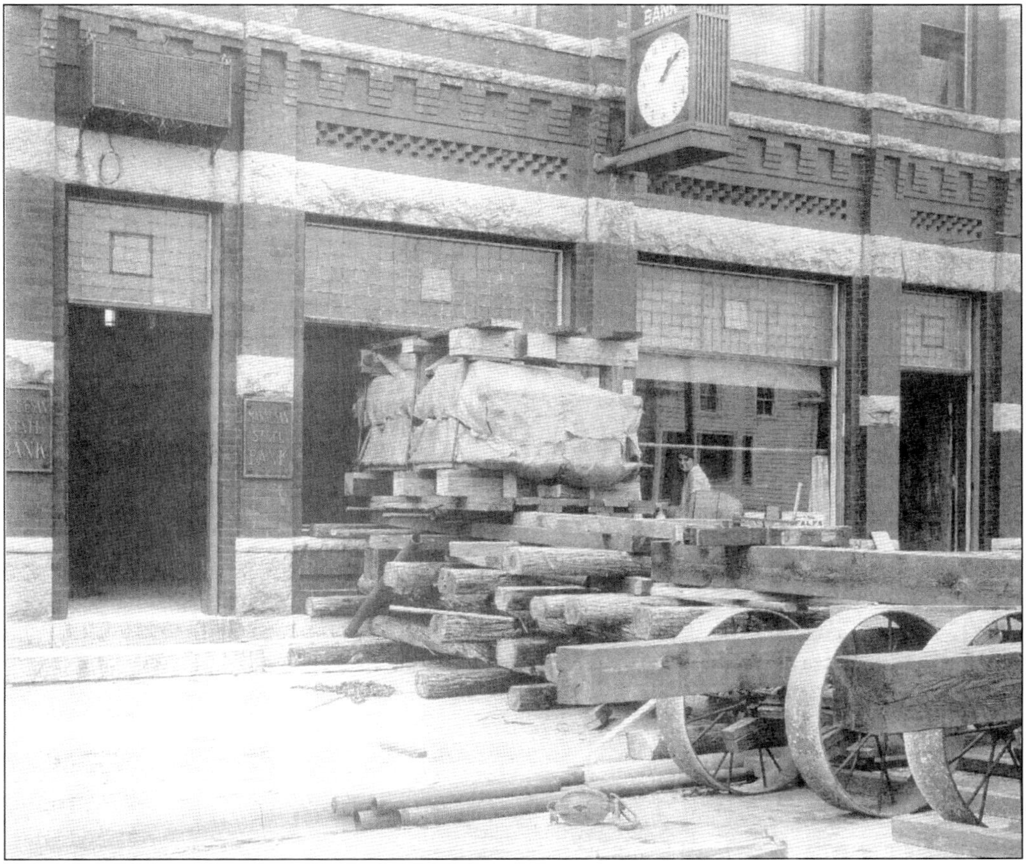

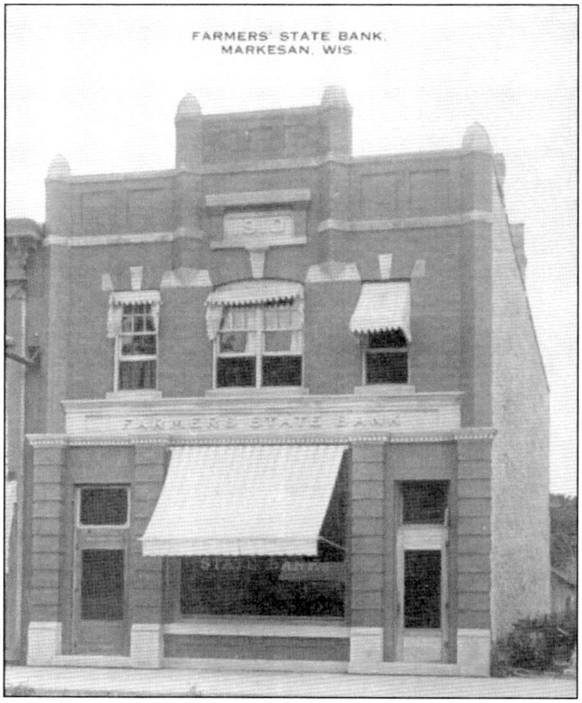

The Farmers State Bank was established on January 20, 1910, under the direction of Henry Friday. This June 23, 1915, photograph shows the front of the main office on Bridge Street. The bank was relocated to its present site on the corner of High and Water Streets in 1969. A new building was constructed to allow for more space for services and parking.

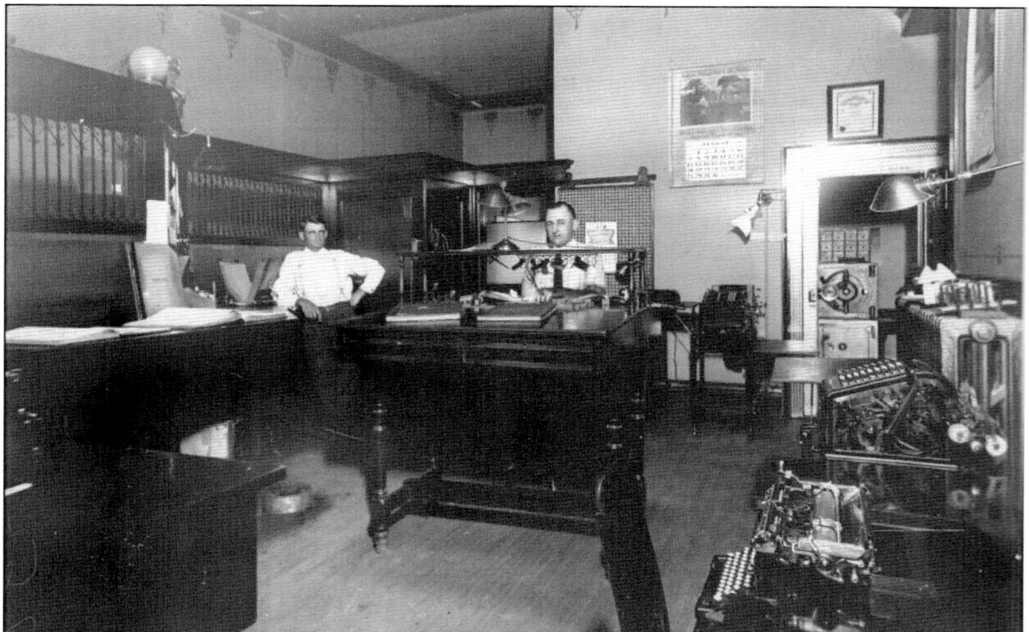

This picture, taken sometime in late 1920s, shows the interior of Farmers State Bank. The men standing in the bank are Harley Dillie and Hugh Miller. Dillie started his career at the bank in 1919 and ended his career in 1943. Miller started working at the Farmers State Bank in 1924 and concluded his time there in 1929.

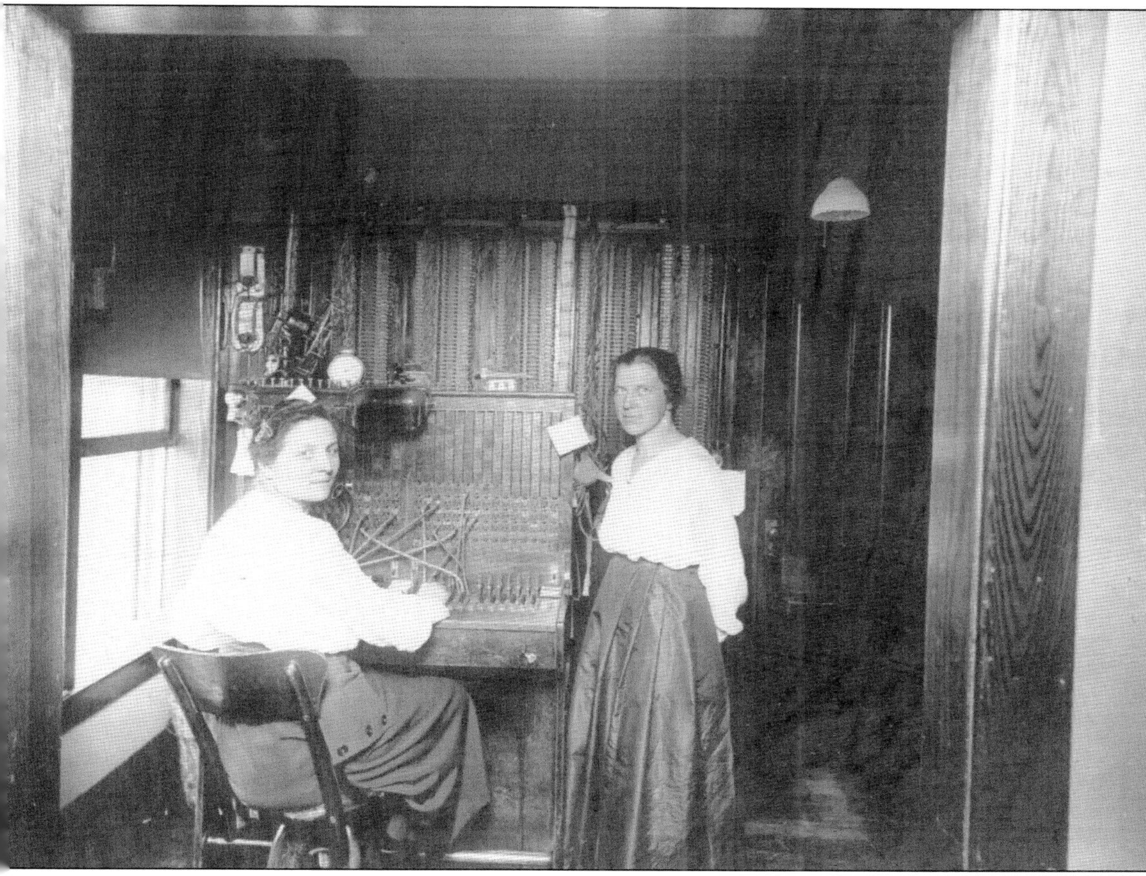

This undated photograph shows two women working as operators for Markesan Telephone Company switchboard. The woman seated is identified as Evelyn Lieske. Her job would have included putting calls through to people in town or transferring calls to the correct out-of-town lines. Being a telephone operator was a common job for women; Lieske was one of many Markesan ladies to work with the company.

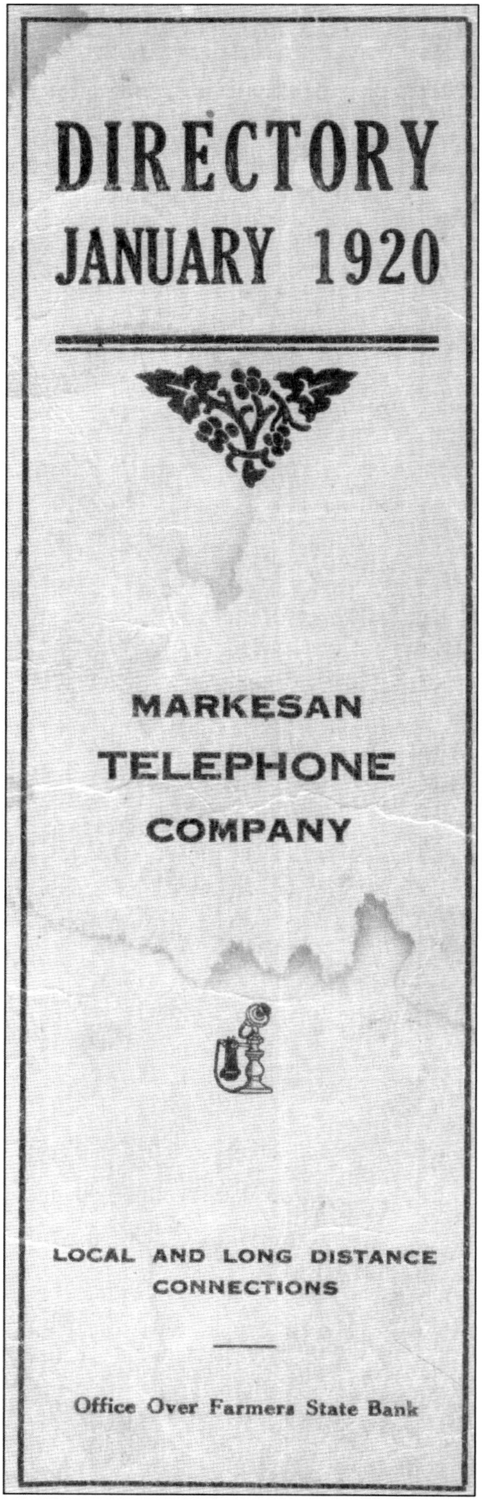

This 1920 phone directory for the Markesan Telephone Company gives the rules, regulations, and rates as well as the names of all the area residents subscribed to the phone service. The office for the telephone service was located in the top office of the Farmers State Bank on Bridge Street. The manager of the company was Harry Price, and the chief operator was Lone Evans. Phone calls were limited to five minutes and could not be made between the hours of 10:00 p.m. and 5:00 a.m. The monthly telephone rate for residents in town line was $2, and a monthly rural line was $5.15 for three months.

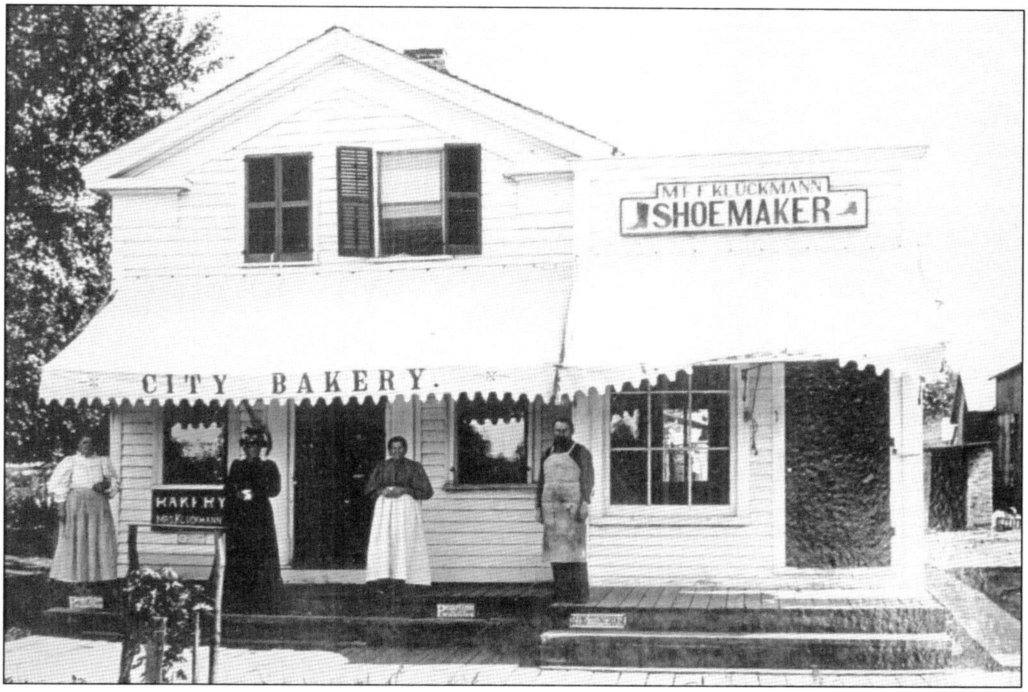

Ferdinand and Louise Kluckman were local business owners in the early days of Markesan. Ferdinand ran a shoe repair shop that was connected to his wife's bakery. Both were German immigrants who eventually made their way to Markesan where they resided and operated businesses. Their daughter-in-law Laura (Heidel) Kluckman would later operate Kluckman Millinery, selling women's hats and fine clothing.

On July 22, 1881, a boy named George Larke started his own newspaper at the age of 12 called the *Markesan Herald*. The first newspaper was eight inches by five inches, and George even carved the wood himself to create the headlines. This 1897 picture shows the *Markesan Herald* printing office under the ownership of C.W. Ludtke. The newspaper would continue to report the news of the community of Markesan until 1996.

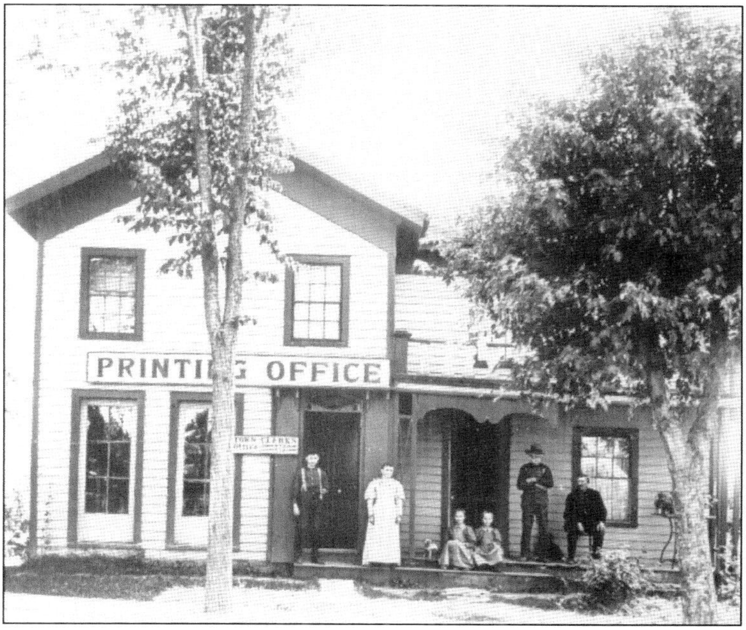

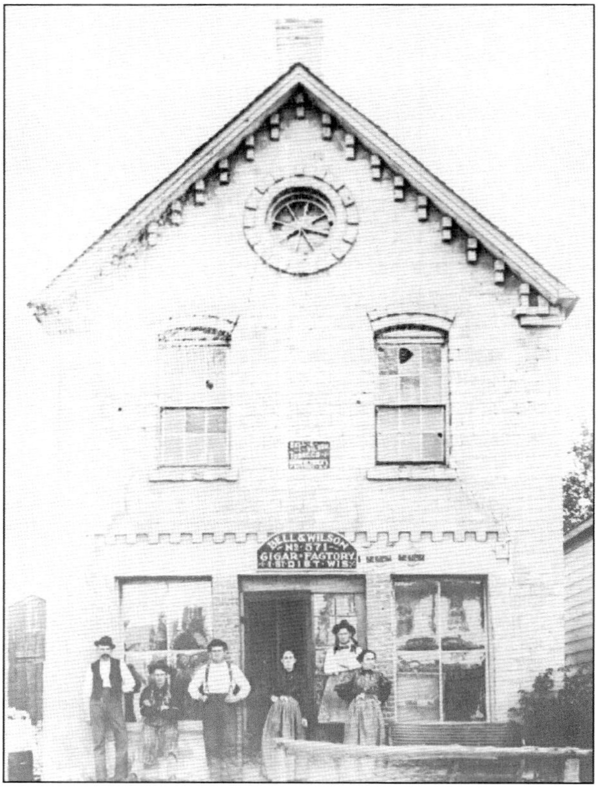

Markesan had its own cigar factory in the early days, as this 1897 picture shows. Gust Hoffman started the factory in this building located on East John Street. In 1908, Clarence G. Lockwood joined the business and eventually took over ownership. When Lockwood ran the business, he relocated to Bridge Street, where he operated his cigar factory in the back of a building and had a retail store in the front.

This 1900 photograph shows the newly built Butenhoff Black Shop. It was owned and operated by Herman Butenhoff (second from the left). His two-story shop served as his business on the ground floor and living quarters on the second floor. Butenhoff was skilled in horse shoeing as well as carriage repair, and he also sold farm equipment. The old blacksmith building was demolished in 1967.

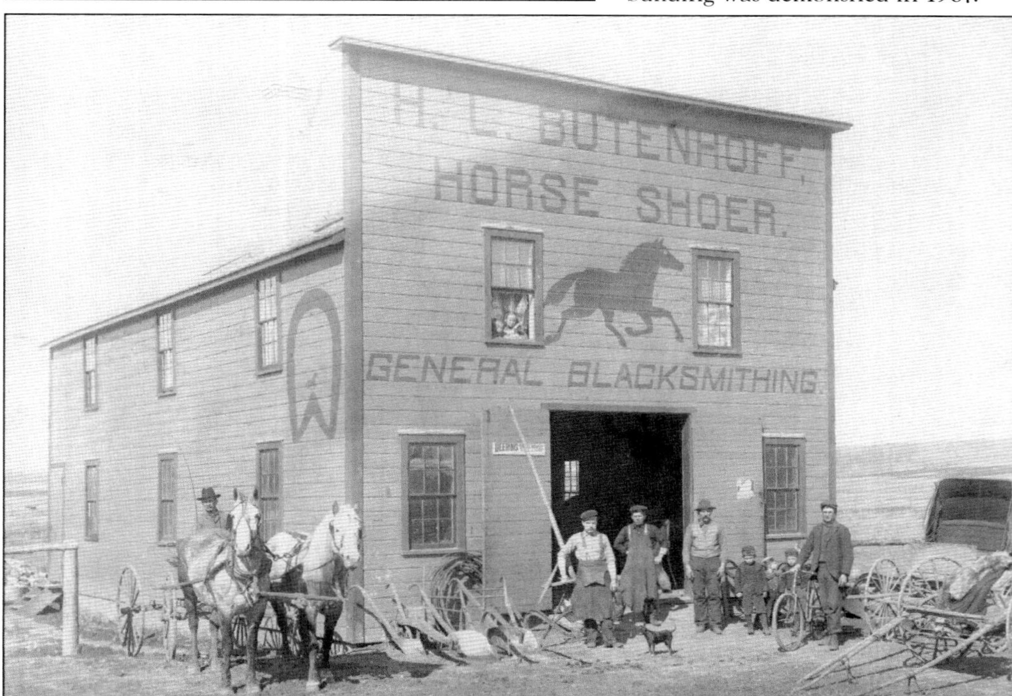

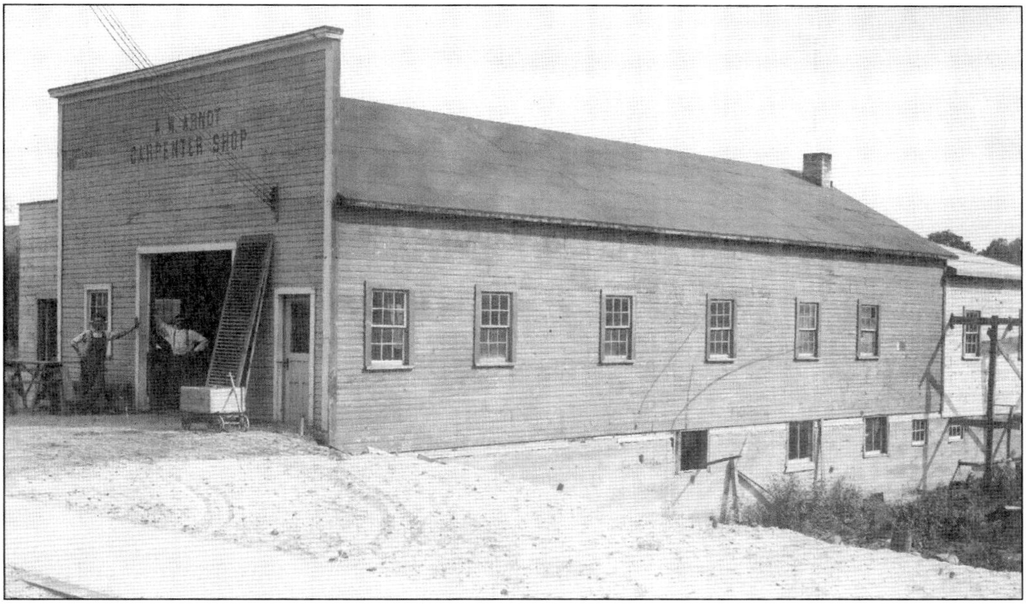

Pictured here is August Arndt's carpentry shop. He was born in Germany in 1873, and his family moved to the United States shortly after. He eventually found his home in Markesan around 1900 and then set up a business. Many buildings in Markesan and the surrounding areas were erected by Arndt, and it was jokingly said that he built Markesan. This structure was situated on the present site of the Grand River Valley Museum and home to the Markesan Historical Society.

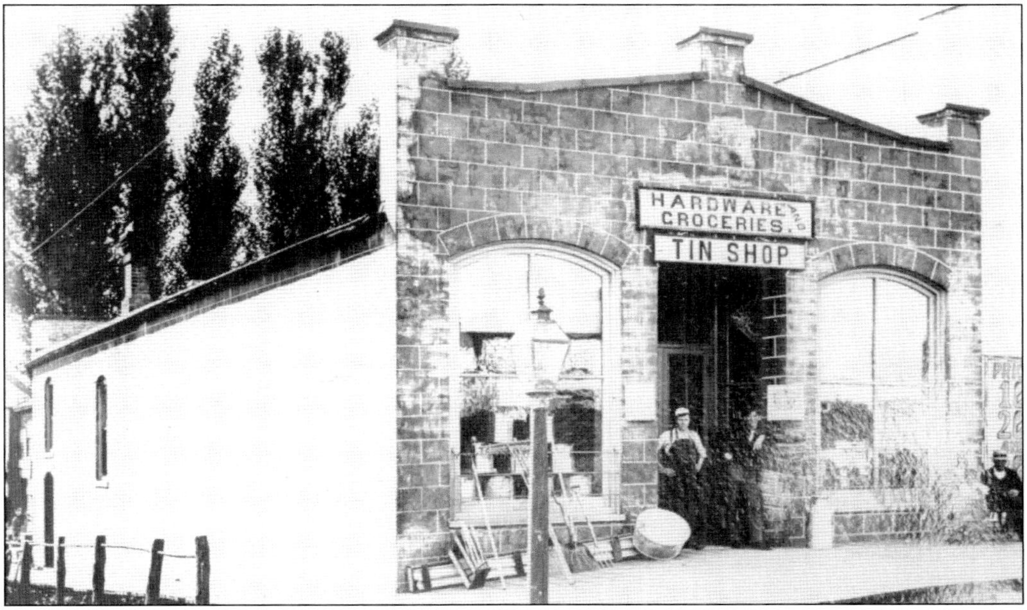

This 1897 photograph shows the hardware store of Rumsey Evans. Evans started his career as a cheese maker; later, he operated a stable until finally opening his own hardware store. He also served as a sheriff in Green Lake County. His son Thomas Evans, born in Markesan in 1876, managed the hardware store. Evans Hardware Store was located on northwest corner of John and Bridge Streets. Today, Markesan Auto Home and Farm occupies the building.

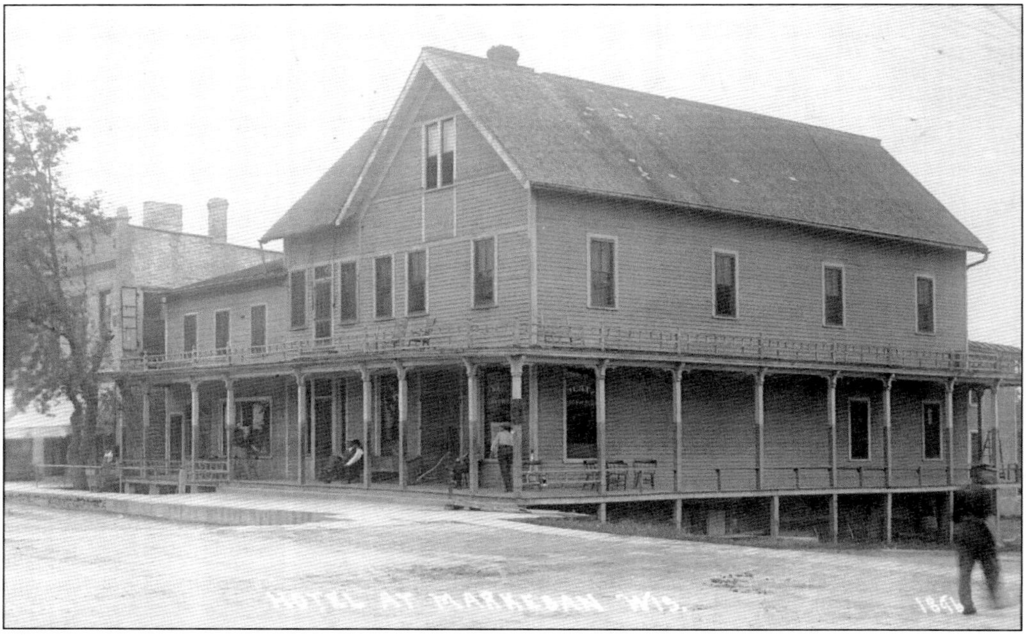

The Yosemite House was a landmark in downtown Markesan. The hotel was operated by George McCracken and his wife. It was originally named McCracken Hotel, but a trip to the Yosemite Valley in California awed the McCrackens, and they named their magnificent hotel after it. A taxi service ran from the train station to the hotel for travelers. The hotel met its fate in 1918 when a fire broke out, and the building was destroyed.

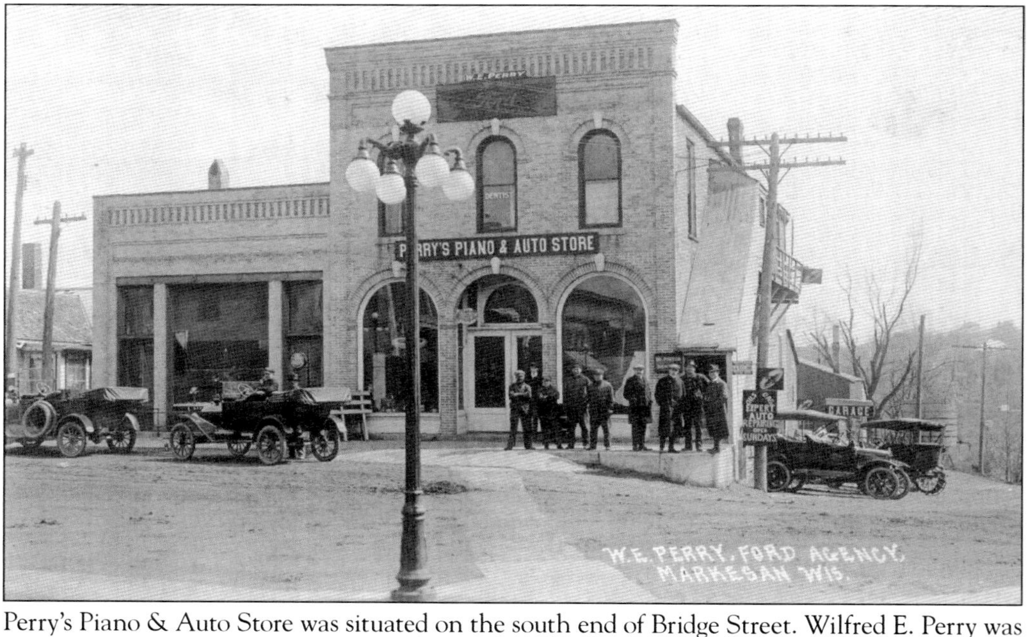

Perry's Piano & Auto Store was situated on the south end of Bridge Street. Wilfred E. Perry was the proprietor of the store. One part of it featured new Ford automobiles on the show floor; under the store was a garage where customers could bring their cars to be serviced or repaired. The other section of his store was a showroom of brand-new pianos.

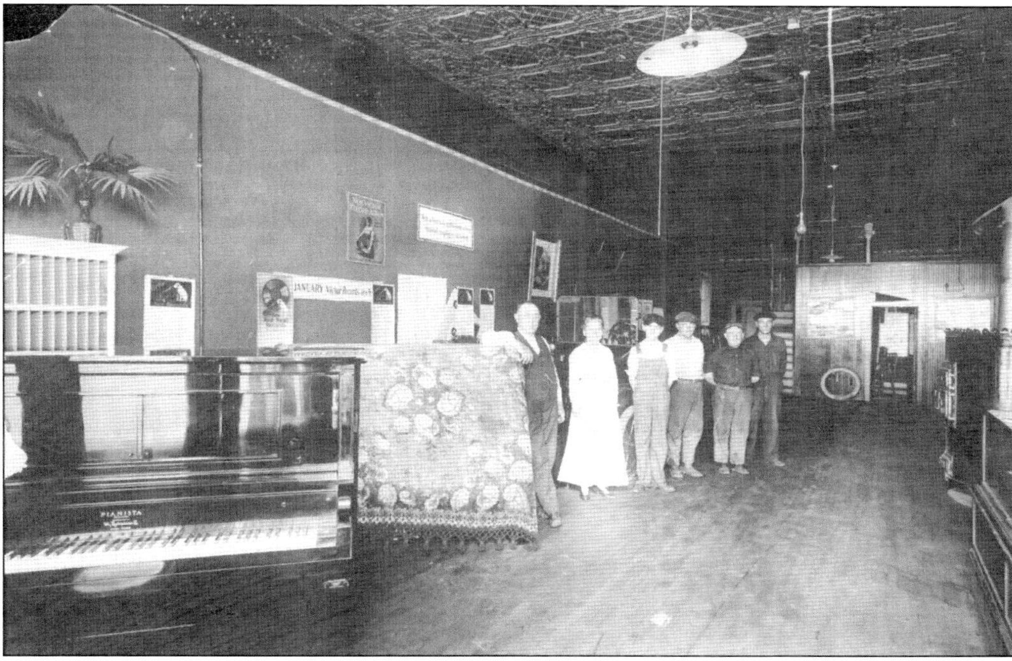

This undated picture shows the interior of Perry Piano & Auto Store, where a Pianista piano is seen in the foreground. Piano lessons were also offered at Wilfred Perry's business. New Ford automobiles are seen in the background behind the staff. Perry also sold Harley-Davidson motorcycles and Victor-Victrola phonographs.

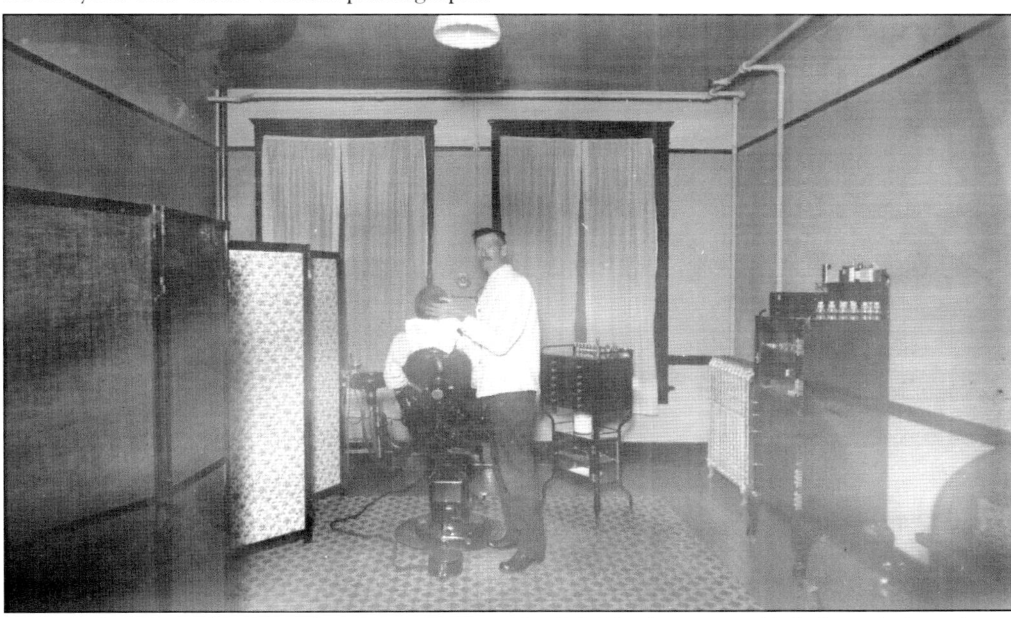

Here, a dentist is shown working on a patient. Dr. E.J. Hughes opened Markesan's first dentist office in 1880. Dr. Hughes studied dentistry in Le Seuer, Minnesota, before opening his practice in Markesan. He had offices in both Markesan and Fox Lake. He made monthly visits to the area communities of Kingston and Randolph as well.

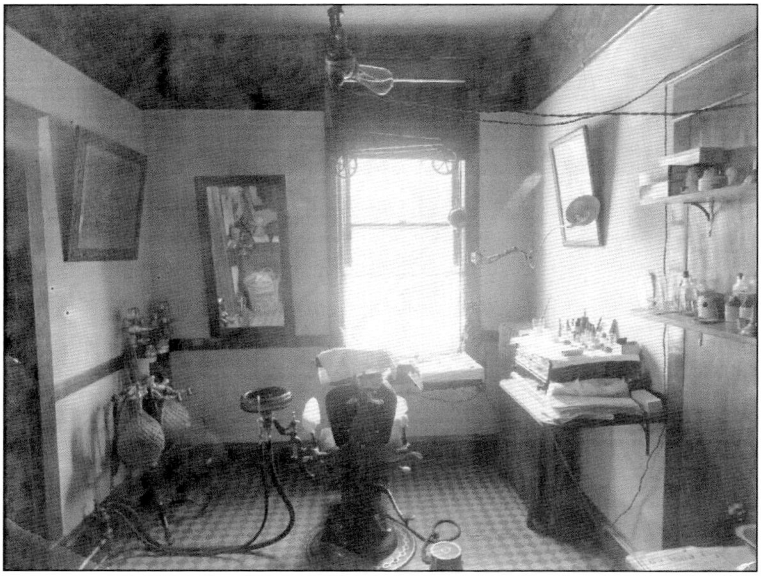

This is the interior of the dental exam room. In the left foreground, the water lines for the rinsing fountain can be seen. Next to that appears to be the air tanks, used to operate the pneumatic tools used by the dentist. On the right, medicines and cleaners are sitting on the shelves, and the swiveling exam light can be seen attached to the window frame.

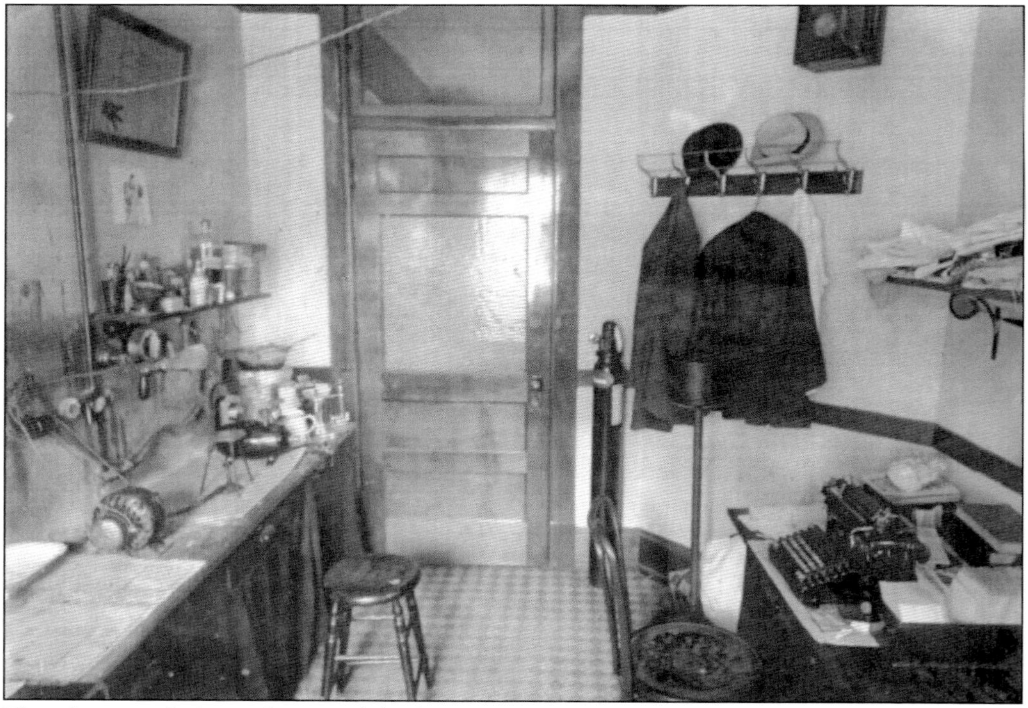

This photograph shows the rest of the dentist's exam room and his office. In the left background are the substances to concoct painkillers and anesthetics for patients. An electric motor can be seen in the left foreground, used for sharpening dental instruments. On the right is the dentist's desk, where his typewriter and record system were kept. The dentist office was located in different places in Markesan throughout the years; it was once above Perry's Piano & Auto Store as well as the Markesan State Bank.

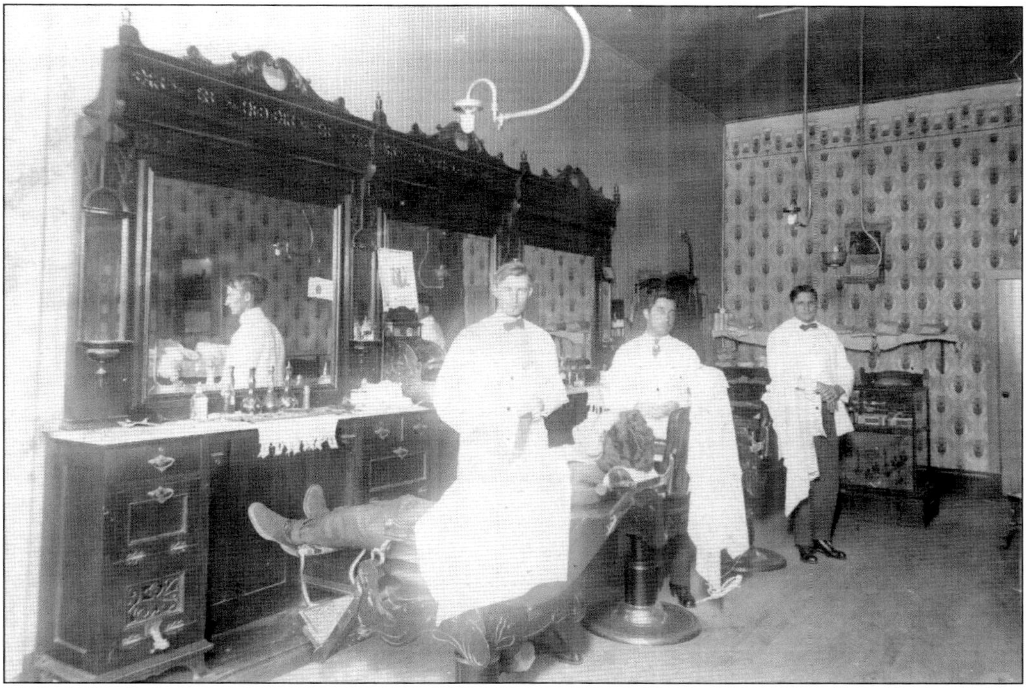

An undated photograph shows the interior of Evans Barber Shop, which was operated by Edmund L. Evans. Evans was born in Markesan in 1873, and upon completing high school, he learned the barber's trade and opened his own business in town in 1897. He continued his trade until his retirement in 1946.

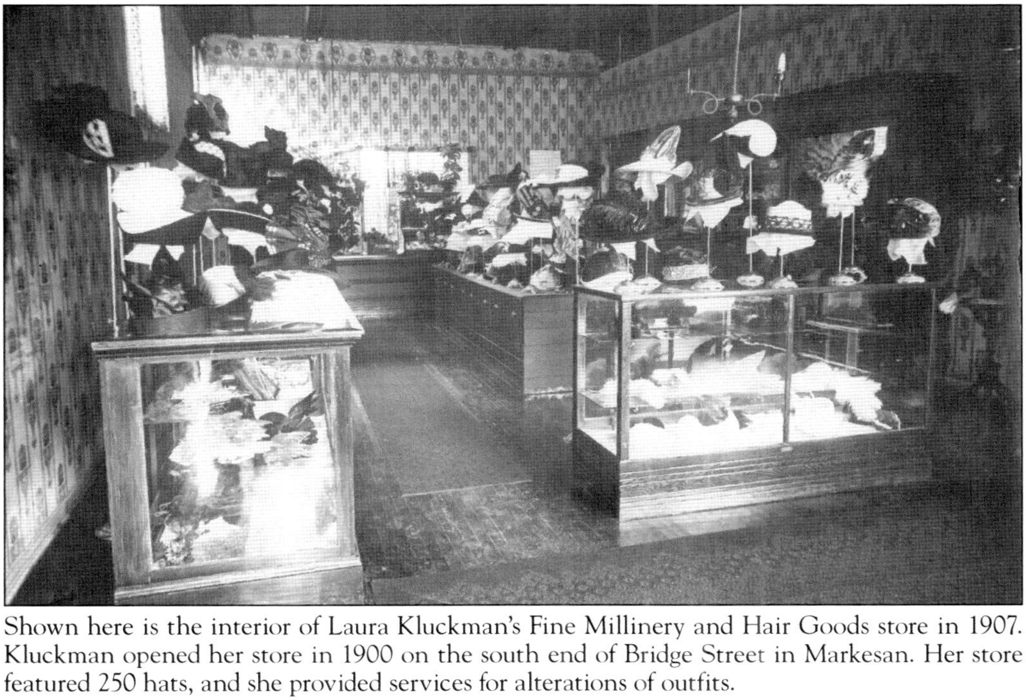

Shown here is the interior of Laura Kluckman's Fine Millinery and Hair Goods store in 1907. Kluckman opened her store in 1900 on the south end of Bridge Street in Markesan. Her store featured 250 hats, and she provided services for alterations of outfits.

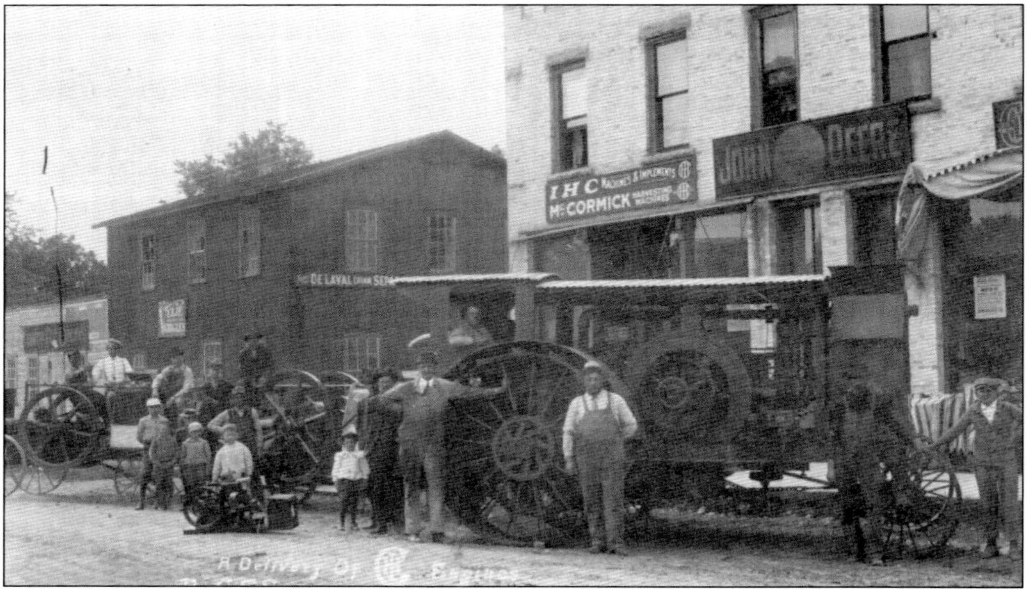

This 1910 picture shows the delivery of two brand-new steam engines delivered to Schraeder Motor Company. Charles F. Schraeder opened a hardware store in Markesan in 1902, and shortly after he began selling Chevrolet automobiles and International Harvester agricultural equipment. His business was handed over to his son Austin Schraeder upon his retirement 1945. The business was located on the northeast corner of John and Main Streets.

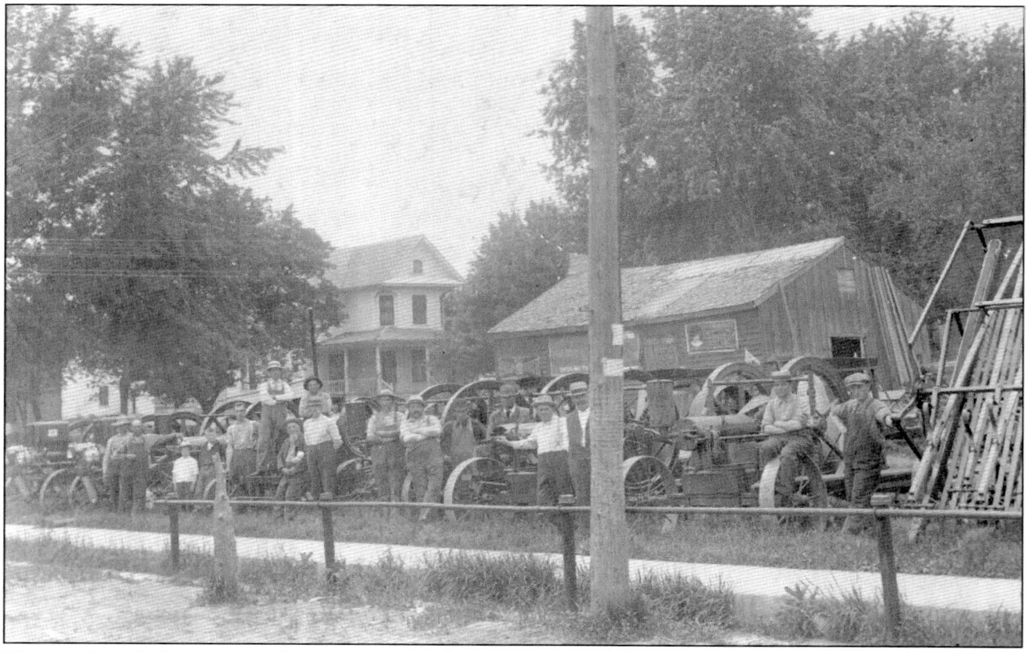

This undated photograph shows the agricultural equipment lot of C.F. Schraeder Motor Company. The lot was situated to the west of the main building on John Street. The implement division of Schraeder's business was one of the first in Markesan. He offered a full line of International Harvester steam engines and tractors, McCormick harvesting machines, and John Deere implements.

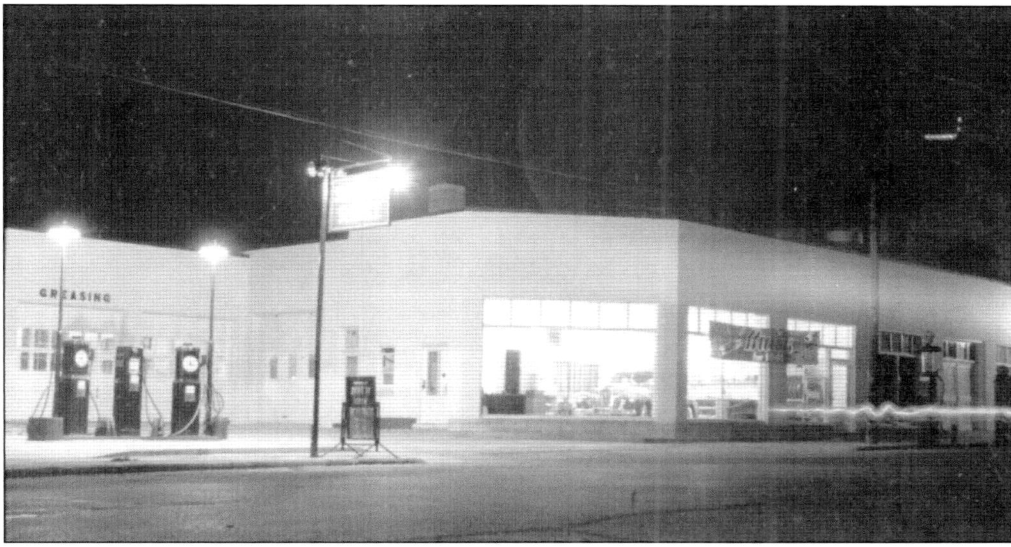

An early 1940s picture shows a new addition to Schraeder Motor Company. Austin Schraeder partnered with his father's business in 1936, and later, he purchased the John Street building from his father in 1939. The dealership was moved to a new building on the southwest corner of John Street and Margaret Street in 1965. Schraeder would continue to operate as a Chevrolet and Buick dealership until his retirement in the early 1970s.

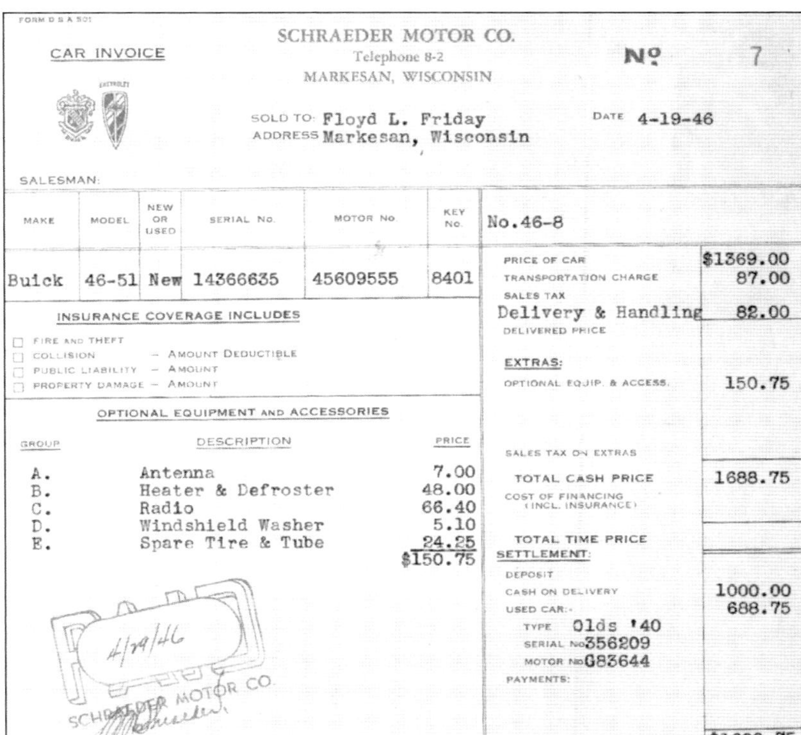

FORM D S A 501

CAR INVOICE

SCHRAEDER MOTOR CO.
Telephone 8-2
MARKESAN, WISCONSIN

Nº 7

SOLD TO: Floyd L. Friday
ADDRESS Markesan, Wisconsin

DATE 4-19-46

SALESMAN:

MAKE	MODEL	NEW OR USED	SERIAL No.	MOTOR No.	KEY No.
Buick	46-51	New	14366635	45609555	8401

No.46-8

INSURANCE COVERAGE INCLUDES

- FIRE AND THEFT
- COLLISION — AMOUNT DEDUCTIBLE
- PUBLIC LIABILITY — AMOUNT
- PROPERTY DAMAGE — AMOUNT

OPTIONAL EQUIPMENT AND ACCESSORIES

GROUP	DESCRIPTION	PRICE
A.	Antenna	7.00
B.	Heater & Defroster	48.00
C.	Radio	66.40
D.	Windshield Washer	5.10
E.	Spare Tire & Tube	24.25
		$150.75

PRICE OF CAR	$1369.00
TRANSPORTATION CHARGE	87.00
SALES TAX	
Delivery & Handling	82.00
DELIVERED PRICE	
EXTRAS: OPTIONAL EQUIP. & ACCESS.	150.75
SALES TAX ON EXTRAS	
TOTAL CASH PRICE	1688.75
COST OF FINANCING (INCL. INSURANCE)	
TOTAL TIME PRICE	
SETTLEMENT: DEPOSIT	
CASH ON DELIVERY	1000.00
USED CAR: TYPE Olds '40 SERIAL No. 356209 MOTOR No. G83644	688.75
PAYMENTS:	
TOTAL	$1688.75

4/19/46
SCHRAEDER MOTOR CO.

This invoice, dated April 19, 1946, is a sales receipt for a new Buick sold to Floyd Friday for $1,688.75. Friday bought his new Buick from Schraeder Motor Company with a trade-in. The slip indicates that Friday traded a 1940 Oldsmobile for $688.75 and gave $1,000 out of pocket for the new car.

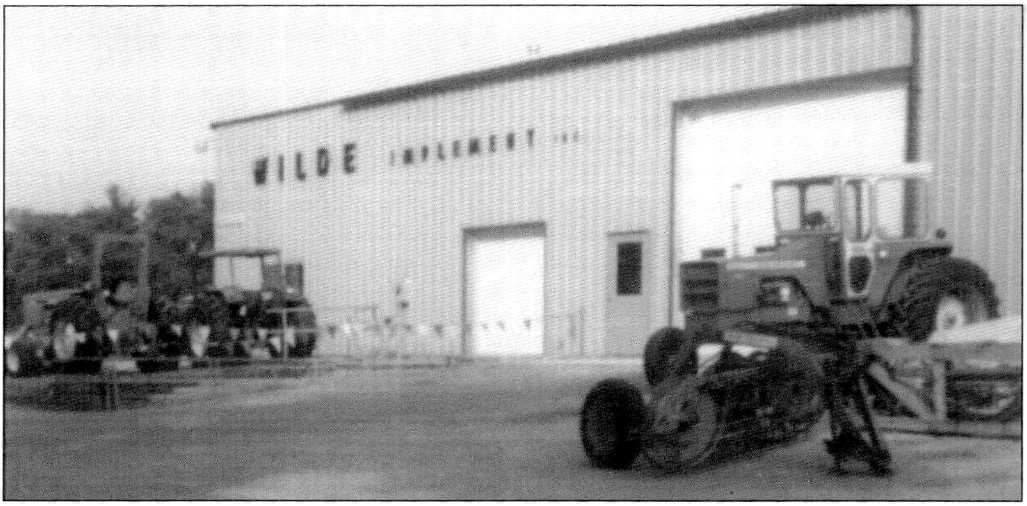

Because of the large amount of farming in the area, many implement dealerships opened in Markesan with the advent of the tractor. Seen here is the exterior of Wilde Implement Inc. for the grand opening of its new store on April 6, 1978. The dealership had once been located on John Street near the downtown area, but the need for more room required relocating and rebuilding just out of town on Highway 44. (Courtesy of the Wilde family.)

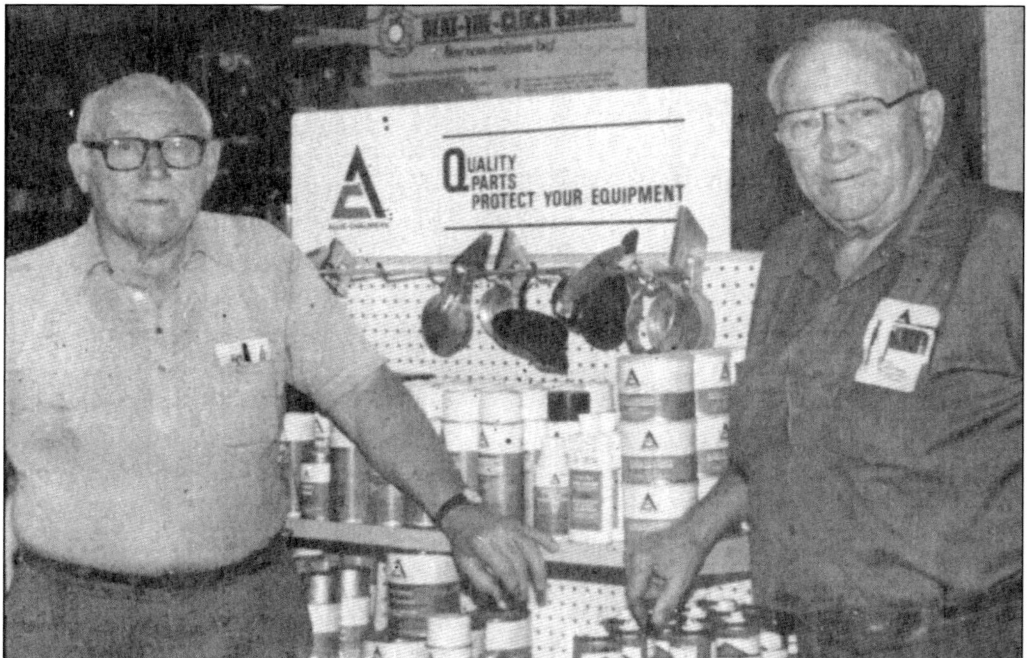

Pictured here are Raymond Wilde (left) and his brother Leslie Wilde in their dealership. The two brothers entered the farm-machinery business with their father, Elmer Wilde, in 1945 upon their return from military service in World War II. It became known as E.W. Wilde and Sons when the brothers formed a partnership with their father. The business was specifically an Allis-Chalmers brand dealership in the beginning, but over the years other brands were added. The family-run business served Markesan-area farmers for almost 50 years before closing in 1986.

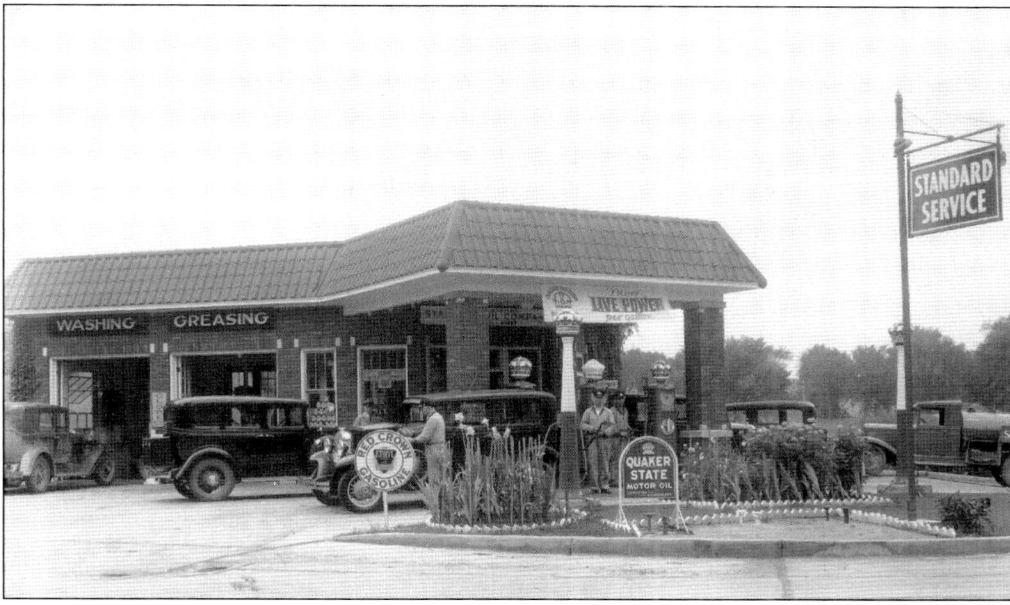

The Zanto fueling station was built by Gustave Zanto and was operated for many years by his sons. Their station offered fueling services as well as a garage for repair and maintenance. This 1931 photograph shows the busy activity at the fueling station. The business was located on the southeast corner of Margaret and John Streets.

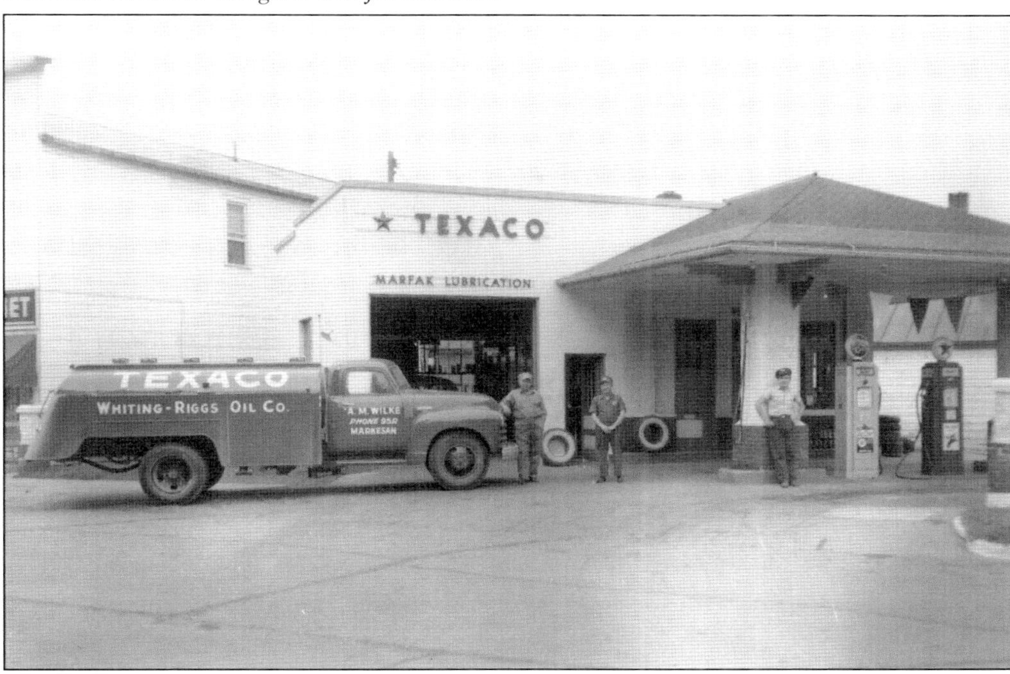

Heine's Texaco was owned and operated by Henry Schultz. Schultz bought the station from Herb Mohr on May 19, 1947, and operated it until his retirement in 1973. The filling station was located on the corner of John and High Streets. The men pictured here are, from left to right, Amos Wilke, Henry Schultz, and Norm Schweder.

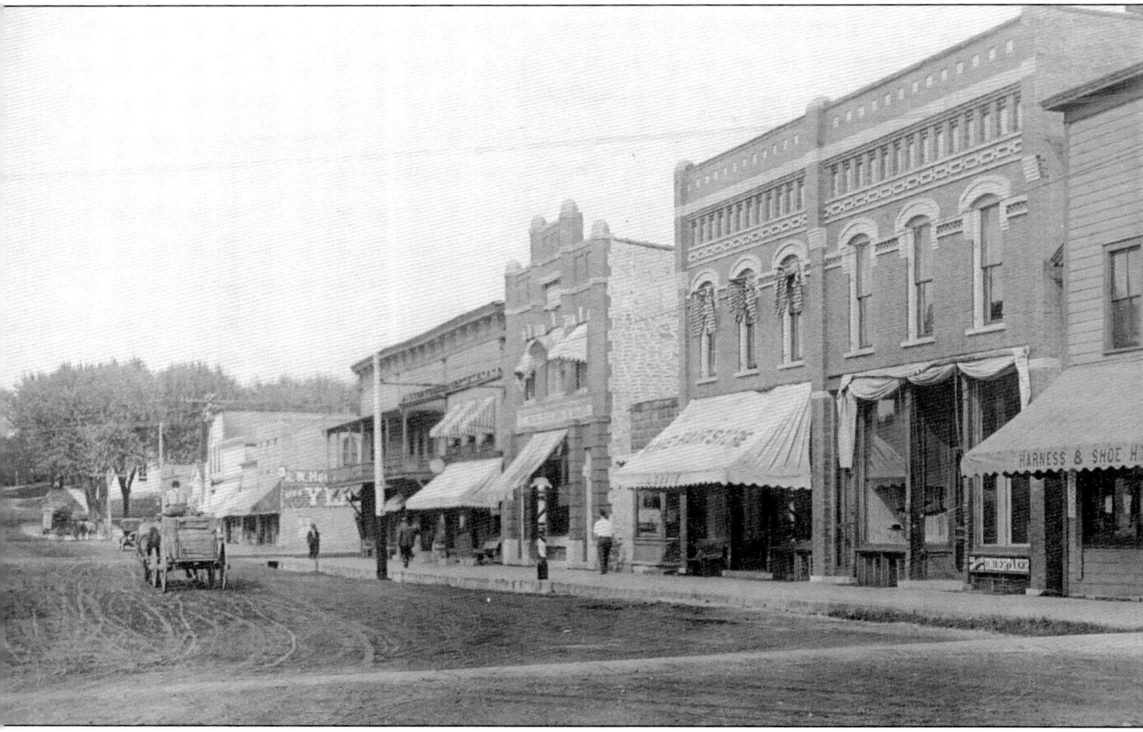

Markesan's downtown area of Bridge Street is the symbol of Markesan trade and economic activity. This 1910s photograph shows the businesses on the southeast end of Bridge Street. The businesses identified are, from left to right, a saloon (operated by Edward Geidel), the Henninger Jewelry Store, Farmers State Bank, The Fair Store (operated by Jacob Davis), Spitzer Millinery (owned by Emma Spitzer), H.R. Kopitzke Undertaker, and the Harness and Shoe Hospital. Though these businesses have since closed or moved, the buildings where they once operated still stand to signify the flourishing commercial district of Markesan's past.

Five

Railroad and Industry

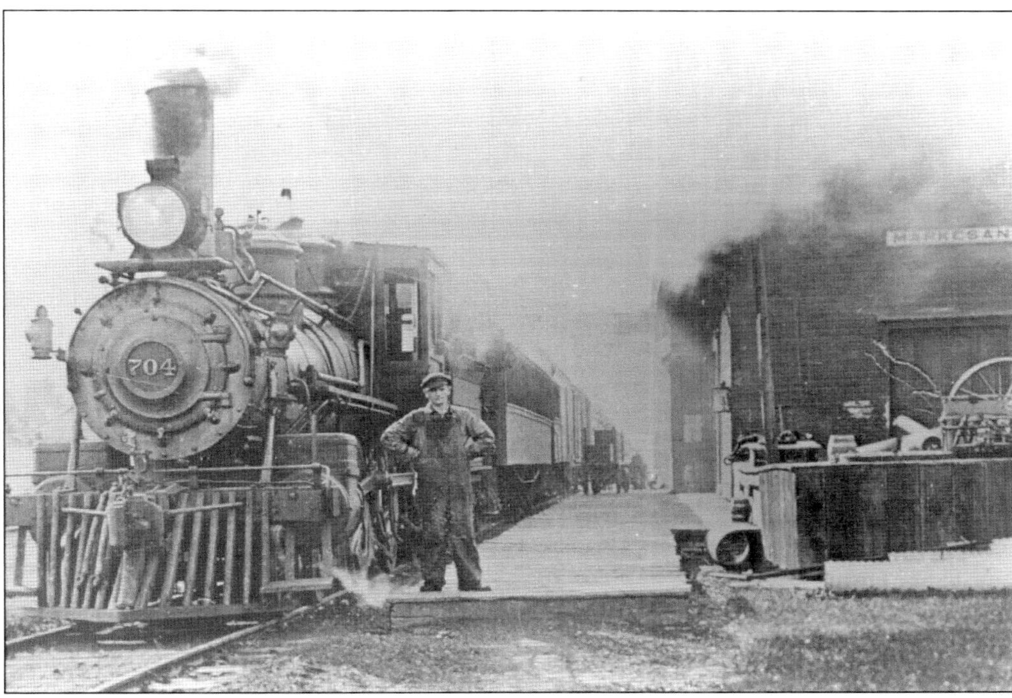

The addition of a railroad spur line coming to Markesan ensured the growth and prosperity of the community. It established connections of the markets in Markesan to the rest of the country. It also produced a line of transportation to allow the movement of people in and out of town. This undated picture shows railroad worker Bradley Ruback posing by engine No. 704 at the Markesan railroad station.

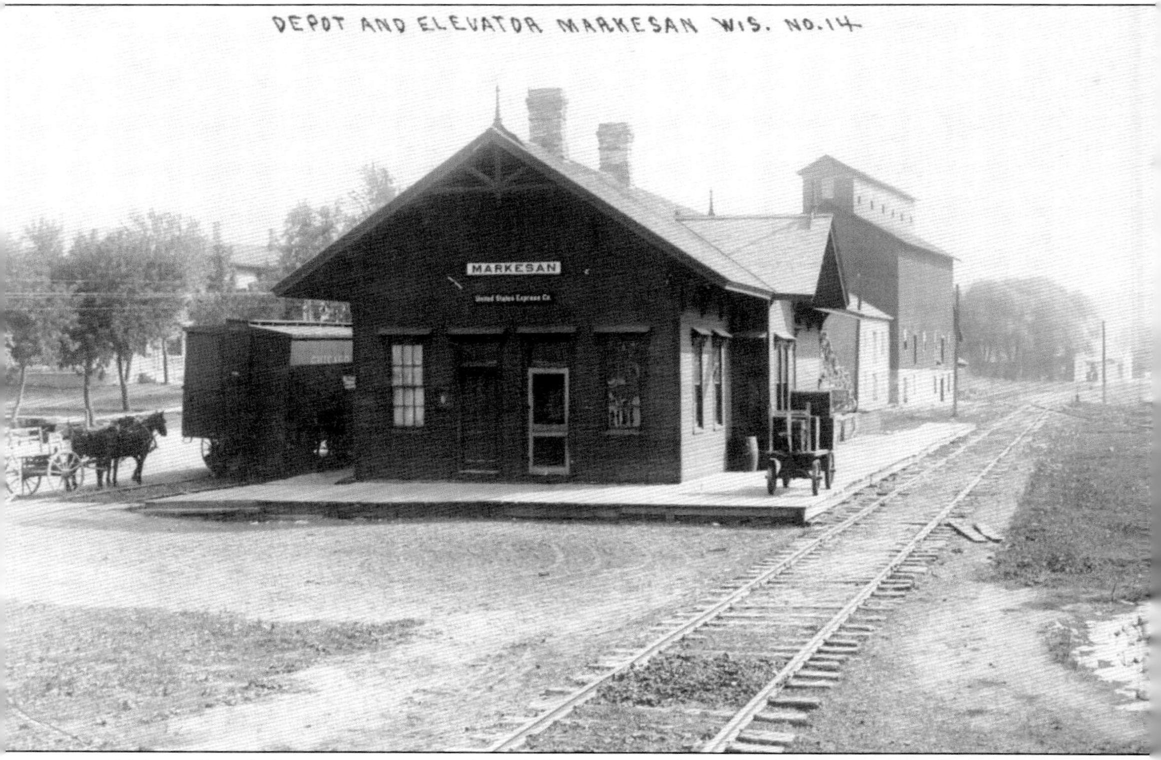

This undated photograph shows the Markesan train depot looking west on John Street. Behind it is the M.B.M. Peacock Mill. Getting the railroad line to Markesan was no easy task. James Densmoor Sr., who headed the project, was relentless in his pursuit, and in 1881 he and John Laper found granite in an area east of Markesan known as Pine Bluff. In 1882, the granite proved to be valuable, and a rail line was established to the quarry operations. Densmoor struck a deal with the Chicago, Milwaukee, and St. Paul Railroad Company, and a railroad ran to Markesan by the end of the year. By 1884, trains were making regular trips in and out of town.

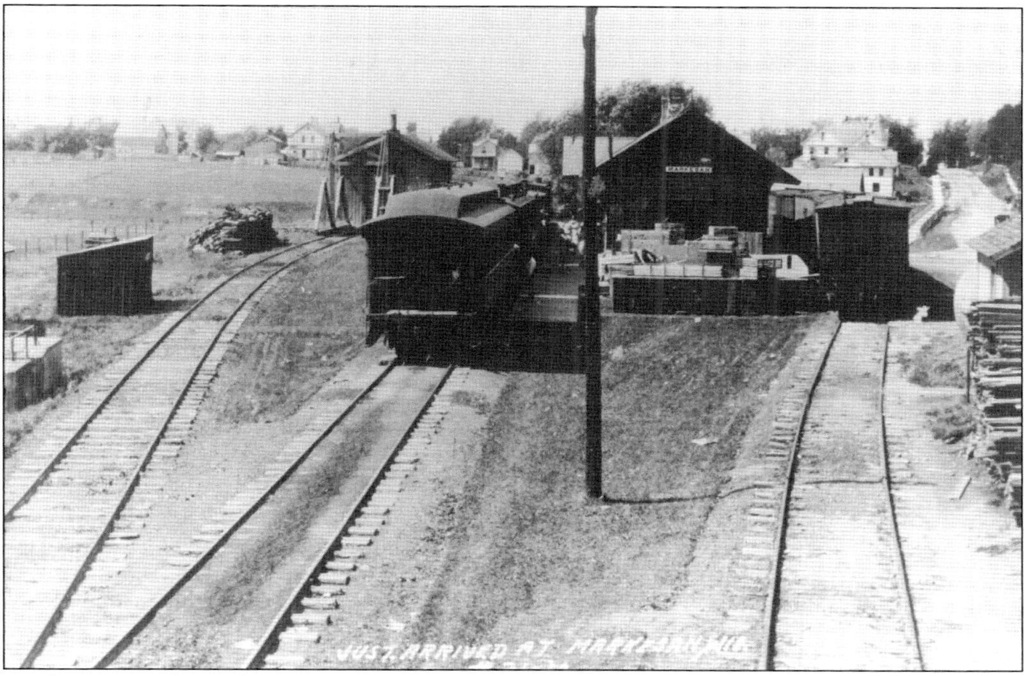

Markesan was the end of the line, and the engine would have to be turned around for its trip back. When the train arrived at the station, the engine uncoupled from the train and was driven to a switch track with a turntable. The engine was turned around and was then re-coupled to the train to be sent back.

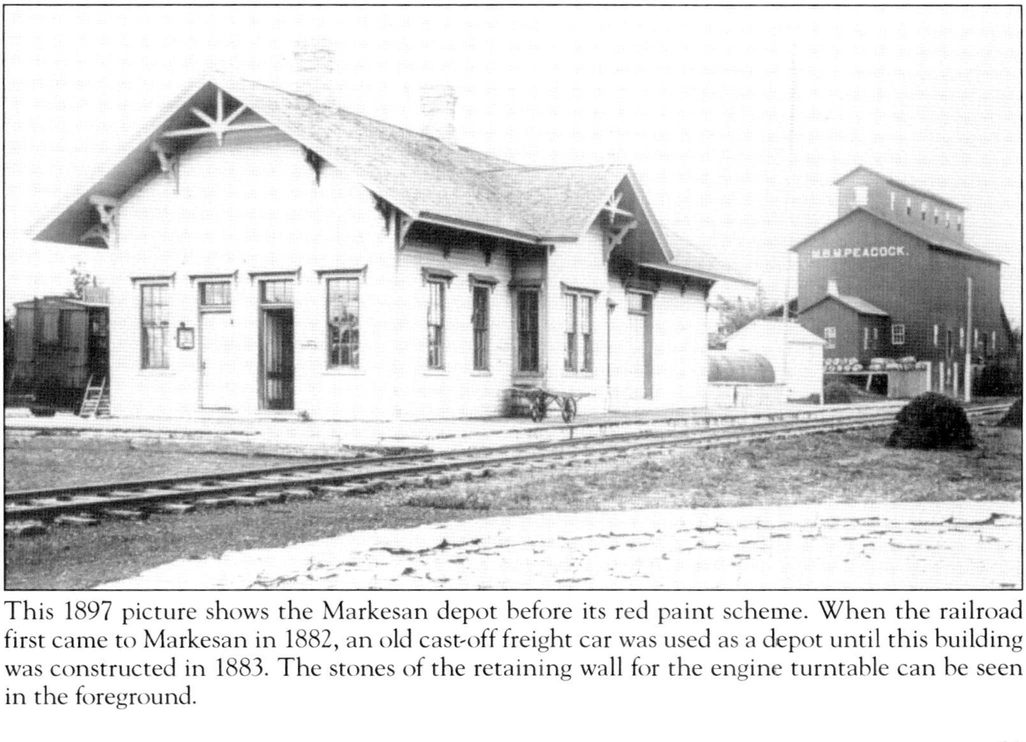

This 1897 picture shows the Markesan depot before its red paint scheme. When the railroad first came to Markesan in 1882, an old cast-off freight car was used as a depot until this building was constructed in 1883. The stones of the retaining wall for the engine turntable can be seen in the foreground.

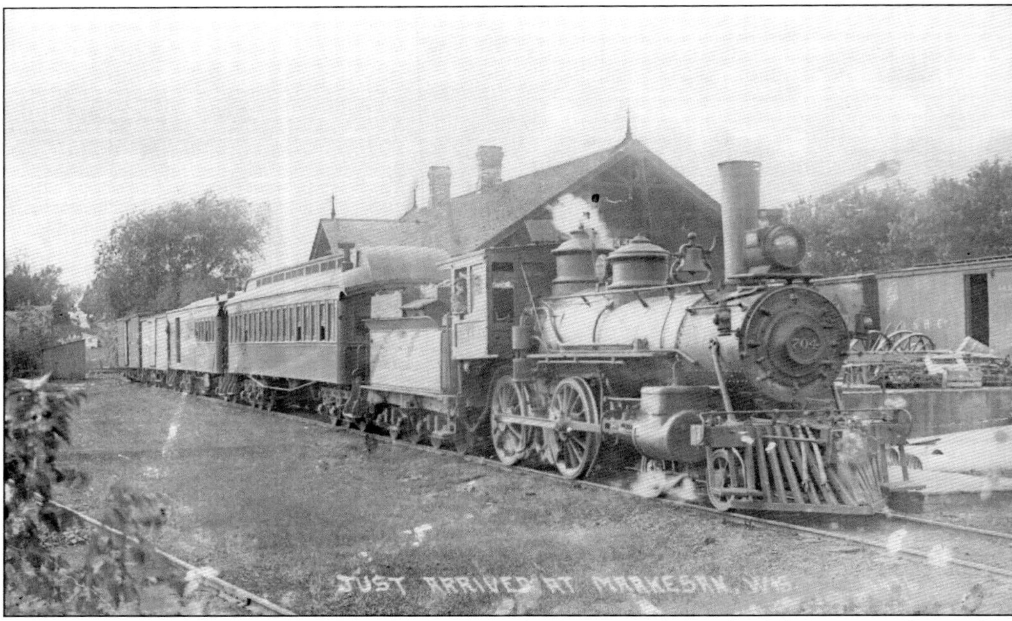

Here, engine No. 704 has been turned around and coupled to the back of the train and is ready to depart from Markesan. When the train was turned around at the Markesan station, the conductor would go through the passenger cars and flip the benches around so passengers would not have to ride backwards on the way back to the main line.

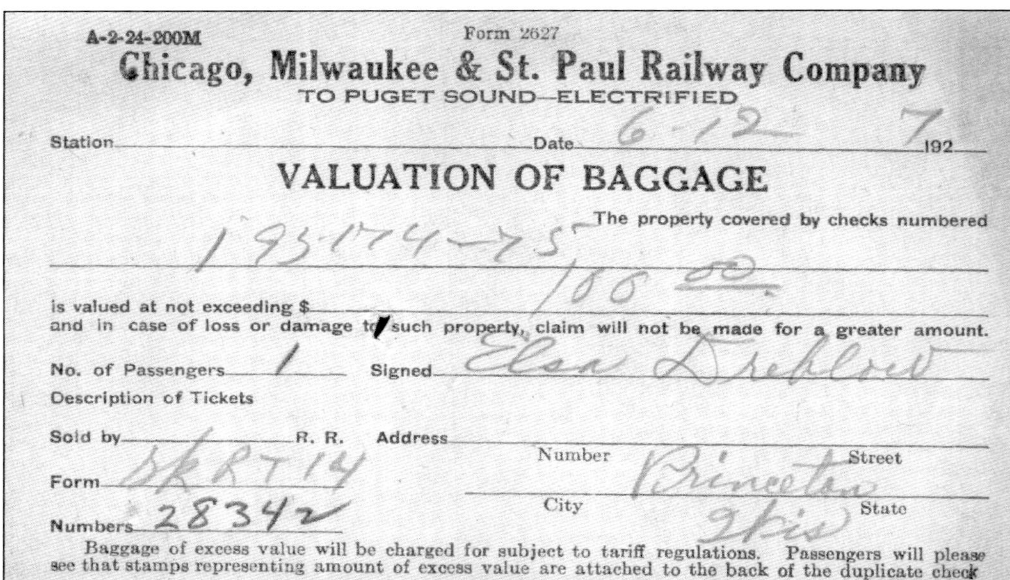

A-2-24-200M

Form 2627

Chicago, Milwaukee & St. Paul Railway Company

TO PUGET SOUND—ELECTRIFIED

Station ________ Date 6-12 192 7

VALUATION OF BAGGAGE

The property covered by checks numbered 193174-75

is valued at not exceeding $ 100.00

and in case of loss or damage to such property, claim will not be made for a greater amount.

No. of Passengers 1 Signed Elsa Dreblow

Description of Tickets

Sold by ________ R. R. Address ________

Number Street

Form SKRT 14 Princeton

City State

Numbers 28342 Wis

Baggage of excess value will be charged for subject to tariff regulations. Passengers will please see that stamps representing amount of excess value are attached to the back of the duplicate check

This baggage ticket, dated June 12, 1927, was issued at the Markesan railroad station, which assessed the value of the luggage that an Elsa Dreblow carried. Baggage was given a ticket with an address on it in case it was misplaced or damaged during the trip. This particular baggage was covered for $100 worth of damage.

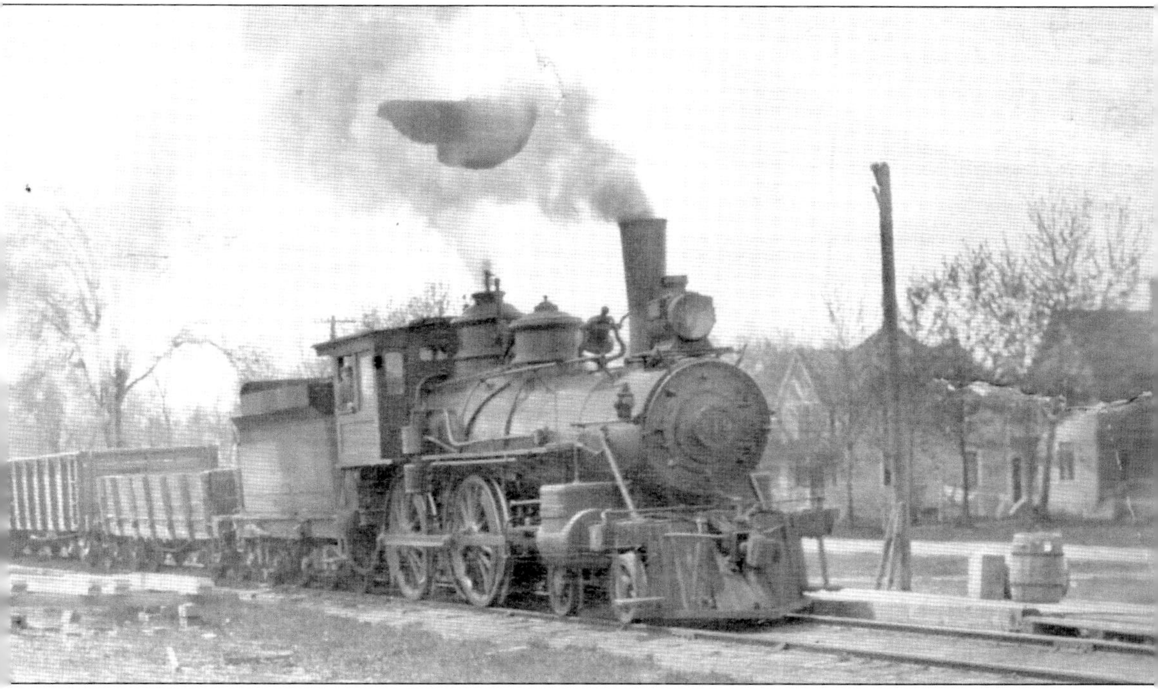

This undated photograph shows engine No. 519 on its way out of Markesan. The train looks as though it was hauling some sort of heavy cargo into town. Passenger cars can faintly be seen coupled at the rear of the train.

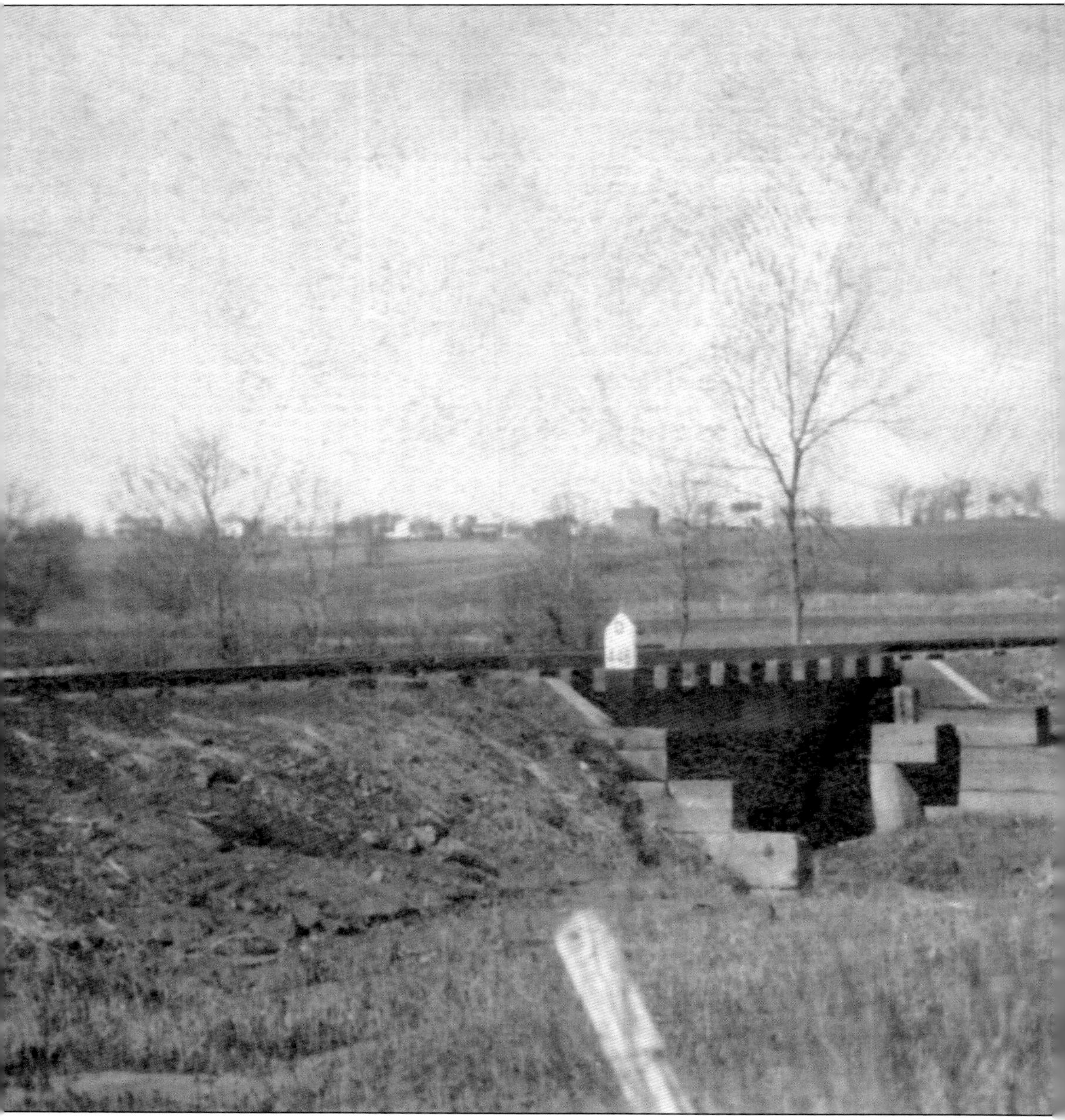

Pictured here is engine No. 519 on a passenger run on the Markesan rail line. When the line was finished, the *Brandon Times* reported, "The grand celebration of the opening of the Markesan railroad will take place . . . one of the features of the occasion will be the presentation of a $250

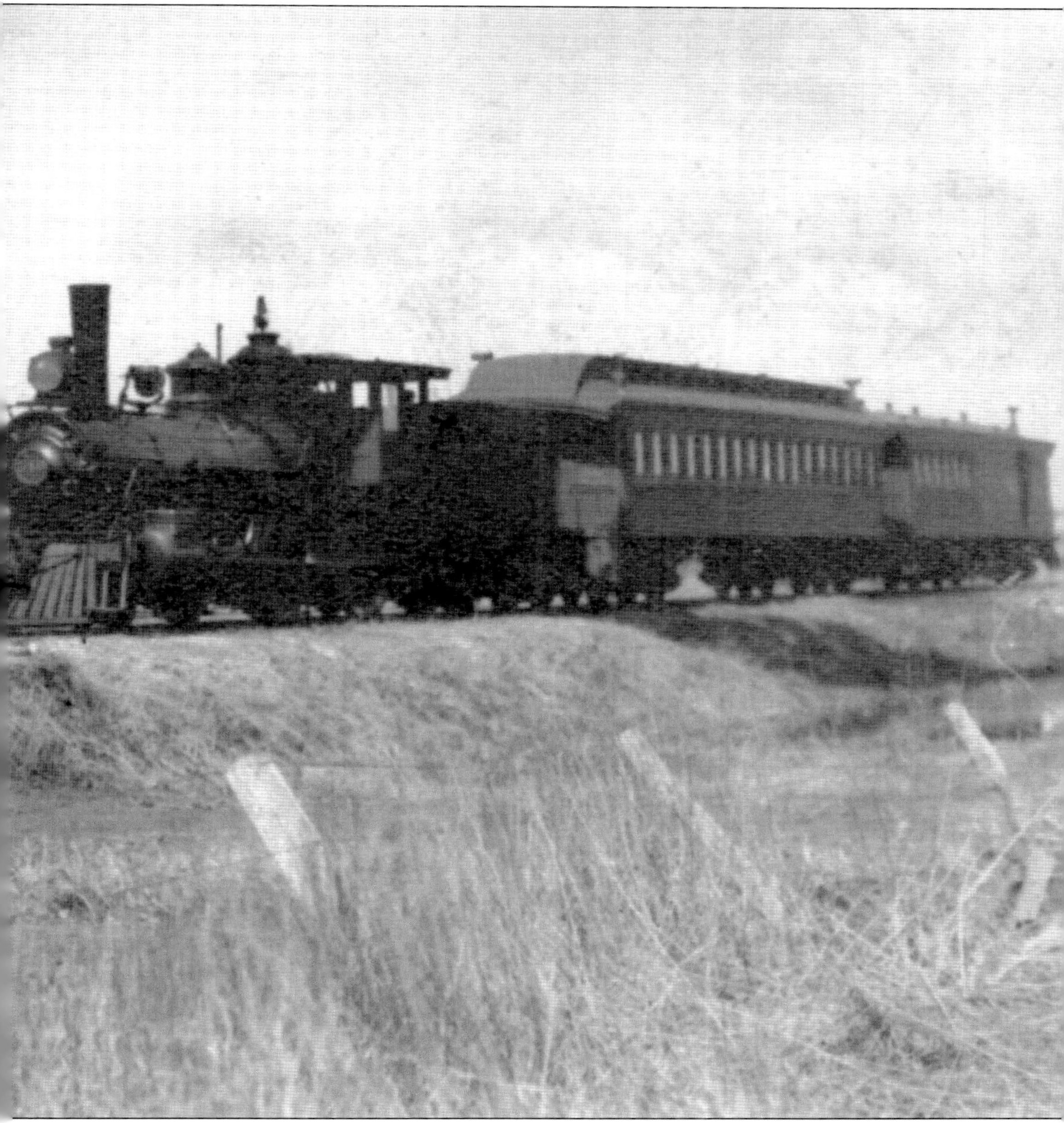

gold watch and chain to James Densmoor Sr., by the residents of Markesan and the vicinity as a recognition of his services in securing the road." With people coming in and cargo going out, Markesan began to grow and prosper.

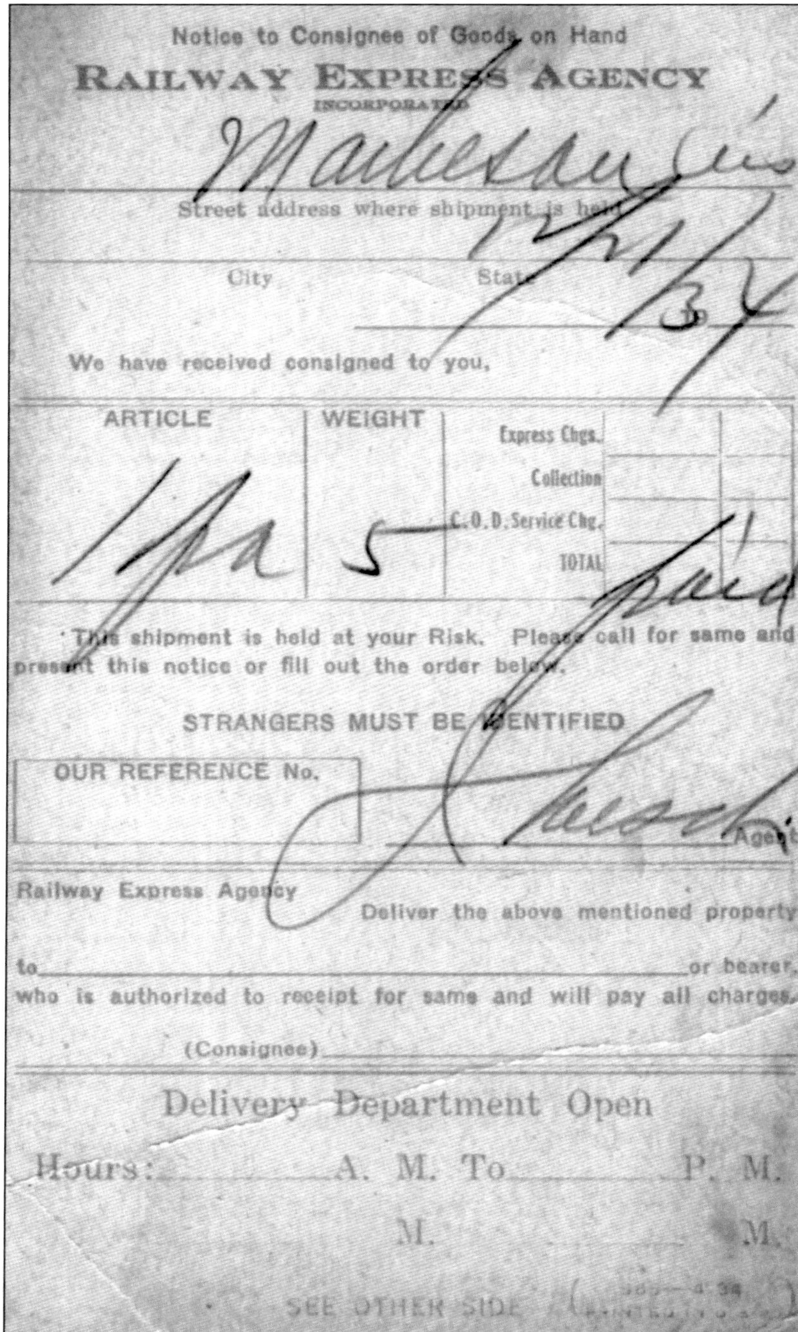

Notice to Consignee of Goods on Hand

RAILWAY EXPRESS AGENCY

INCORPORATED

Street address where shipment is held

City State

19

We have received consigned to you,

ARTICLE	WEIGHT		
		Express Chgs.	
		Collection	
		C.O.D. Service Chg.	
		TOTAL	

This shipment is held at your Risk. Please call for same and present this notice or fill out the order below.

STRANGERS MUST BE IDENTIFIED

OUR REFERENCE No.

Agent

Railway Express Agency

Deliver the above mentioned property

to ____________ or bearer, who is authorized to receipt for same and will pay all charges.

(Consignee) ____________

Delivery Department Open

Hours: ______ A. M. To ______ P. M.

M. M.

SEE OTHER SIDE

This postcard was sent to Markesan-area resident Otto Zuehls in 1934. The Railway Express Agency was notifying him of a cargo shipment that came in at the railroad yard. Local businesses and farmers found the railroad very important when it came to sending their finished goods or harvested crops to market. The railroad also served an important role of bringing in large cargo and mail to the area.

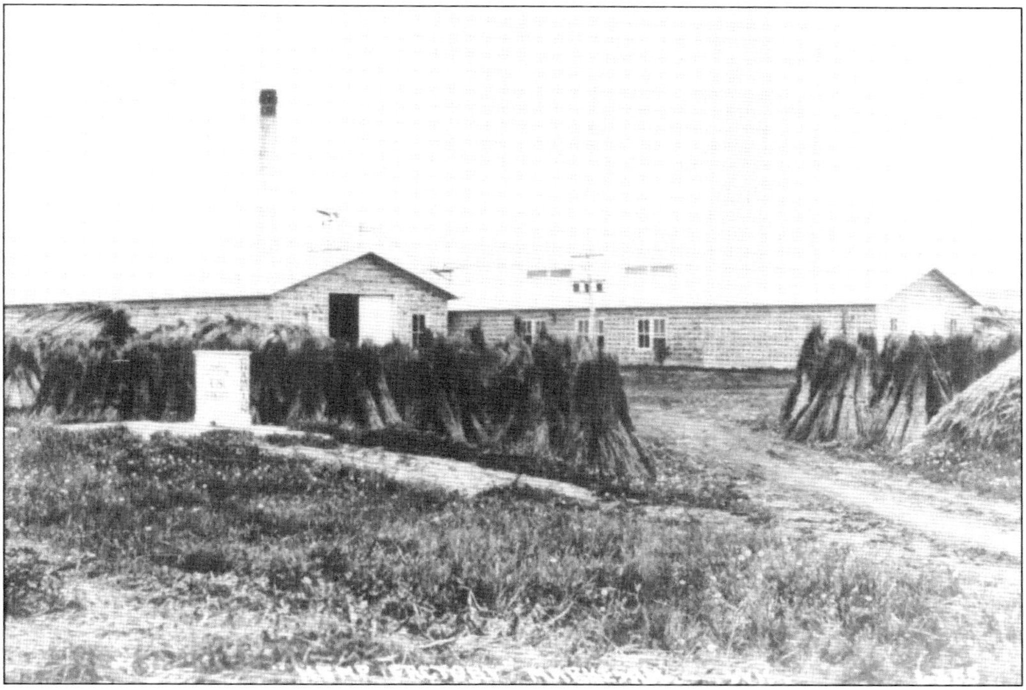

Hemp was a popular crop in the rural Markesan area for a number of years. William Sink, who formerly owned the M.B.M. Peacock Mill, started the Markesan Hemp Company around 1920. In 1940, Sink sold the mill to Matthias Rens Sr. Rens operated the Markesan Hemp Company mill, as well as many other hemp mills in the area.

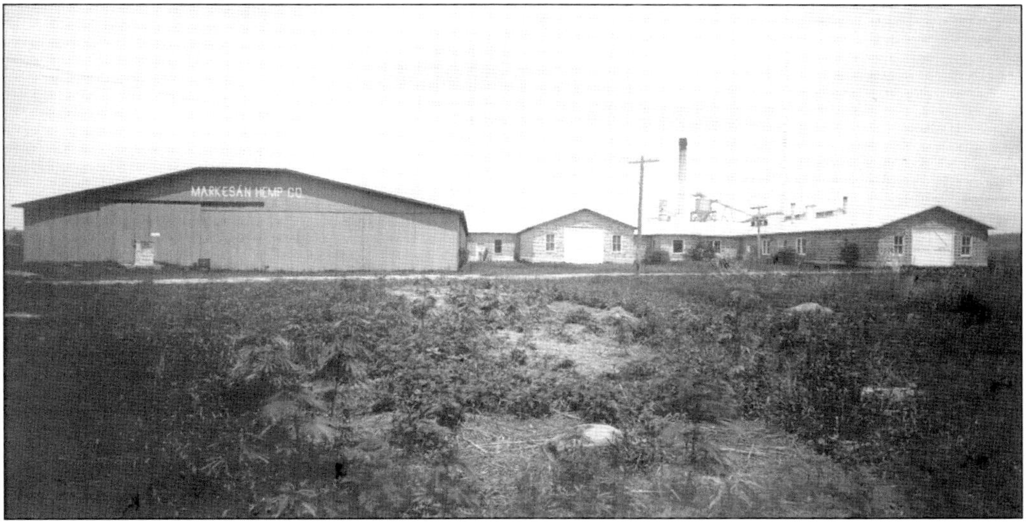

The hemp grown by area farmers was harvested and shipped to the Markesan Hemp Company for drying and processing. The cleaned and processed hemp fibers were sold to larger firms that produced goods using the fibers. Hemp became a wartime crop during World War I and World War II, but when the war ended so did growing hemp. In 1952, the Markesan Hemp Company ceased operations, and the building was sold. Today, the former hemp building is occupied by Robin II Incorporated.

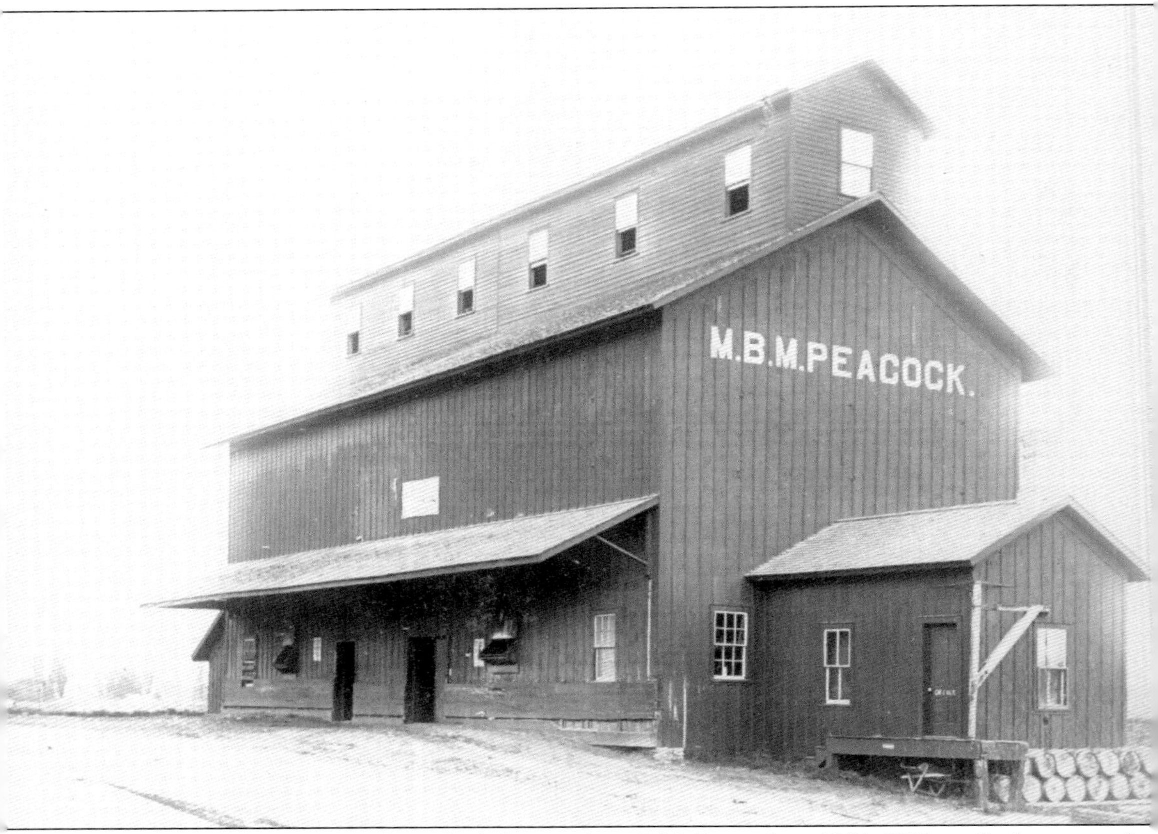

The M.B.M. Peacock Mill was built by Matthew B.M. Peacock in 1884. William Sink managed the mill for Peacock for several years and then eventually bought it. Sink owned and operated the mill for a number of years until he sold it to John M. Hull in 1914. After the acquisition by Hull, it was renamed the Hull Mill. It was said that farmers lined up to High Street on Saturday afternoons so they could bring in their grain for storage and sale. Hull operated the mill until his death in 1941. The building then became part of the Grand River Co-Operative and served as its feed mill until it was destroyed by a fire in 1962.

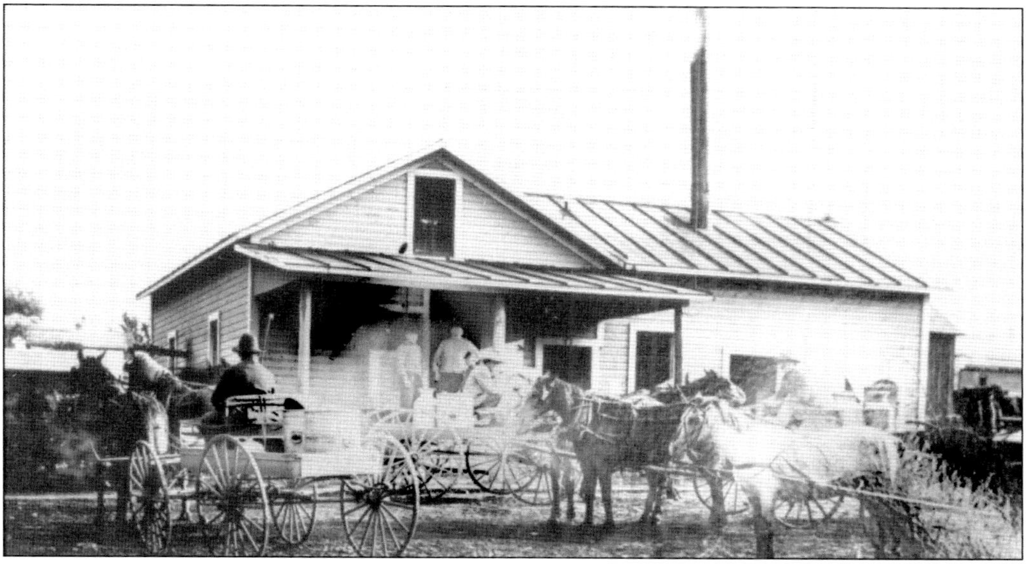

The Markesan Creamery was founded in 1892 by Henry P. Friday. Friday operated his creamery until 1912, when Edward Seaman bought it. Seaman turned the business over to Johnson and Guderian in 1915 and then regained ownership around 1921. This photograph is dated 1897, when Friday was the owner and operator.

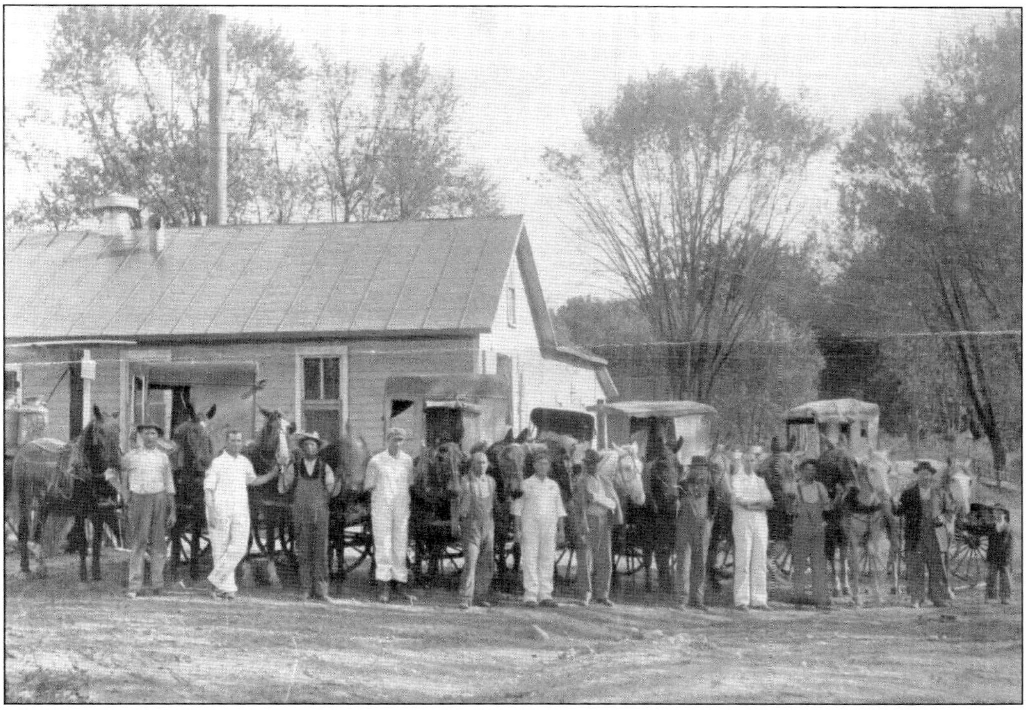

This 1910 picture shows the workers of the Markesan Creamery. The creamery was located on the northeast corner of Main Street and Water Street. Fine butter, cheese, and ice cream were once produced there. Friday's slogan was, "Put up in any style package. Full weight and honest test. Deliver good milk, I'll do the rest!"

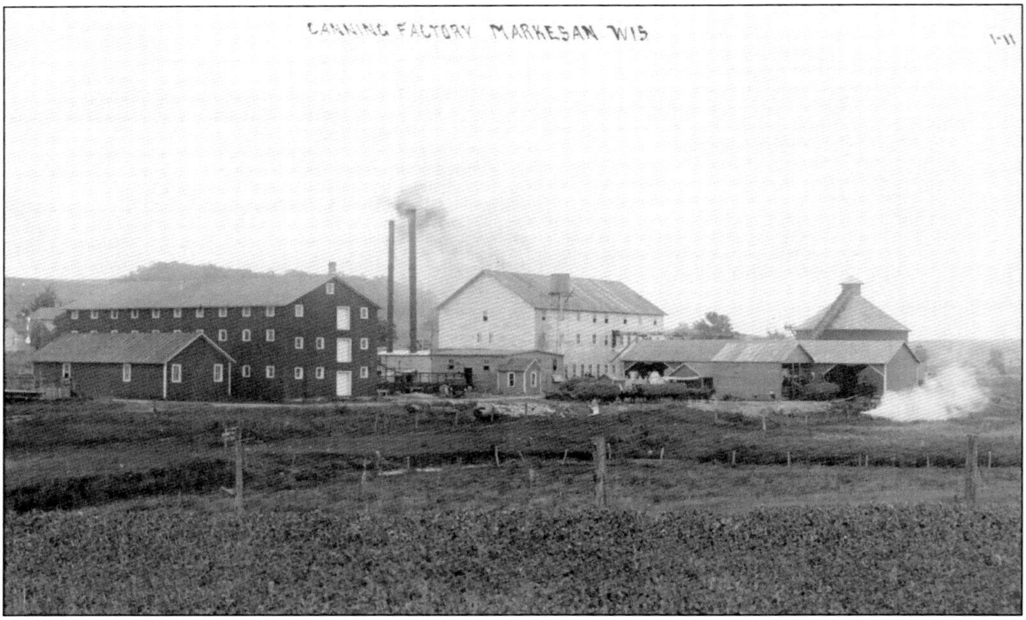

The Markesan Canning Company was formed in 1902 and set up operations on the Chicago, Milwaukee, and St. Paul Railroad line stretching to Markesan. Early operations included canning corn and tomatoes. Soon after, pea canning replaced both tomatoes and corn for a number of years before corn was then canned at the plant again.

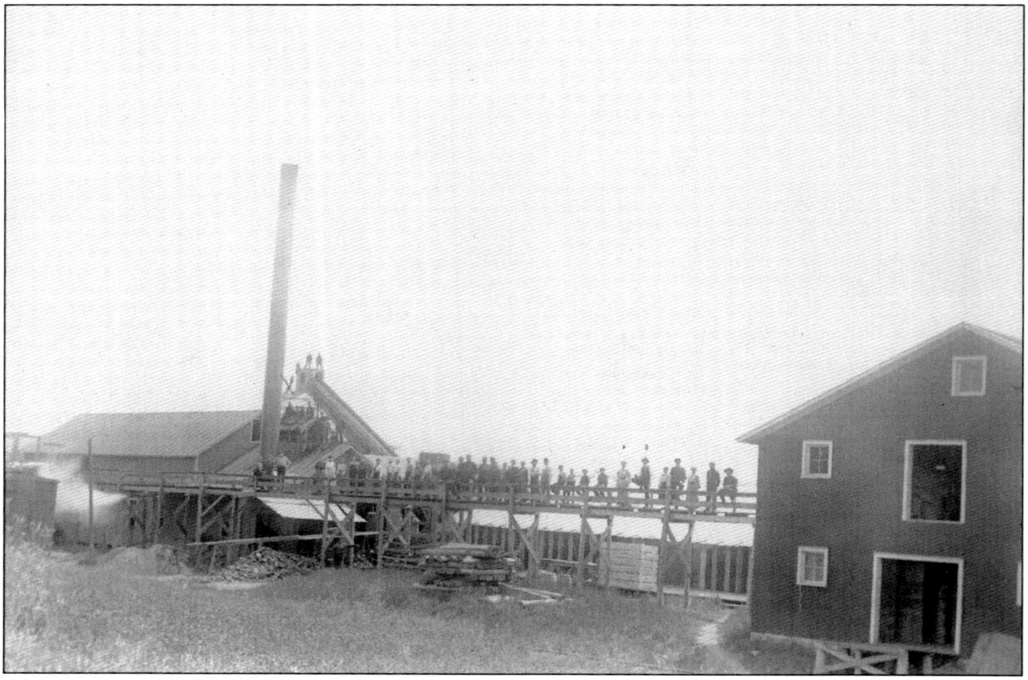

This 1905 picture shows the crew at the Markesan Canning Company canning corn or peas. Workers used a walkway from the packinghouse to move the canned vegetables to storage in a shed.

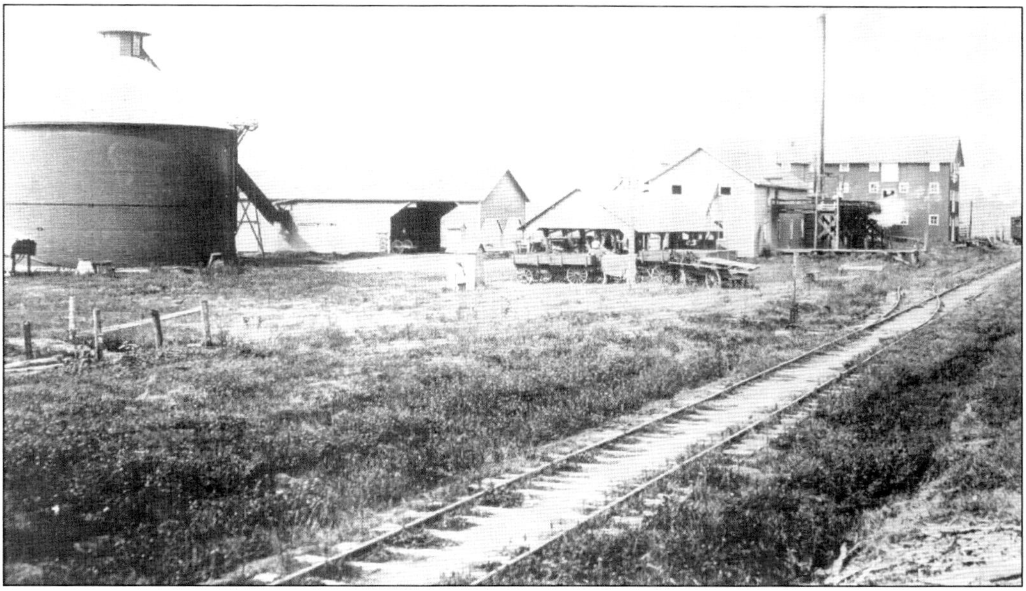

Photographed here are factory grounds at the Markesan Canning Company. Seen on the far left is the silage silo that was erected in 1906. The silo was constructed to take the husks and any other debris from the corn cleaners and hold it for later use of feed.

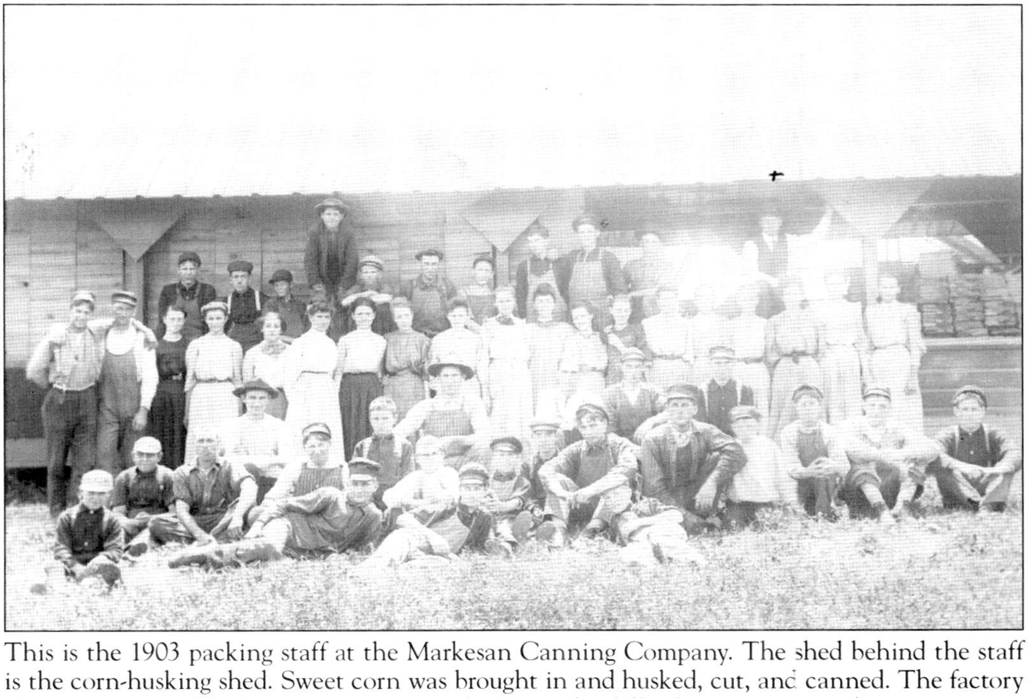

This is the 1903 packing staff at the Markesan Canning Company. The shed behind the staff is the corn-husking shed. Sweet corn was brought in and husked, cut, and canned. The factory also experimented with canning tomatoes; however, the difficulties in growing the tomato crops forced the company switch to canning peas.

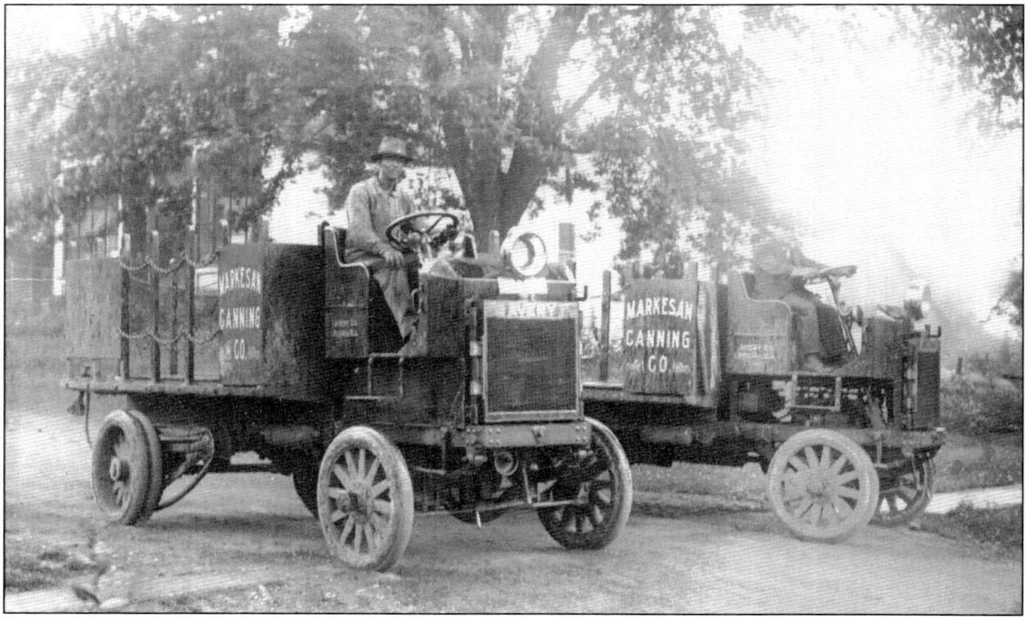

Here, two men are pictured driving Avery trucks for the Markesan Canning Company. The trucks were used to haul heavy loads of canned corn and peas either to storage or loading on railroad cars. These early trucks had hard rubber tires rather than pneumatic ones.

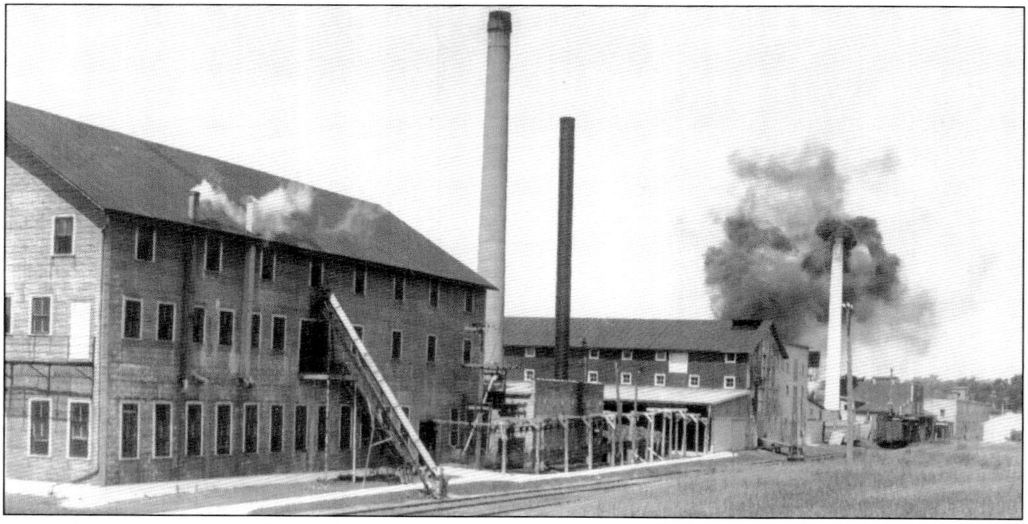

As technology advanced, the factory updated to keep up with demands. For example, a bigger storage house and packing department were built. Markesan Canning Company remained in operation for 58 years until the merger with California Packing Company in 1962. Canning of corn and peas eventually ceased, and a new factory was constructed, where beans were then processed and canned.

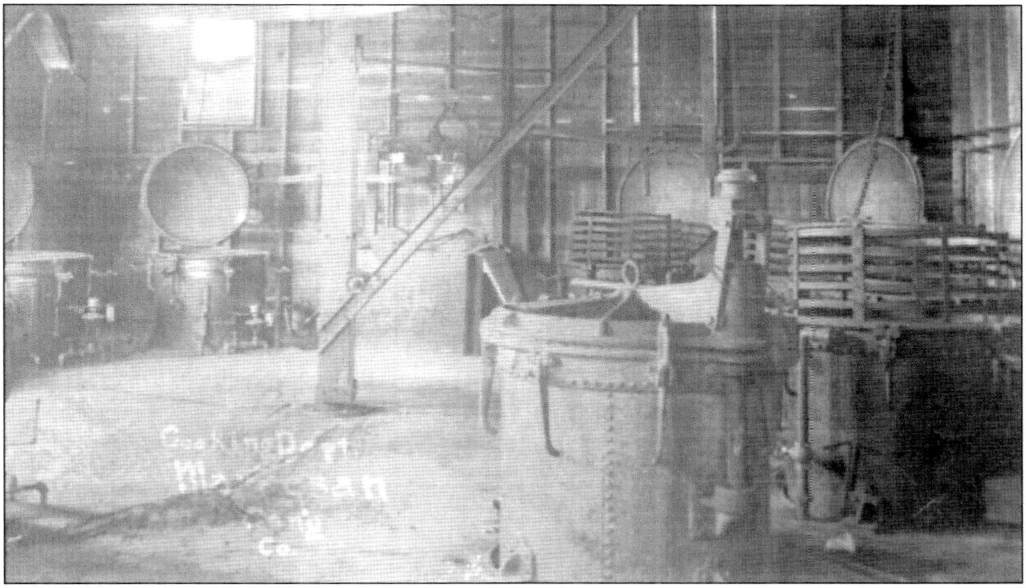

These rare photographs show a glimpse of the inside of the Markesan Canning Company's cooking and packing departments during the early years of operation. After the crop was picked and cleaned, it was sent to the cooking department. Above, produce would be cooked thoroughly to kill any bacteria before being sent over to the packing department. The packing department consisted of a huge machine driven by belts that sealed and labeled the cans. Below, peas and corn were canned and sealed shut to retain their freshness. Belt-driven conveyor lines kept the canned goods moving to the final destination in a storage house.

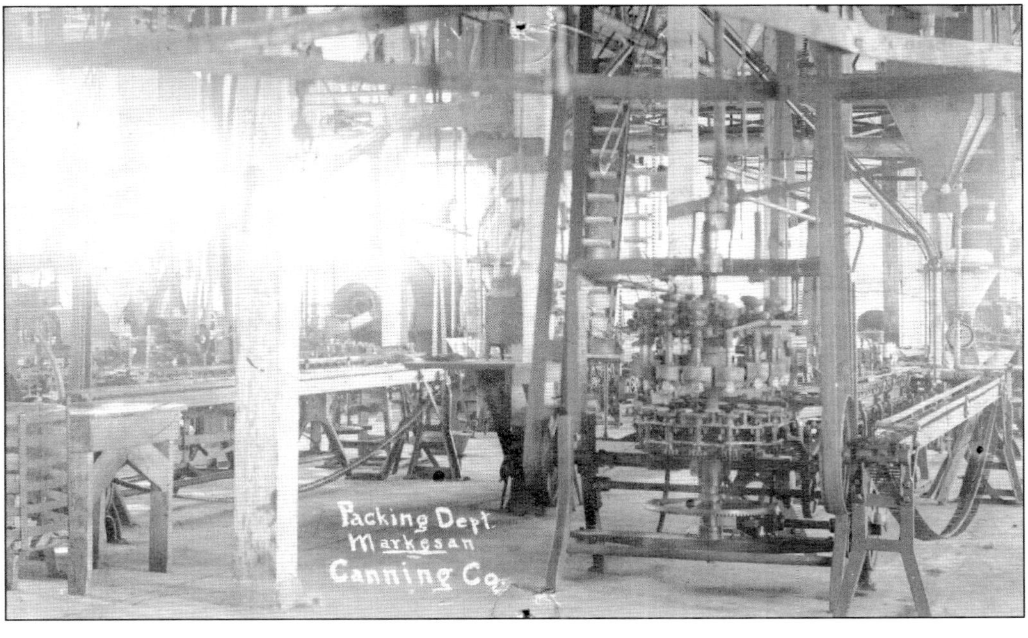

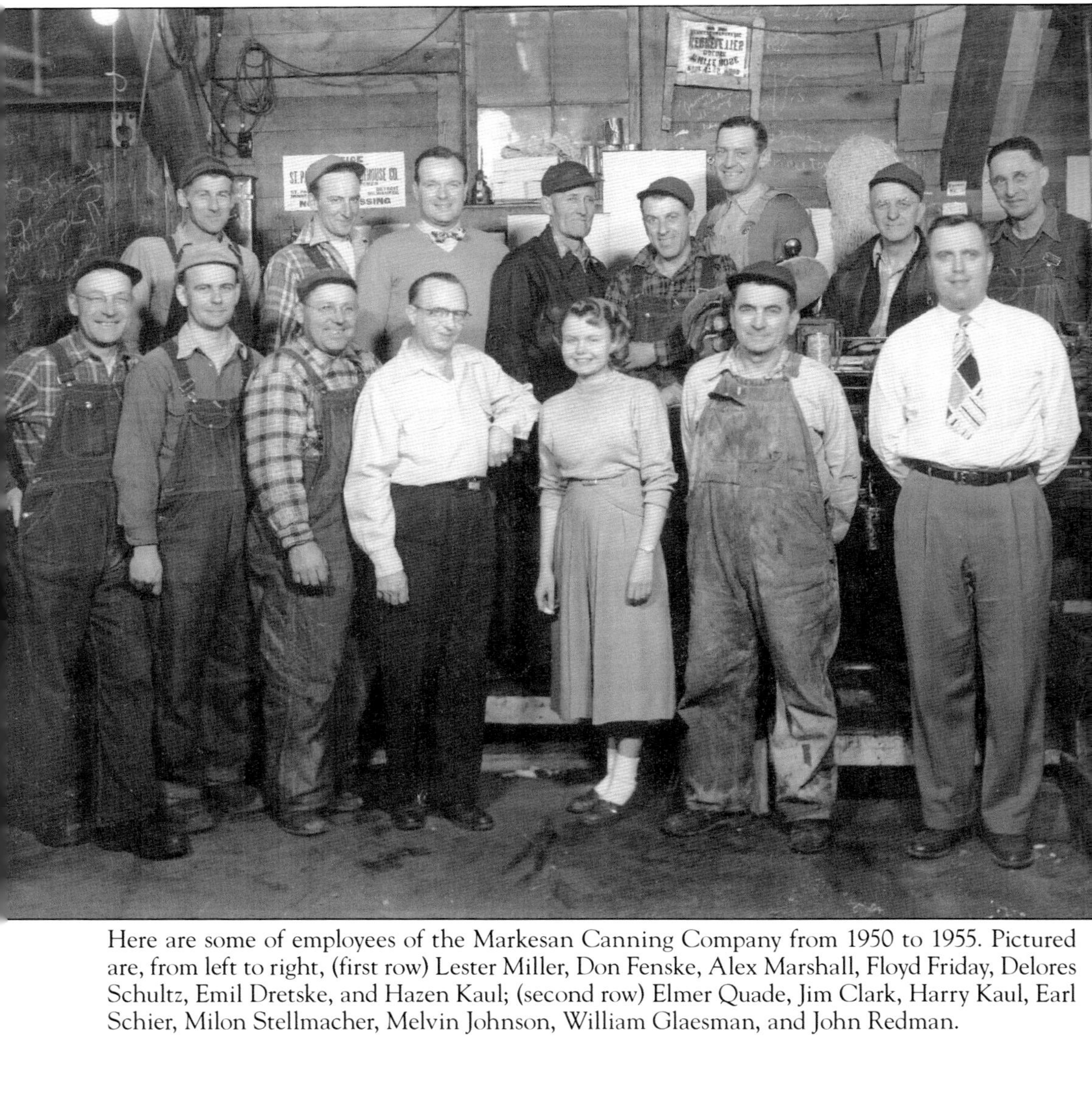

Here are some of employees of the Markesan Canning Company from 1950 to 1955. Pictured are, from left to right, (first row) Lester Miller, Don Fenske, Alex Marshall, Floyd Friday, Delores Schultz, Emil Dretske, and Hazen Kaul; (second row) Elmer Quade, Jim Clark, Harry Kaul, Earl Schier, Milon Stellmacher, Melvin Johnson, William Glaesman, and John Redman.

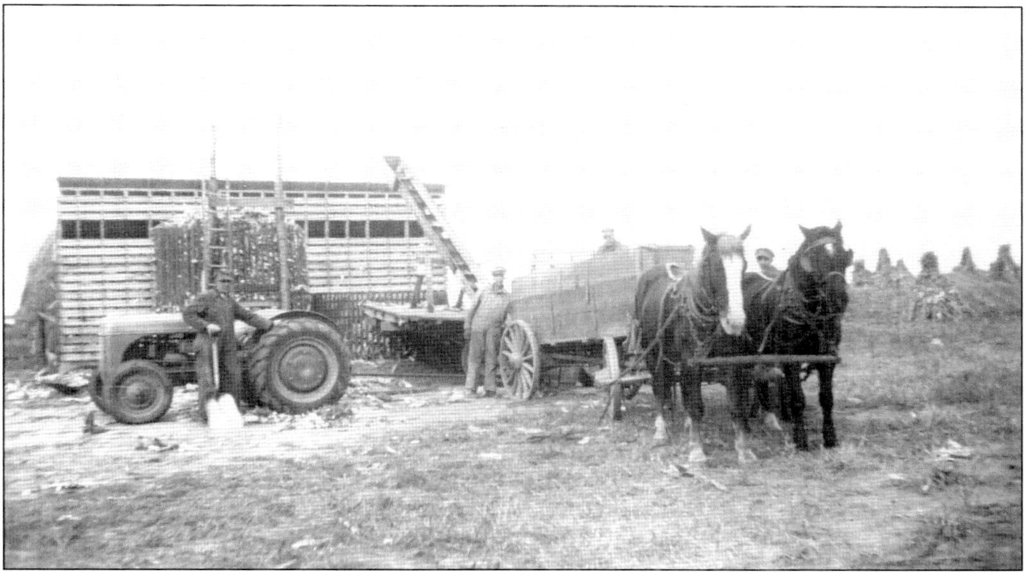

Farming was a staple industry, and it remains so today. Farmers in the area have lush soil that helps produce the best crops, which they are then able to sell for profit. Pictured here is activity on the Larkin family farm near Markesan. The men in this photograph are performing the fall harvest as they crib corn with a tractor.

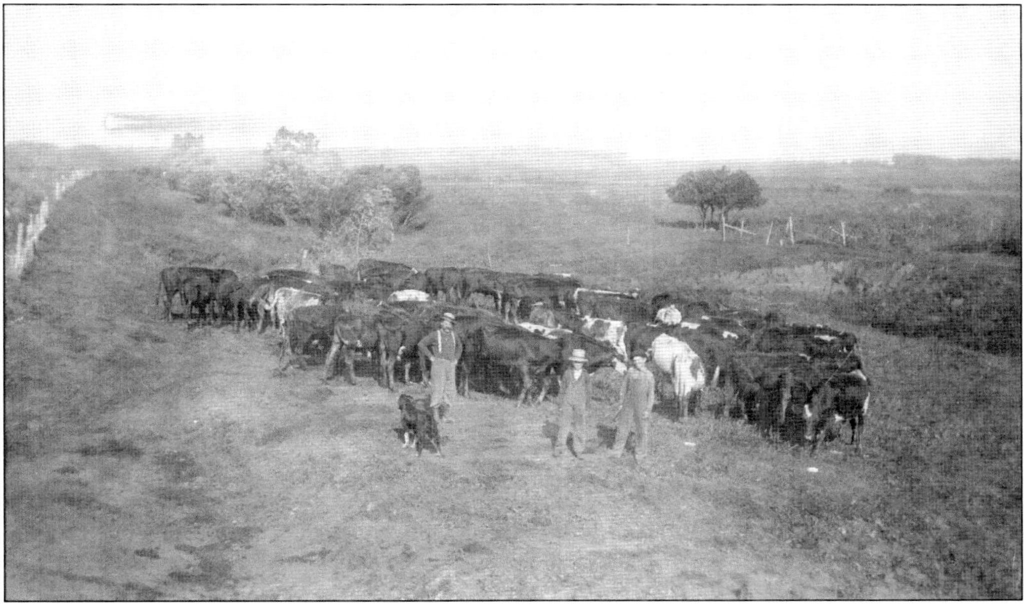

Livestock was an important element on every farm in Markesan. Farmers used horses for all purposes of farmwork and transportation. Before tractors became an important part of operations, horses were the main workforce on the farm. Cows were raised for their milk, which fed the family or was sold at town markets. Farmers were indeed self-sufficient. Here, a group of men poses for a picture with their dairy cattle on a farm near Markesan.

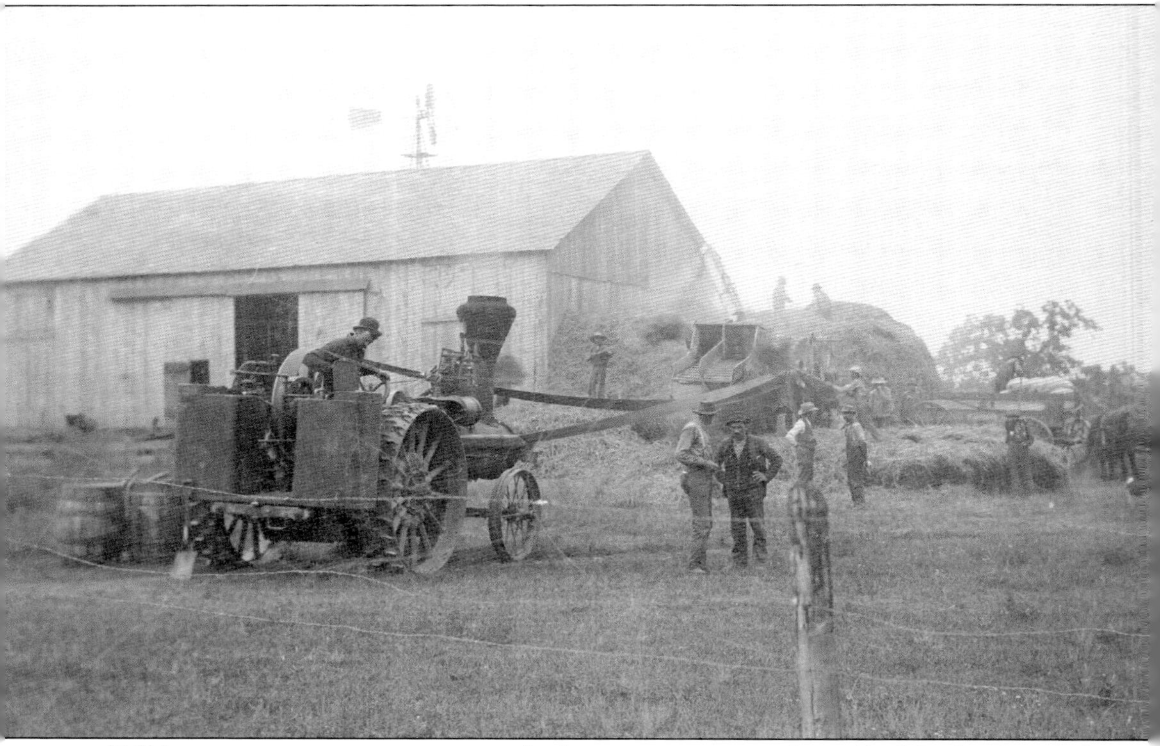

Fall harvest was an important time for farmers near town when all of the hard work from spring tilling and planting would pay off. Pictured here is a threshing crew harvesting grain on a farm near Markesan. Family, friends, and even neighbors would come together to help with the harvest. Farmers would often buy threshing machines together and move them from farm to farm when needed. An early steam-powered tractor was used to operate this threshing machine. The crops were cut and bundled into shocks and then brought to farmyard, where they were sent through a thresher that separated the seed from the rest of the plant. Chaff and other debris were blown into the barn to be used for bedding, while the seed was bagged and used for feed or shipped to market.

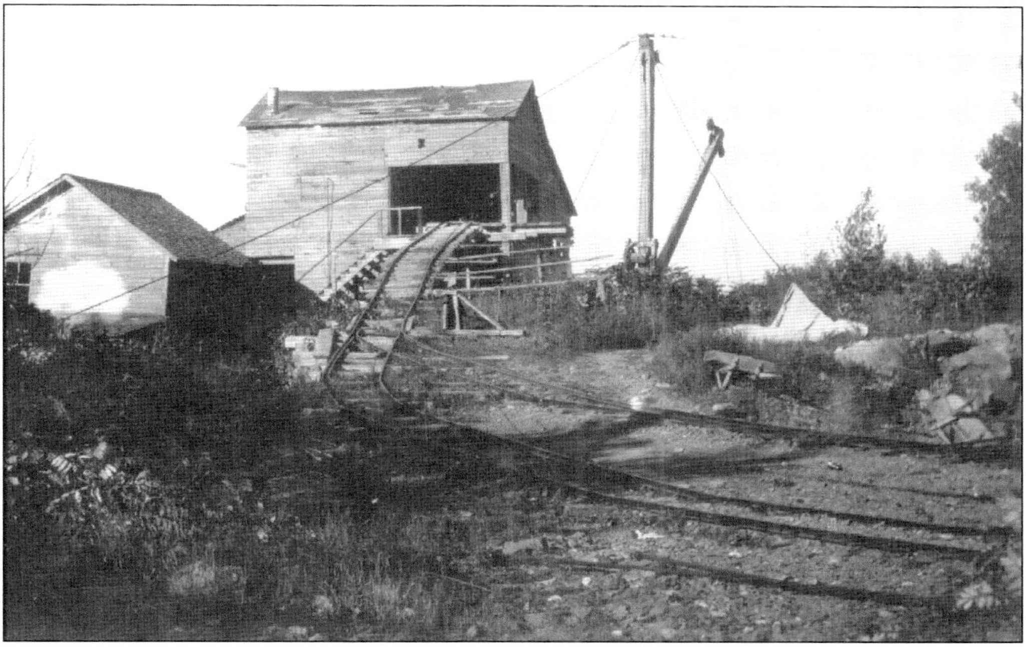

Above is a 1910 photograph of the rock crusher at the Utley granite quarry. Utley was a granite boomtown six miles east of Markesan. Granite was discovered in 1881, and quarrying began immediately thereafter. When the railroad was run to the quarry, the area was named after railroad line assistant superintendent Charles Utley. The area prospered, and a small town sprang up. Most of the granite was shipped to Chicago, where it was used to build streets. Utley met its demise in 1933 when quarry operations ceased. Below, some of the quarry workers pose with their tools.

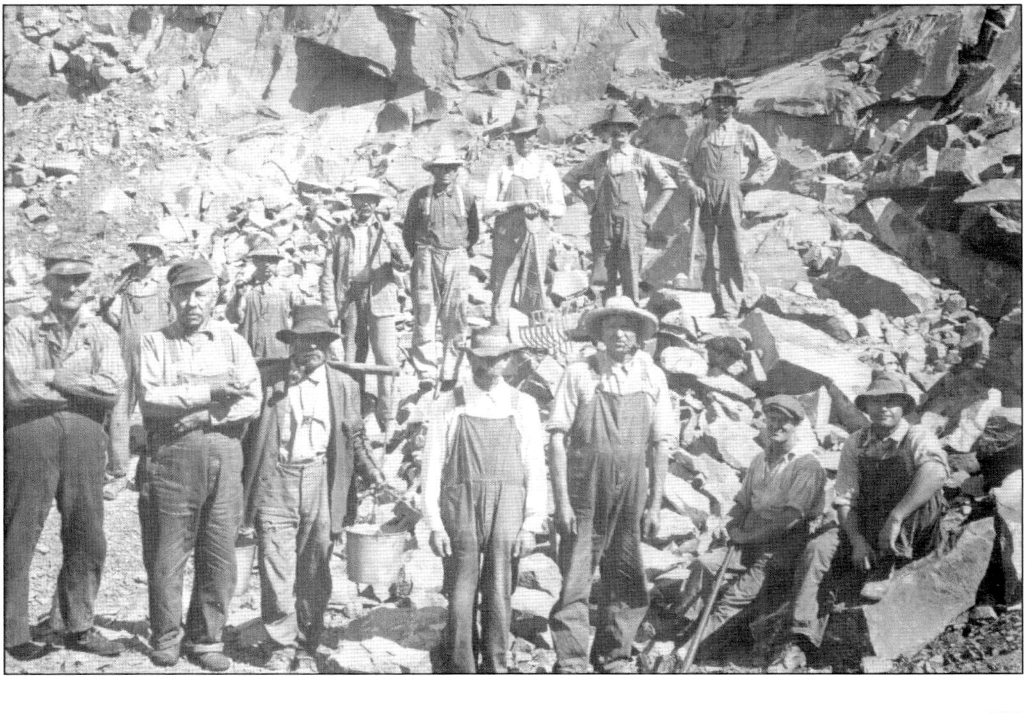

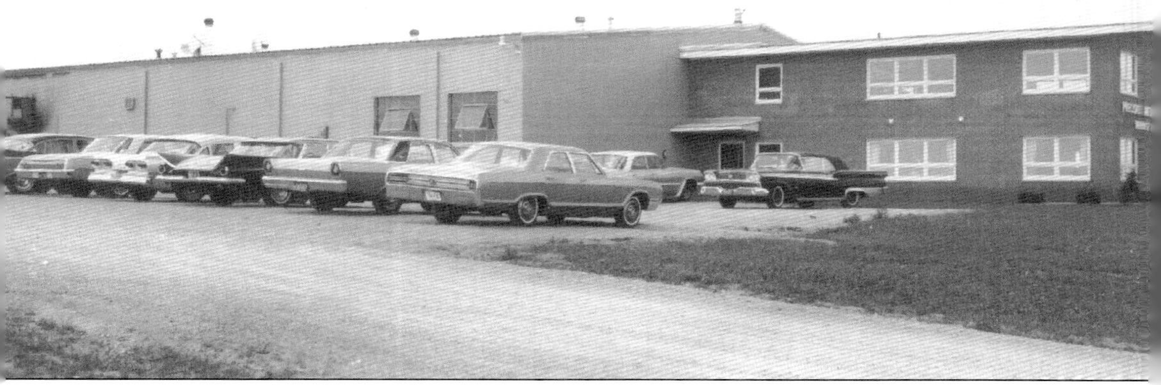

Precision Metalsmiths Inc. (PMI) was an already established company out of Cleveland, Ohio, specializing in metal castings. Former Markesan resident and businessman Robert Miller, who founded and owned the firm, helped bring a branch of the company to Markesan in 1964. The company grew within two years, and additional facilities where added onto the existing factory. A total of eight additions were added to PMI between 1964 and 1980. PMI continues to provide jobs for people in the Markesan area.

Six

Leisure and Celebrations

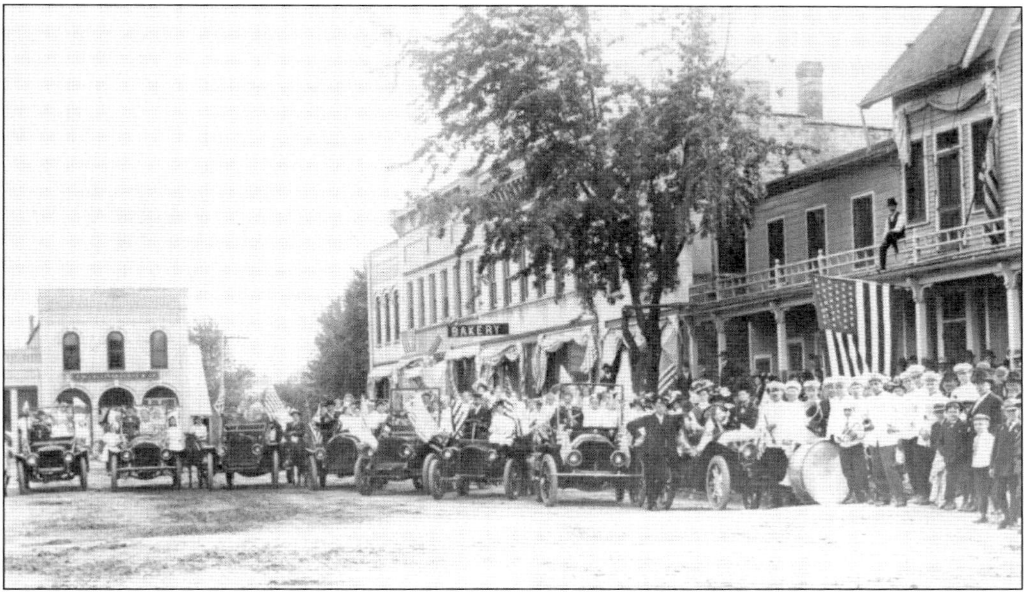

Every little town had its own celebrations and places to relax. Celebrations were important community social events, where work could be set aside for the day to spend time with family and friends. Markesan had places for people to kick back, relax, and have fun. Here, the 1908 Decoration Day (today Memorial Day) celebration is underway on Bridge Street, as the Markesan Band plays its tunes. People showed up by foot or by automobile for the grand spectacle downtown.

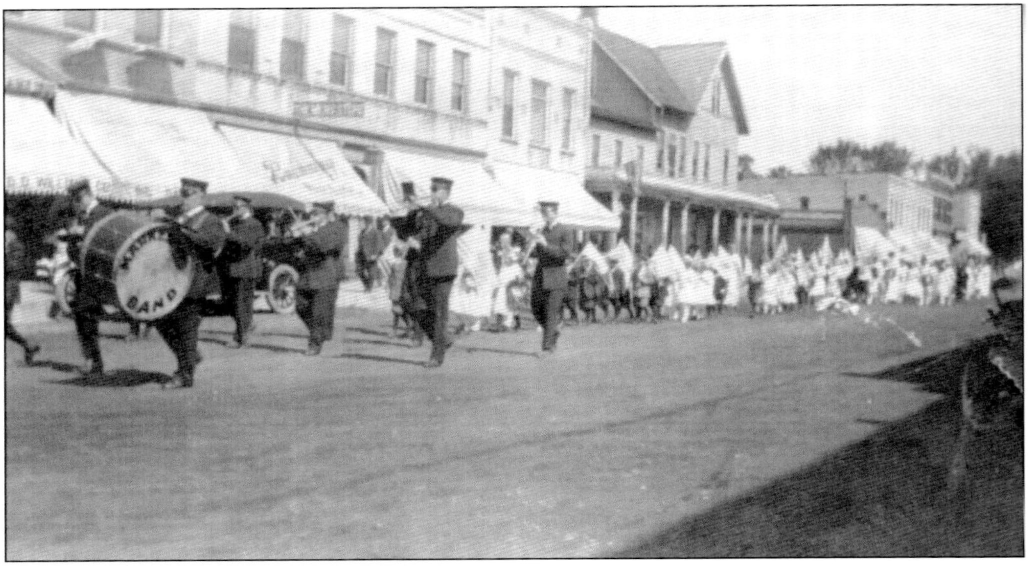

A parade is seen above going downtown with the Markesan Band marching by, as children with flags follow them. This could be an Independence Day parade, as they were common in the early days of Markesan. Cannons were brought in and fired at dawn and dusk to celebrate the birth of America. The day was followed with a parade, picnic, church services, and fireworks at dusk. The celebrations were held in the park near the John Millard home. Pictured below is the Independence Day parade in 1929. It was also quite common for races of different kinds to be held on holidays. In the early days, sack races and foot races were popular, but later horse and bicycle races gained popularity. These competitions were held on a track just west of town.

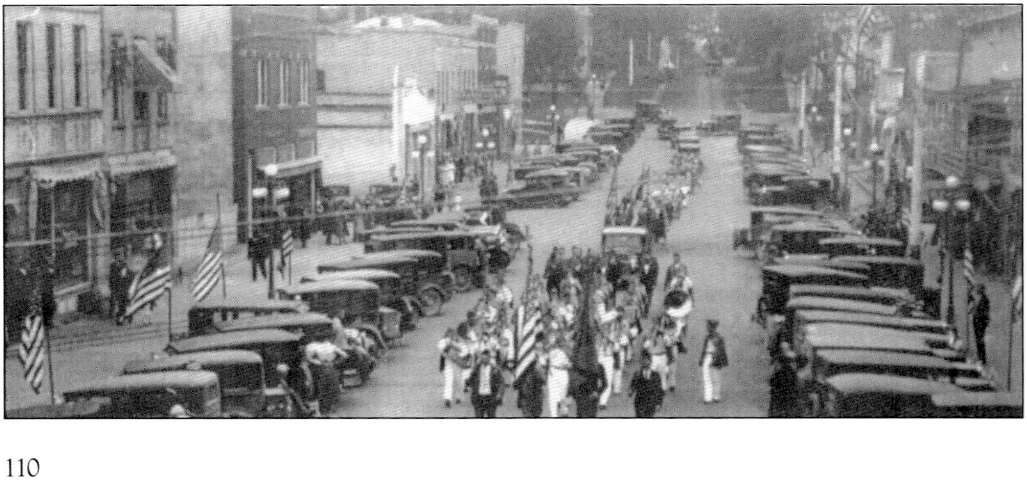

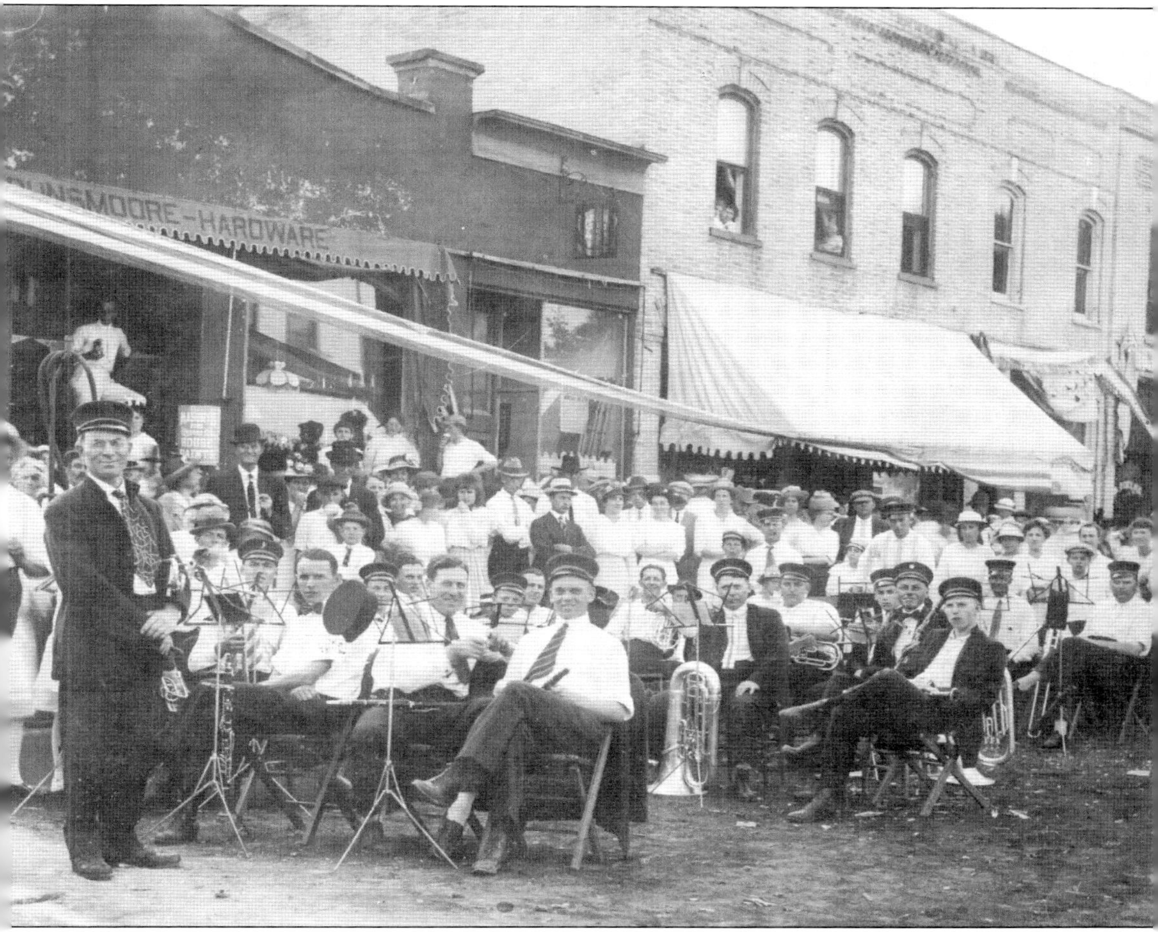

The Markesan Band consisted of people of all ages. It was not uncommon for the band to have afternoon performances in the park on weekends, at sporting events, or for special celebrations. This one appears to be a patriotic holiday judging by the streamers directly above the crowd. This particular performance was held on the corner of John and Bridge Streets in front of William F. Dunsmoore Hardware Store. Note the infant sitting in the window second from the left on the upper level of the building next door.

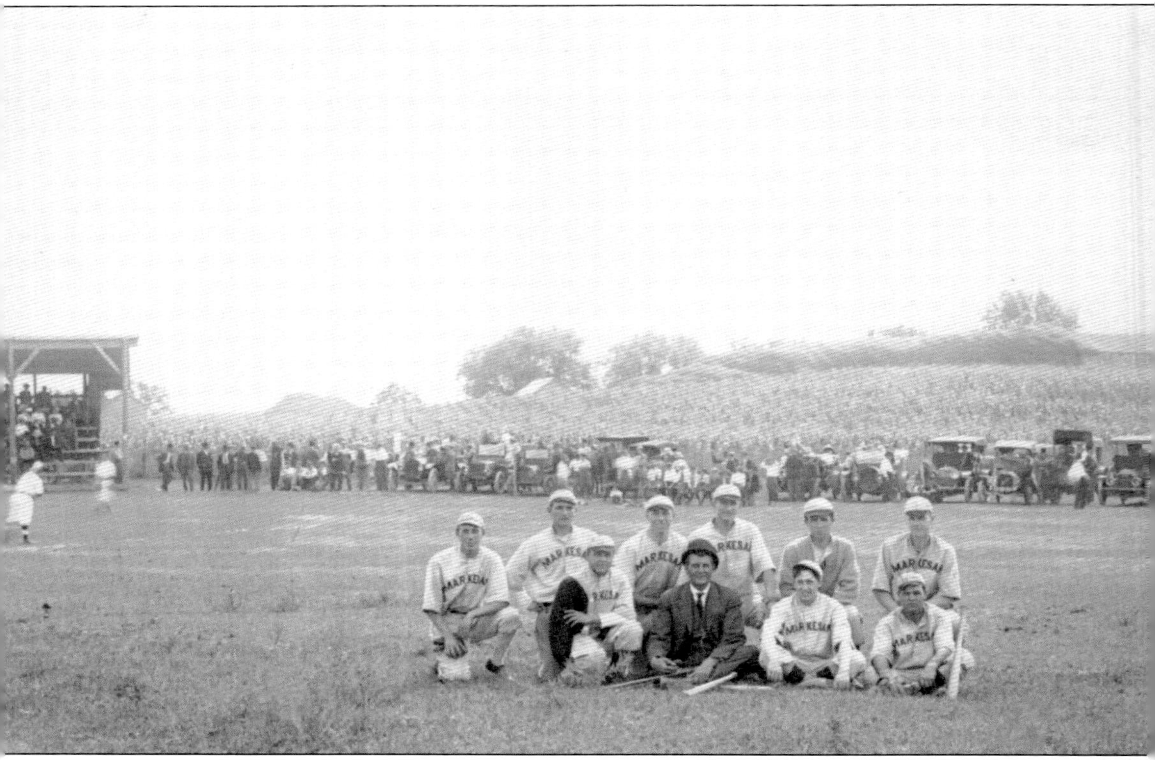

Baseball was a favorite past time of men, young and old, in Markesan. It is said that Markesan had been known as a baseball town for many years. The Markesan team won many championships and also started a few rivalries. This picture, dated 1934, was taken the same day that the Markesan baseball team won the Mid-State Championship game. The men who played in Markesan were very good—so good that one man got a big break in the majors. A *Markesan Herald* article, dated July 29, 1937, explains how resident Walter Zuehls had signed a one-year contract with the Chicago White Sox as a pitcher.

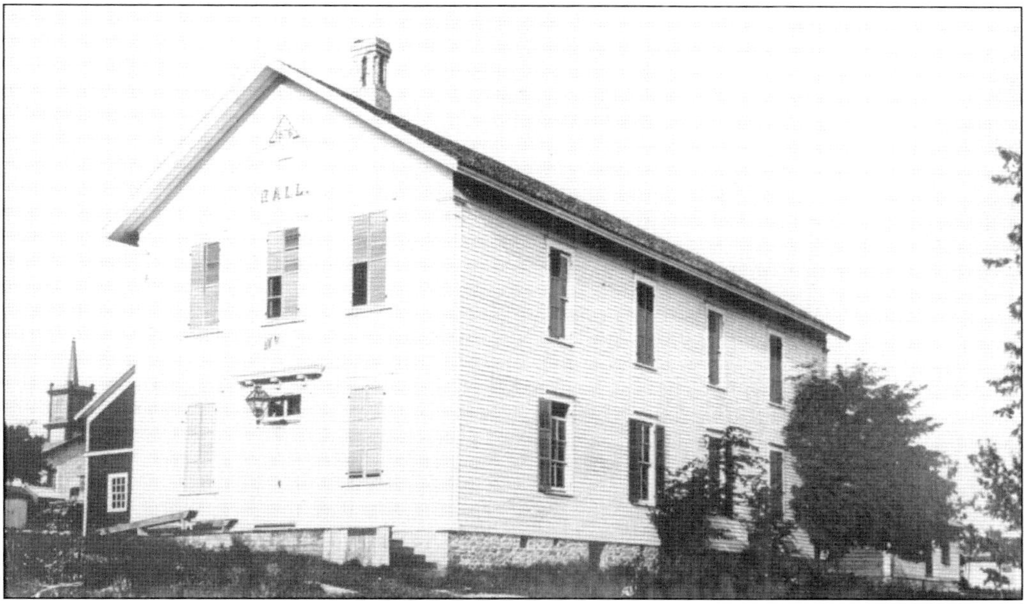

The Temple of Honor, above, was built in 1876 by the Good Templars Lodge, which organized in Markesan in 1874. It was built on the corner of Bridge and Charles Streets. When the organization was disbanded, the building was sold to the Markesan Masonic Lodge in 1910, and the hall was then known as the Masonic Hall. The building was used for all kinds of social events as well as school events. Meetings and gatherings were held in the hall; the picture below shows a meeting of the Farmers Institute dated February 26, 1937. The Masonic Hall was used for about 80 years until it was demolished in 1955, and a new brick building was erected in its place. Today, it serves as the building for the meetings of American Legion.

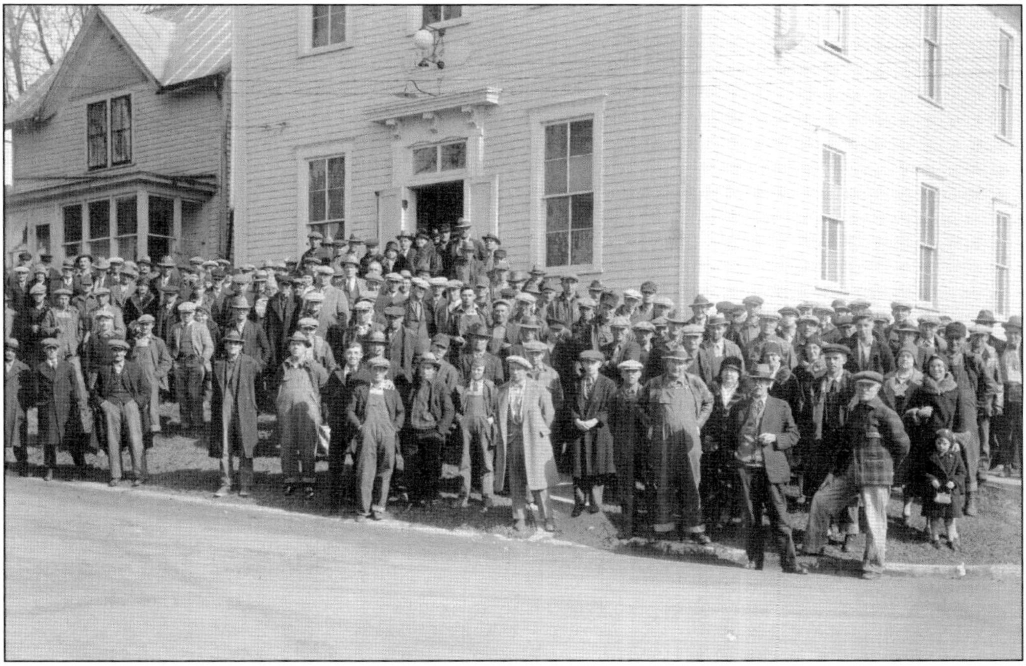

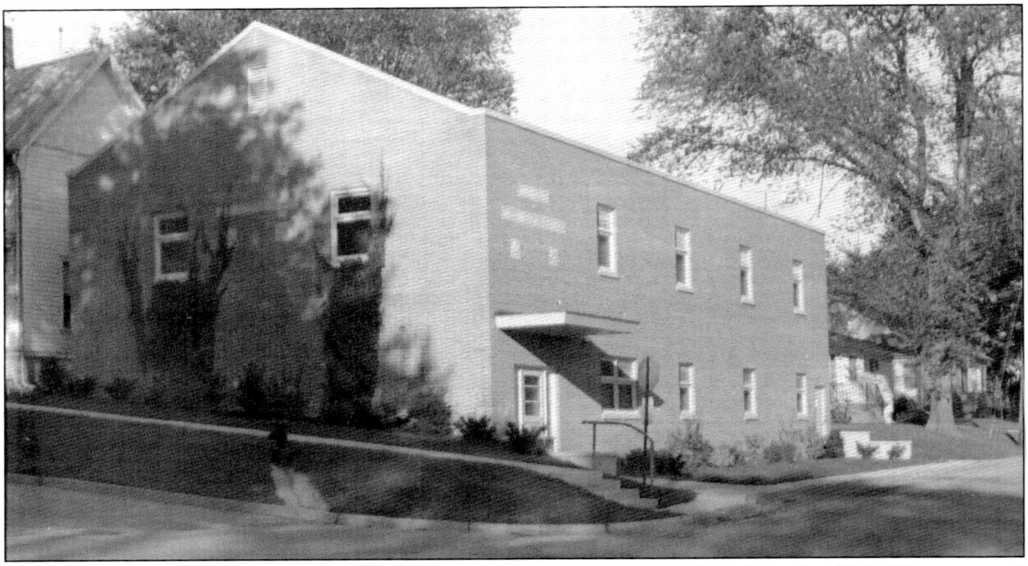

The American Legion Post No. 282 of Markesan was chartered on July 9, 1920. The original name for the post was the Franklin Abendroth Post in honor of Abendroth's service and sacrifice during World War I. In 1946, another name was added to the post, and it became the Abendroth-Connolly Post No. 282. This was in honor of Keefe Connolly, who lost his life December 7, 1941, onboard the USS *Arizona*, where he remains entombed to this day. The legion bought the former Masonic Hall in 1990, and it is now used as the meeting hall and gathering place for the Abendroth-Connolly Legion Post.

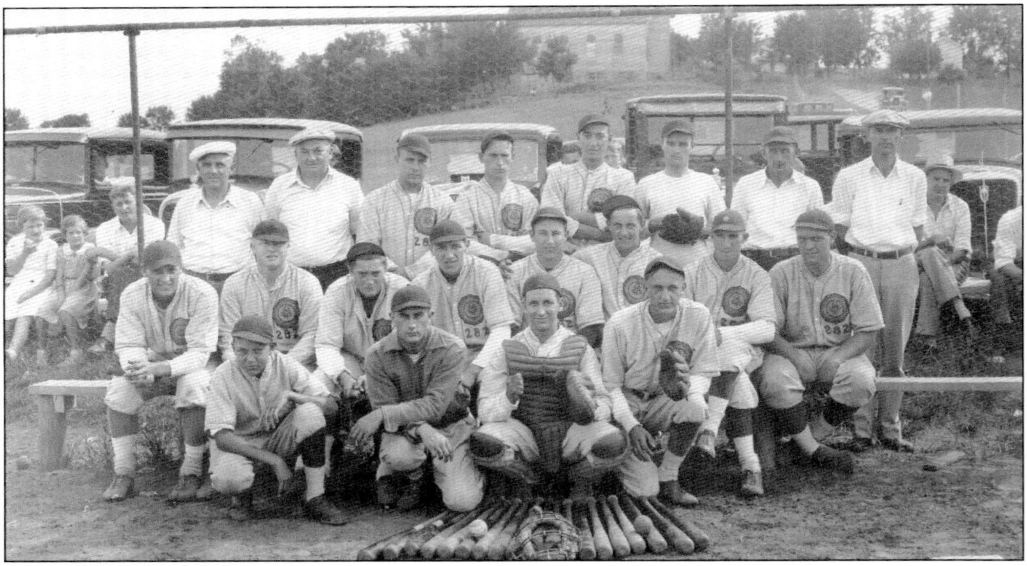

The legion also sponsored social events and recreational activities. Shown here is the 1933 Markesan Legion No. 282 baseball team. Pictured are, from left to right, (first row) Myron Woehlke, Merle Froehlich, Ray Lemke, and Walter Zuehls; (second row) Jack Miller, Red Allen, "Tille" Wittenburg, Dale Long, Fred Stamm, George Zuehls, Ira Radel, and Melvin Johnson; (third row) Mace Dunsmoor, Bill Woehlke, Bob Henninger, Gerald Westover, Gordun Hull, Clarence Dumdey, Flick Cahoun, and Chet Horn.

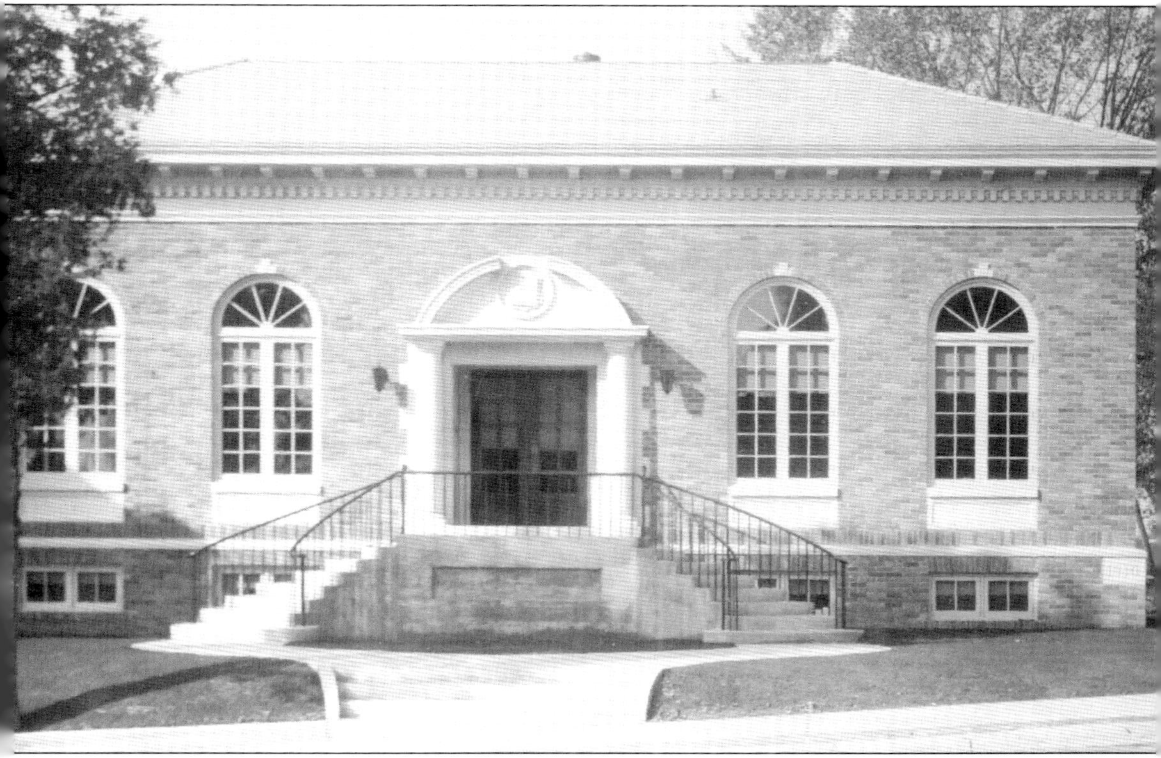

The Markesan Public Library was formed on August 28, 1900, when 10 people from the community met to discuss the organization of a library association. The first form of the library was located in the upstairs of the old D.D. Williams Daylight Store building on Bridge Street. By the late 1920s, the association bought land on the corner of Bridge and Charles Streets, and the library was constructed there in 1930 with monetary donations from the citizens of Markesan. The Markesan Public Library underwent remodeling and updating in 1999, and a new addition was added onto the west portion of the building.

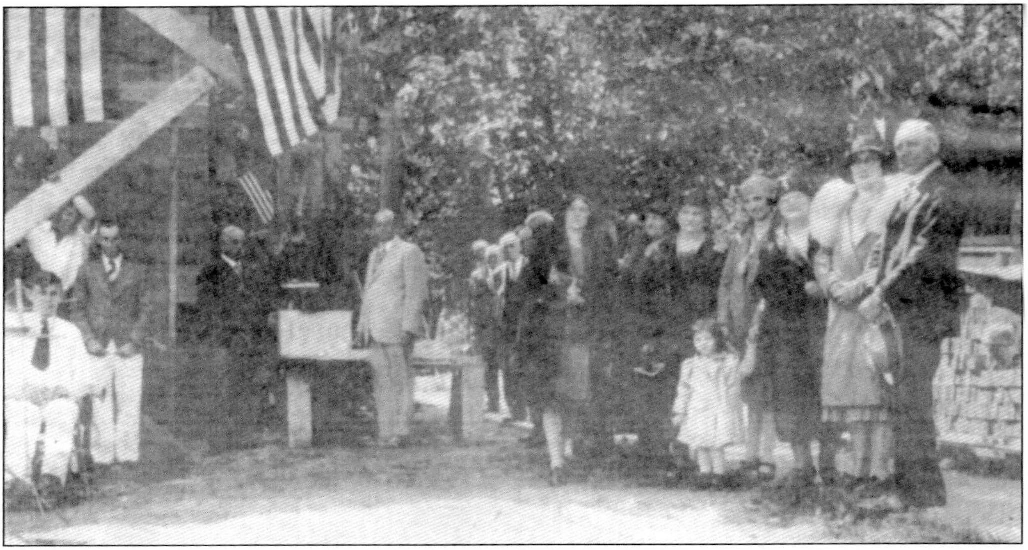

Construction of the library commenced in 1930. Here, the cornerstone is being put in place. William Sink (left) and Charles Yunker are pictured standing on either side of the corner stone. They, along with eight others, served on the library board for a number of years.

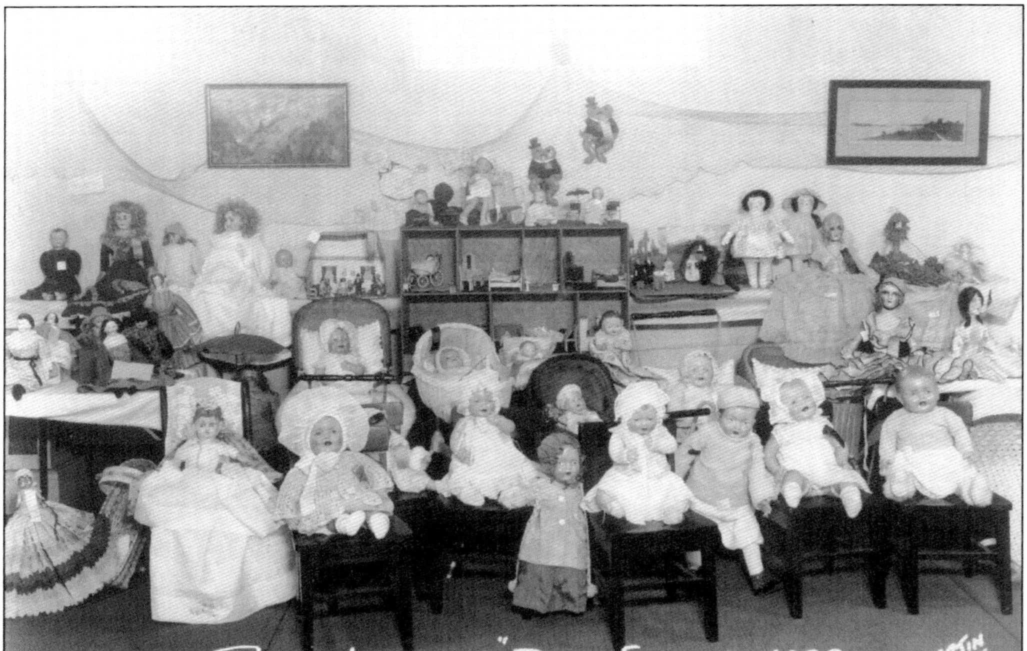

The library was not only a place for recreational reading and education, but it also served as a facility for holding certain community events. This photograph shows a doll show that was held at the library in 1932. Similar displays, such as a flower show, were held at the library for local enjoyment and gave residents a chance to show off their collections.

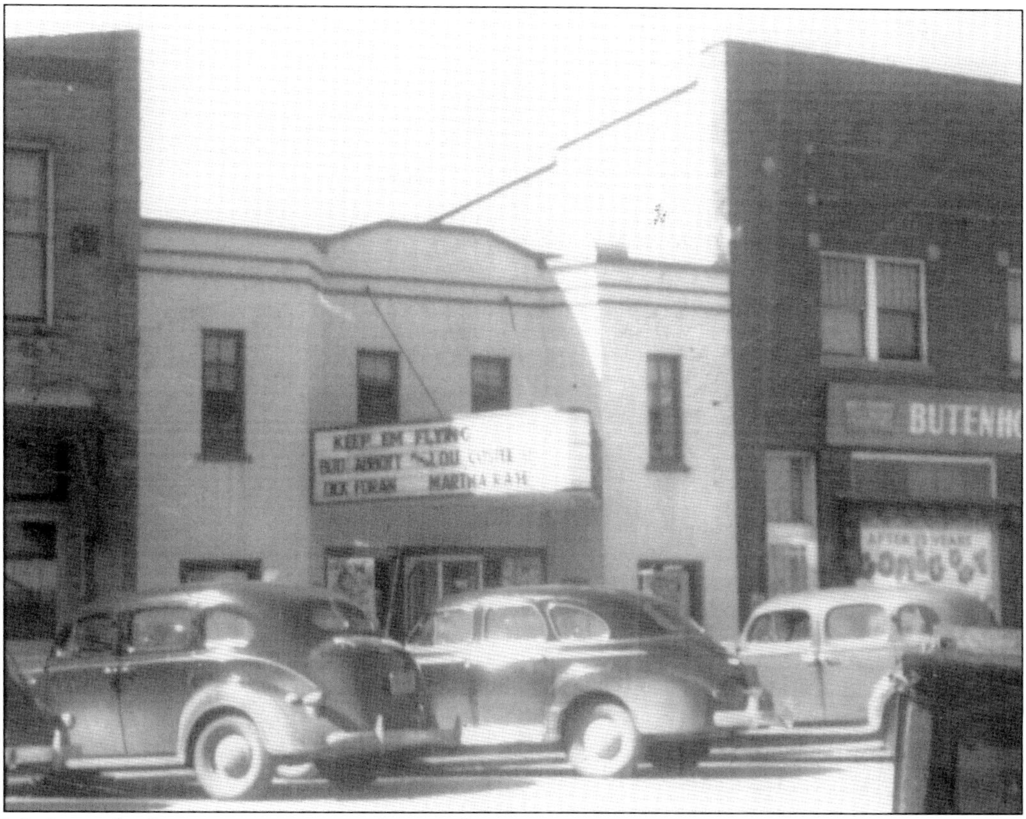

Markesan had its very own movie theater that was located on Bridge Street in the downtown business district, seen above. The theater was started by Henry Pueschner Sr. and his wife, Mabel, in October 1938. The Pueschners operated it until 1970, when it was sold to Kurt Hitzemann. He maintained the theater until 1972, when Henry Pueschner Jr. bought it. Randy Berghammer was the last to manage the theater, and he operated it until it closed in 1975. Kathryn (Laper) Albright poses at right just outside the box office of the theatre in 1940. All sorts of movies where shown at the Markesan Theatre in its 37 years of operation. The original building still stands, although the marquee has long since disappeared. It is now occupied by Grand River Electric and Heating.

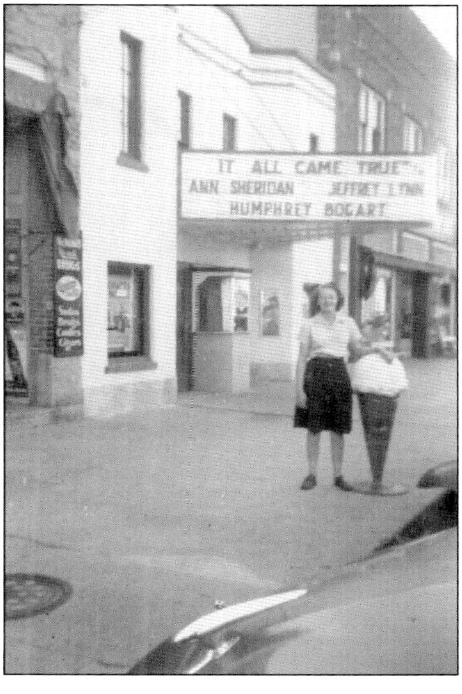

Markesan Theatre

2 Shows Daily at 7 - 9. Matinee Sundays at 2:30.

Friday, Saturday, December 8 - 9
LOUISIANA HAYRIDE with Judy Conova and
TUCSON RAIDERS with Bill Elliott, Geo. Gabby Hayes.

Sunday, Monday, Tuesday, December 10 - 11 - 12
BATHING BEAUTY in Technicolor with Red Skelton
Ester Williams, Harry James Orchestra

Wednesday, Thursday, December 13 - 14
MEET THE PEOPLE
with Lucille Ball, Dick Powell, June Allyson

Friday, Saturday, December 15 - 16
SWING IN THE SADDLE with Jane Frazee and
EVER SINCE VENUS
with Ann Savage, Billy Gilbert, Hugh Herbert

Sunday, Monday, Tuesday, December 17 - 18 - 19
HOME IN INDIANA in Technicolor
with Walter Brennan, Jeanie Crain, Charlotte Greenwood

Wednesday December 20
ONCE UPON A TIME
with Cary Grant, Janet Blair, James Gleason

Thursday, December 21
THE SONG OF BERNADETTE
Matinee at 3 p.m. 1st show at 5:50. 2nd show at 8:40.
Admission—Matinee: Children 40c. Adults 76c.
Admission after 5:50: Children 55c. Adults $1.10

Friday, Saturday, December 22 - 23
SWINGTIME JOHNNY with Andrews Sisters and
THE LAST HORSEMAN with Russell Hayden

Sunday, December 24
HAPPY LAND with Don Ameche, Frances Dee
Harry Carey.

Monday, Tuesday, December 25 - 26
FOUR JILLS IN A JEEP with Martha Raye,
Carole Landis, Francis Dee, Mitzi Mayfair.

Wednesday, Thursday, December 27 - 28
THE ADVENTURES OF MARK TWAIN
with Fredric March, Alexis Smith, Donald Crisp,
C. Aubrey Smith.

Friday, Saturday, December 29 - 30
KANSAS CITY KITTY with Joan Davis.
And LIGHTS OF OLD SANTA FE with Roy Rogers.

The Markesan Theatre posted movie times and showings in the *Markesan Herald* and other community boards. This newspaper posting shows that there were two motion pictures playing daily at 7:00 p.m. and 9:00 p.m.; Sundays the theatre had 2:30 p.m. matinees. Back then, tickets were 55¢ for children and $1.10 for adults, and matinees were 40¢ for children and 76¢ for adults. The last showtime listing for the Markesan Theatre was posted in the *Markesan Herald* in April 1975.

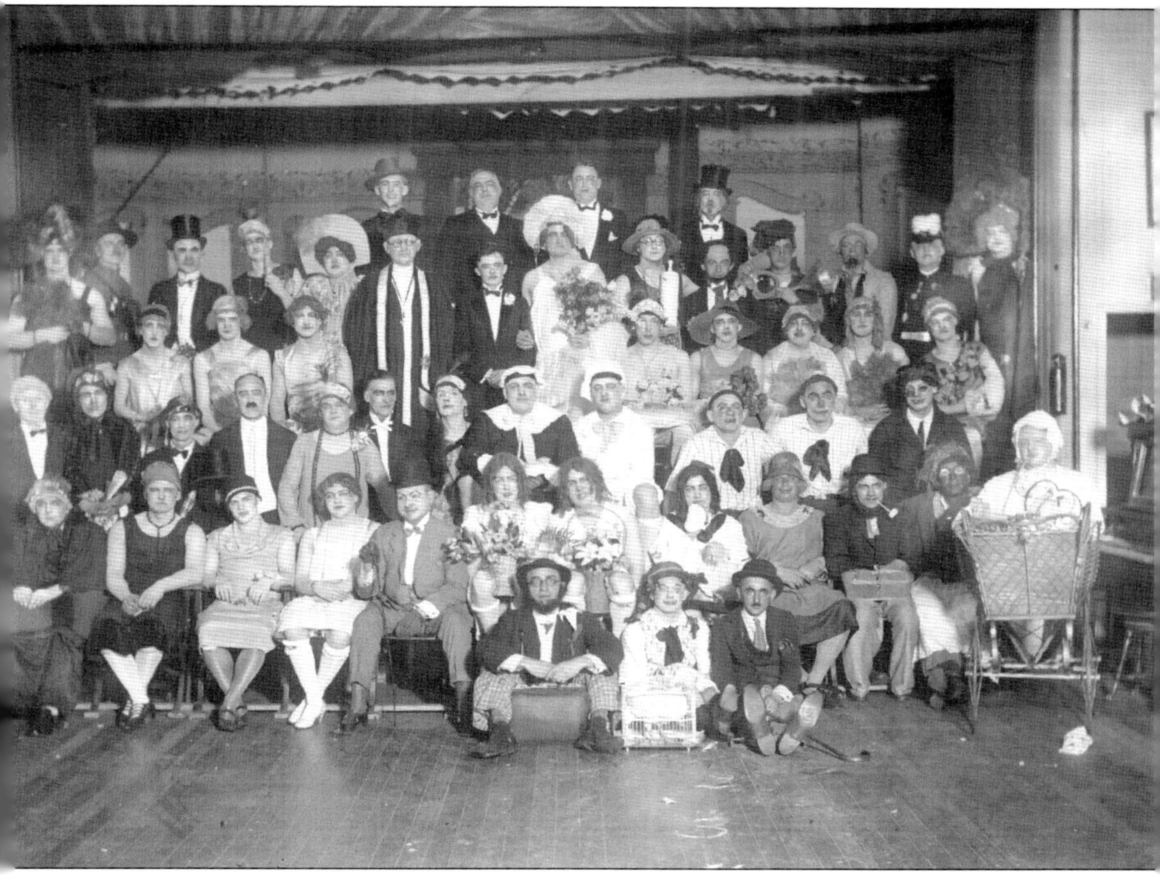

The Markesan Kiwanis Club was organized on May 5, 1947, and a charter was presented on June 16, 1947. The organization adopted the motto "We Build" as it played a major role in charities and other uplifting programs in the community and surrounding area. One of the ways this organization raised money to support its work was by holding a minstrel or variety show. This photograph shows the variety show held on April 2, 1928, in the old Masonic Hall on Bridge Street.

IF YOU CAN'T LAUGH---DON'T COME TO SEE THE

WOMANLESS WEDDING

TO BE PRESENTED AT THE

MASONIC HALL MARKESAN, WIS. Monday and Tuesday **APR. 2 - 3**

By the Sympson-Levie Co. of Bardstown, Kentucky
Sponsored by the Womans Club

60 LOCAL MEN AS CHARACTERS **60**
Screams of Laughter. Funniest Affair Ever Staged in Markesan. Come.

ALL STAR CAST
A. A. KRAUSE
AS LEADING LADY

CAST OF CHARACTERS

Butler—Samuel Cookson.
The Punch Girls—F. L. Friday, Walter Dunsmoor.
The Present Takers—Earl Frei, C. F. Shaw.
Brides Weeping Mother—R. O. Schoen.
Brides Comforting Father—Ed. W. Laper.
Brides Bad Little Brothers—H. Bloedel, Geo. C. Johnson.
The Old Maid Aunt—Dr. E. R. Orrick.
Ikey Rosenstein—B. M. Henninger.
Brides Grandmother—F. M. Dunsmoor.
Brides Grandfather—S. E. Ames.
Charlie Chaplin—Ralph Clark.
Deaf Aunt and Uncle From The Country—H. H. Kaul, E. H. Davidson.
Twin Sisters— Hy Chaimson, O. H. Rasmussen.
Mary Pickford—Chas. Welk.
Groom's Haughty Mother and Father —Blaine Dillie, W. F. Kohls.
Sis Hopkins—Elmo Henninger.
Harry Lauder—Fred Schwandt.
The Fashion Plate—Leo Butenhoff.
The Country Cousin—C. G. Lockwood.
Pat and Rosie O'Grady—B. J. Oelke, Jack Densmoor.

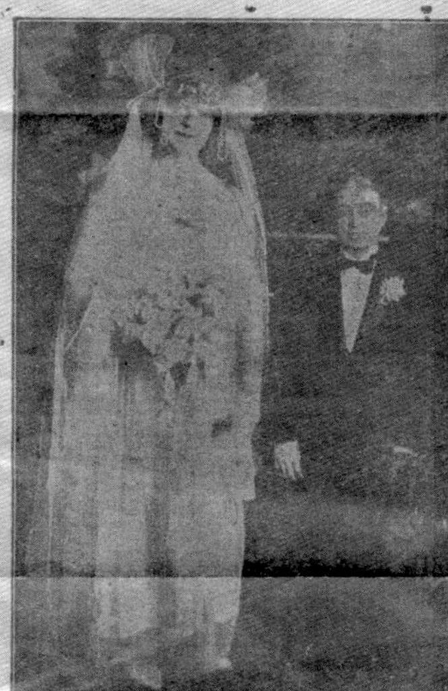

Annie Laurie—Richard Abendroth.
The Henpecked Husband—C. H. Reif.
His Devoted Wife—W. A. Miller.
The Flappers of 1928—Austin Schroeder, A. W. Buzzell.
The Kentucky Colonel and His Lady —A. H. Schleunes, W. E. Geidel.
Mary Garden—Guy M. Folsom.
President and Mrs. Coolidge—Geo. Graf, Dr. M. T. Blewett.
Negro Mammy—J. M. Hull.
Brides Baby Sister—F. H. Allen.
The Village School Ma'am—G. W. Broecker.
General Pershing and Admiral Sims —A. S. Densmoor, Ira Parker.
Theda Bara—Lee Buzzell.

THE BRIDAL PARTY

The Best Man—A. M. Williams.
The Bishop—Hugh Miller.
The Ringbearer—Bill Butenhoff.
Paderewski—L. H. Mumbrue.
Maid of Honor—Stanley Phelps.
Bridesmaids—Kenneth Van Vuren, Clarence Dumdey, Winston Price, Louis Bazeley.
Flower Girls— C. E. Mielke, E. C. Nehring.
Trainbearer—A. W. Sommerfield.
The Bride—A. A. Krause.
The Groom—Guess Who ? ? ?

Show Starts at 8:15 p. m. **Reserved Seats 50c on Sale Friday at Schoen's.**

WARNING This particular play was composed, is owned and produced by the Sympson Levie Company, protected by copyright No. 70971, U. S. Copyright office, Washington, D. C. Any person or organization attempting infringement will be prosecuted to the fullest extent and damages collected.

Other organizations in Markesan were also established to get people, young or old, together to hold social events in town, do community service, or just for social reasons. Markesan Boy Scout Troop 28 was established in 1921. The Columbian Club of Markesan organized in 1891. The Women's Club came in 1916, and the Columbian Club and Women's Club merged to form the Columbian Women's Club in 1955. This poster was advertising the Womanless Wedding show that was to be held at the Masonic Hall, and the Women's Club of Markesan is shown to sponsor the entertainment.

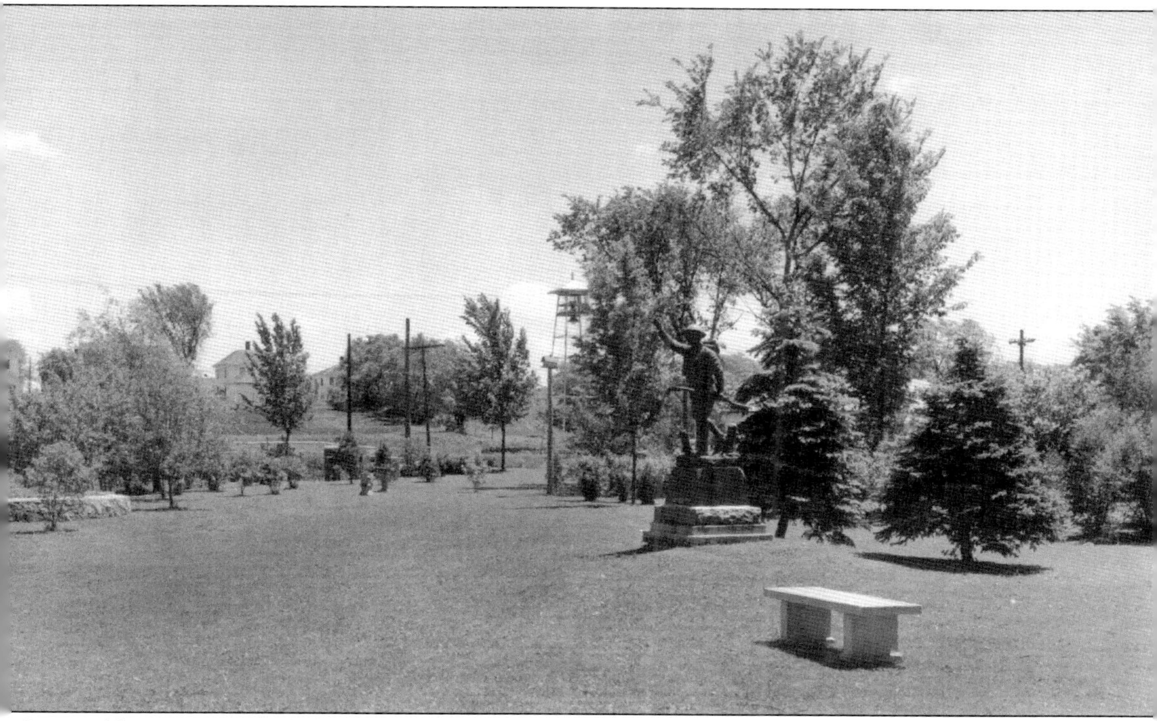

Pictured here is Hein Park, located on Bridge Street near the Grand River. The land and money to landscape it was donated by August Hein in the 1940s, shortly before his death. One of the most interesting pieces to be displayed at the park was the Doughboy statue in honor of World War I veterans. The statue was moved to Grand River Memorial Park in 2007.

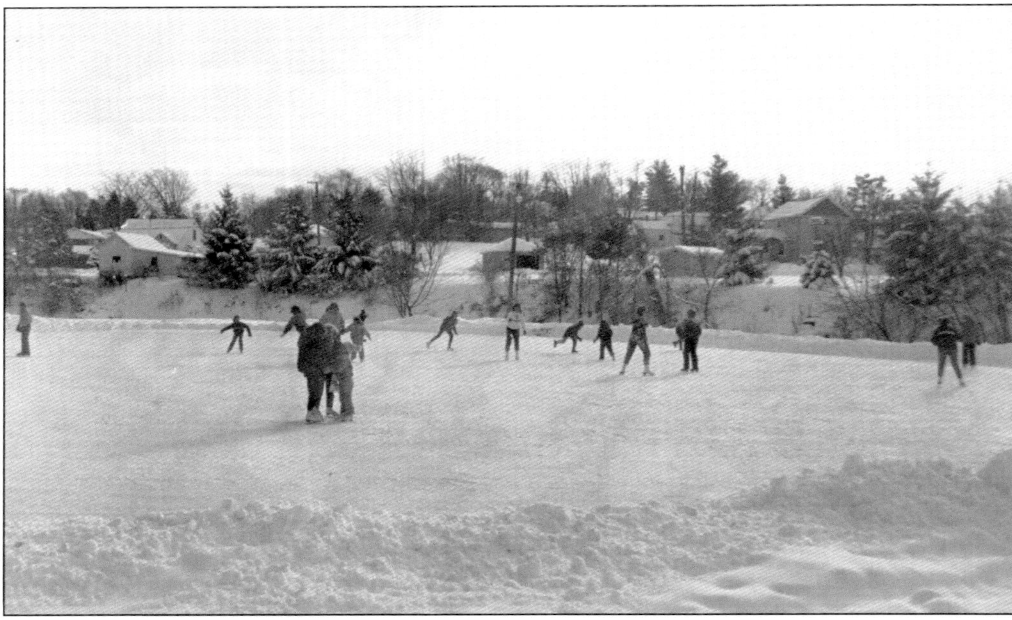

Another area situated across the river from Hein Park is the Kiwanis Park. The park was originally known as Riverdale Park, as it is located next to the Grand River and the former Riverdale Manor, which was built in 1961. The park has many areas for recreation and serves as the city ice-skating rink during winter months.

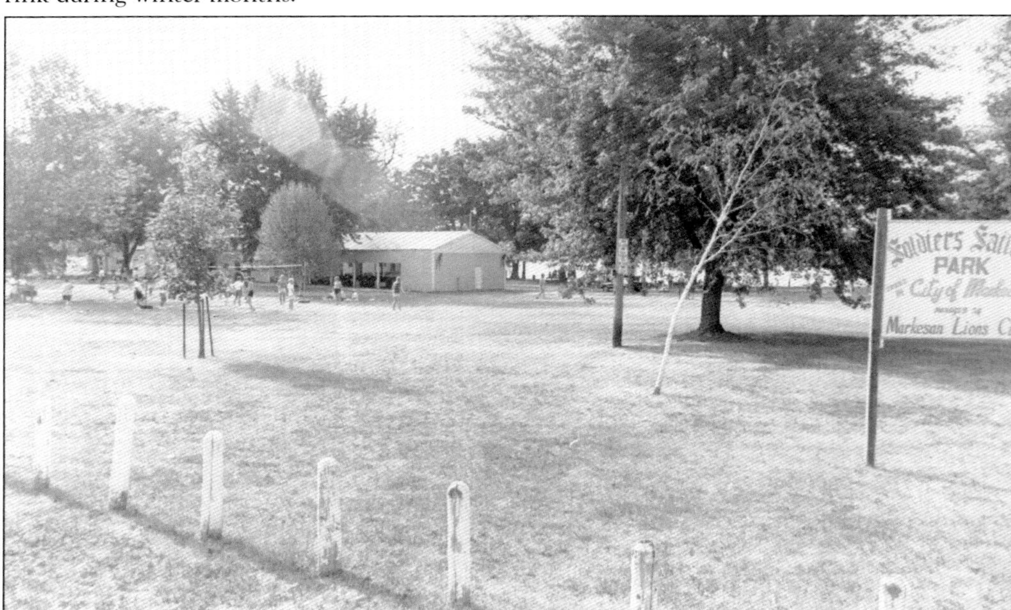

Soldiers and Sailors Memorial Park is located on the south shore of Little Green Lake, just two miles north of Markesan. The park was established in 1928 by the Columbian Club of Markesan. In the 1930s, the Markesan Fire Department maintained the park. It organized and built shelters, fencing, bathhouses, toilets, and a refreshment stand. The first Firemen's Picnic was held around 1937. Markesan purchased the park in 1960 and has maintained it since then.

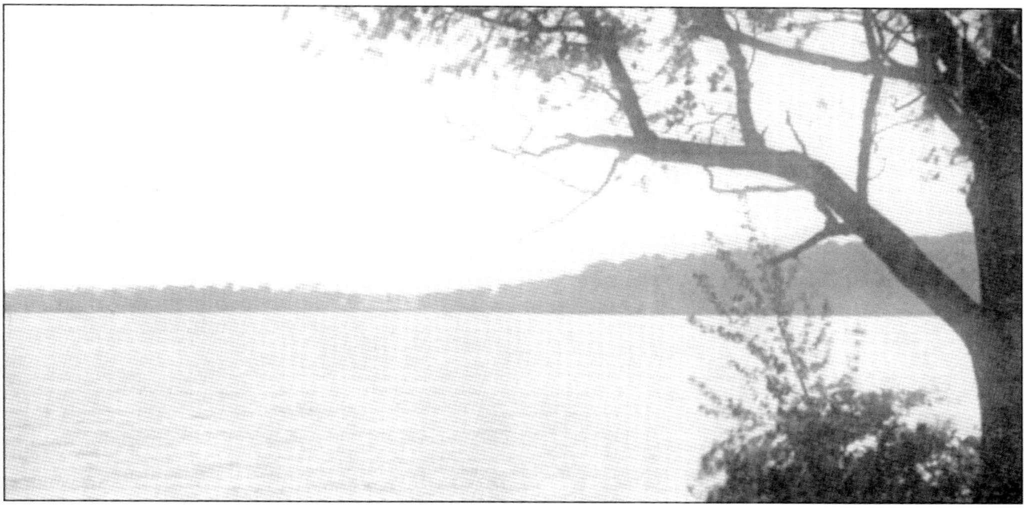

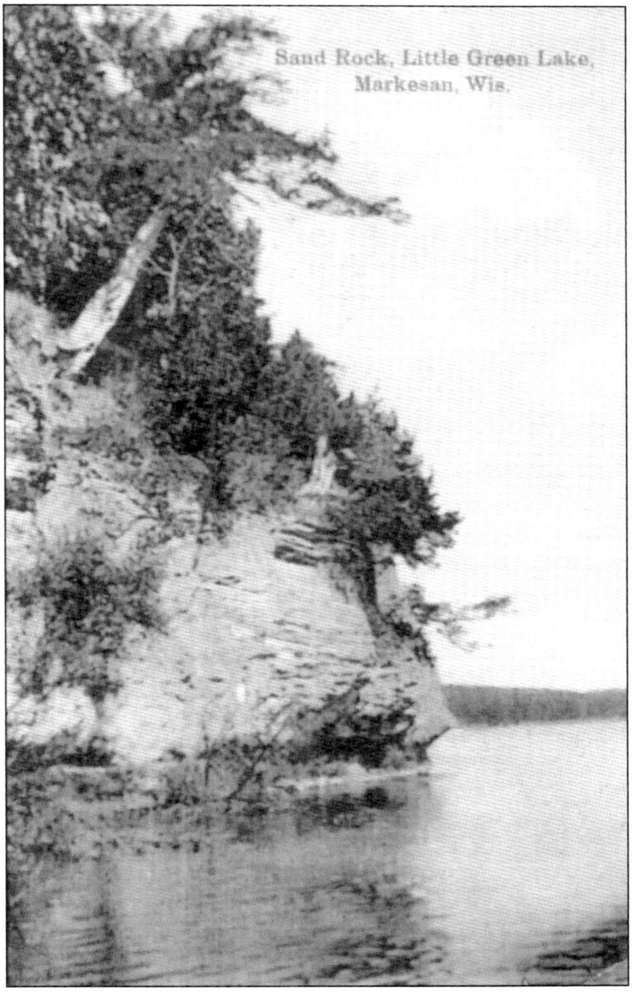

Little Green Lake has always been a spot for rest and relaxation. The shoreline view of the lake seen above is from around 1900. The lake was originally known as Choara Lake, named by Native Americans. Sometime after the area became settled, the body of water was renamed Little Green. At right, it was said that a group of men had a counterfeit money operation in a cave on the north side of the lake sometime between the 1830s and 1840s.

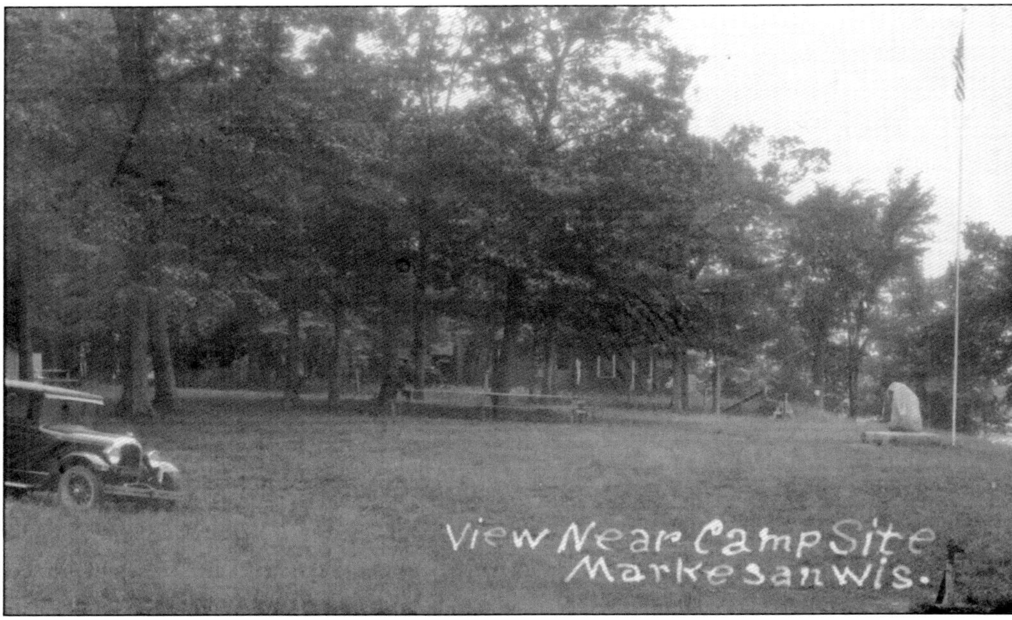

The campsite near the Soldiers and Sailors Park on Little Green Lake was used by the Markesan Boy Scouts. The stone seen in these photographs, placed by the Columbian Club of Markesan, is a memorial to all who served in World War I. The Boy Scout troop was organized in 1921 under the leadership of Anton Hatlestad. During the early years of the organization, the Boy Scouts camped in tents near Little Green Lake. Storms frequently blew the tents away, and insects plagued the boys as they tried to eat, so a cabin was built on the grounds to shelter the troop.

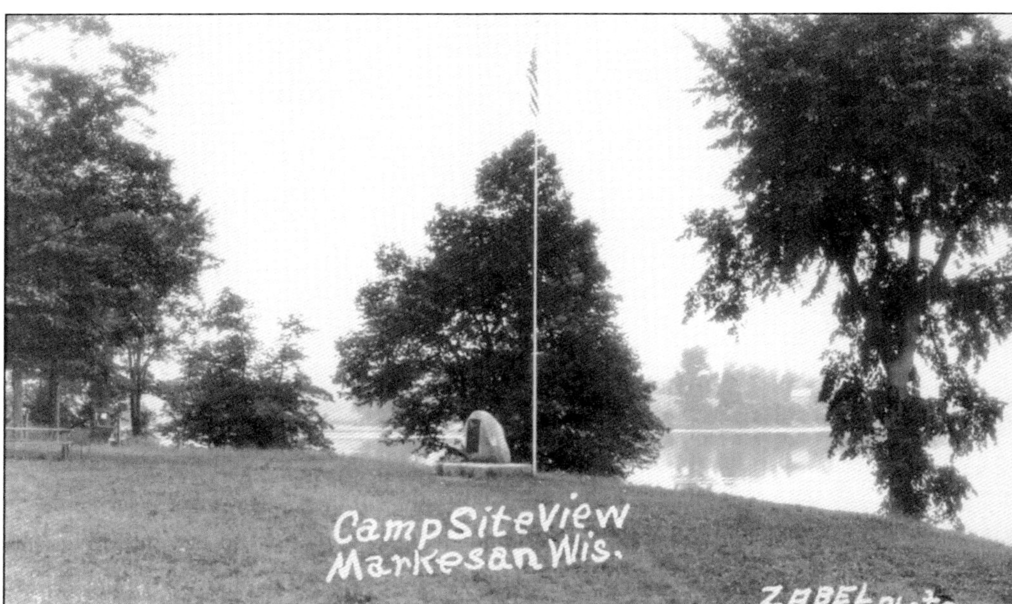

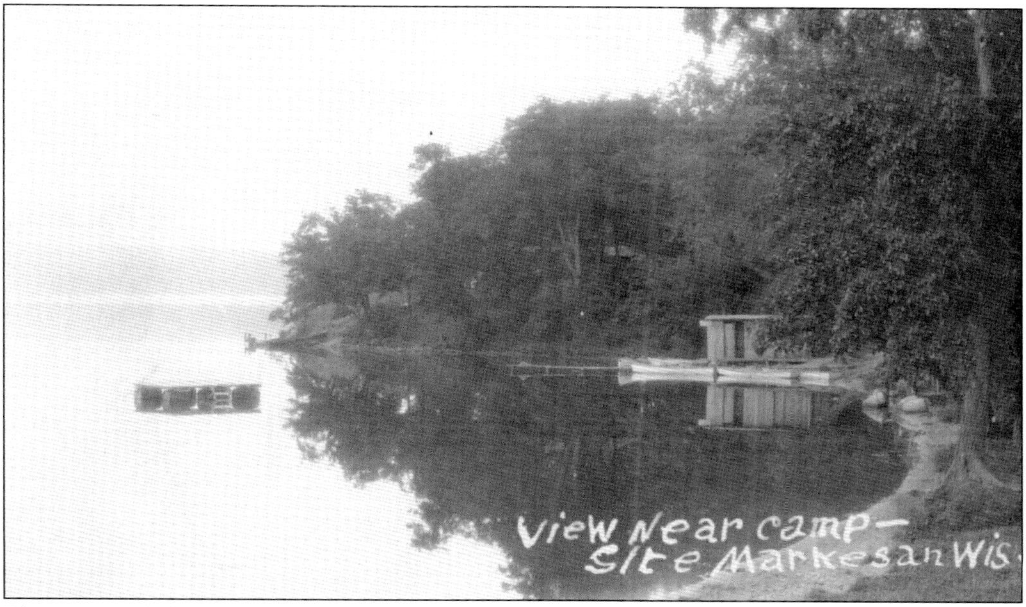

This postcard, dated 1929, shows a camp on Little Green Lake. The message on the back reads, "Dad, I can use a few dollars if you can spare them. Please buy me a bathing suit, Robert took mine. A red and white one with odd designs will suit me. Size 38–40. Am having a wonderful time. Myrtle."

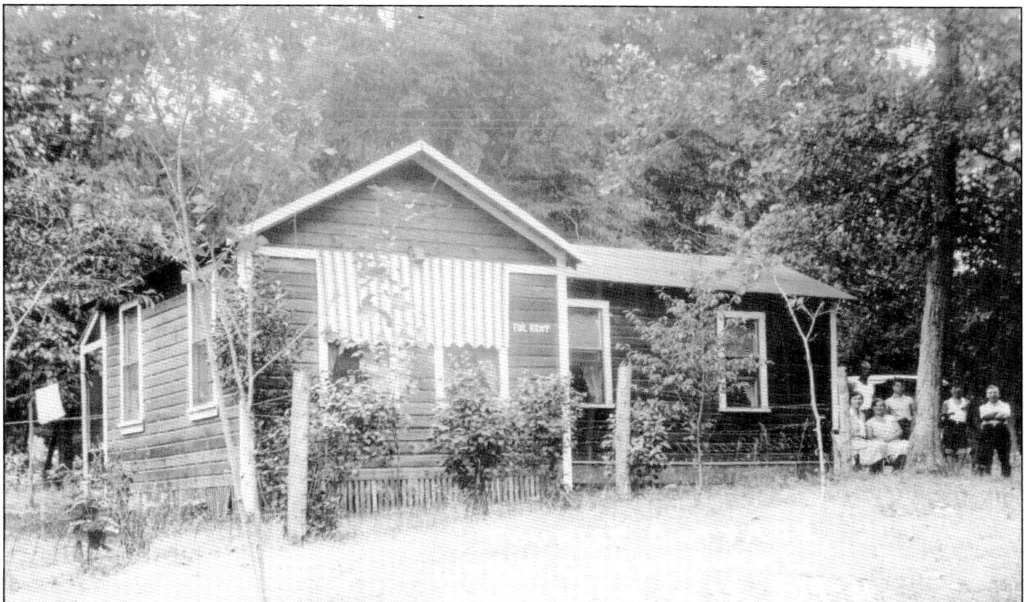

Cottages were rented out to those seeking a retreat on the lake during the summer months. Families took time to relax and enjoy swimming and fishing on the lake. It was said that the Kelm family of Markesan built the first cottage on the lake around 1900. Little Green Lake covers almost 500 acres of land and is near 30 feet in depth.

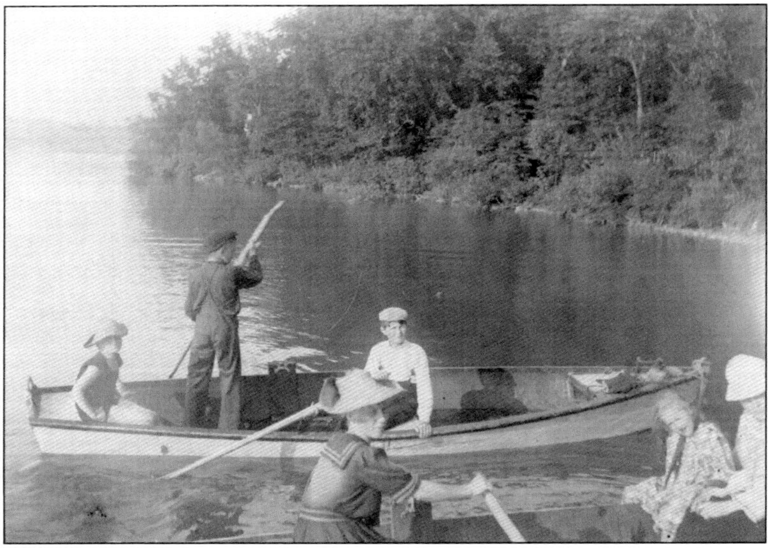

Here is a group of young kids out for a boat ride. Little Green Lake has been a hot spot of summer activity. The Firemen's Picnic was a big hit for many years. Dances, races, picnics, and entertainment were all popular at these gatherings. Today, the lake is dotted with cottages and restaurants; it remains a lively place year-round.

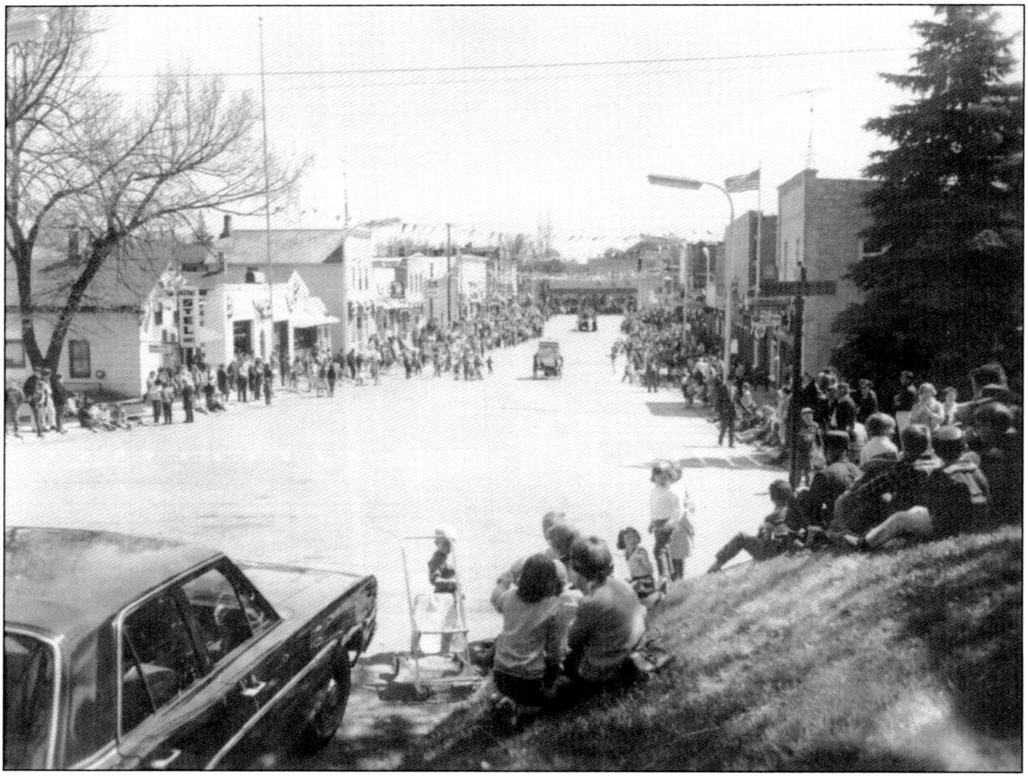

In 1966, Jo Ann Cupery, daughter of Markesan physician Dr. Dowe and Jeanette Cupery, won the Alice in Dairyland competition. In 1967, the District 7 finals were held in Markesan to pick a young woman to continue to the 1967 Alice in Dairyland pageant. Pictured here is the parade on Bridge Street to welcome the contestants and visitors to the event.

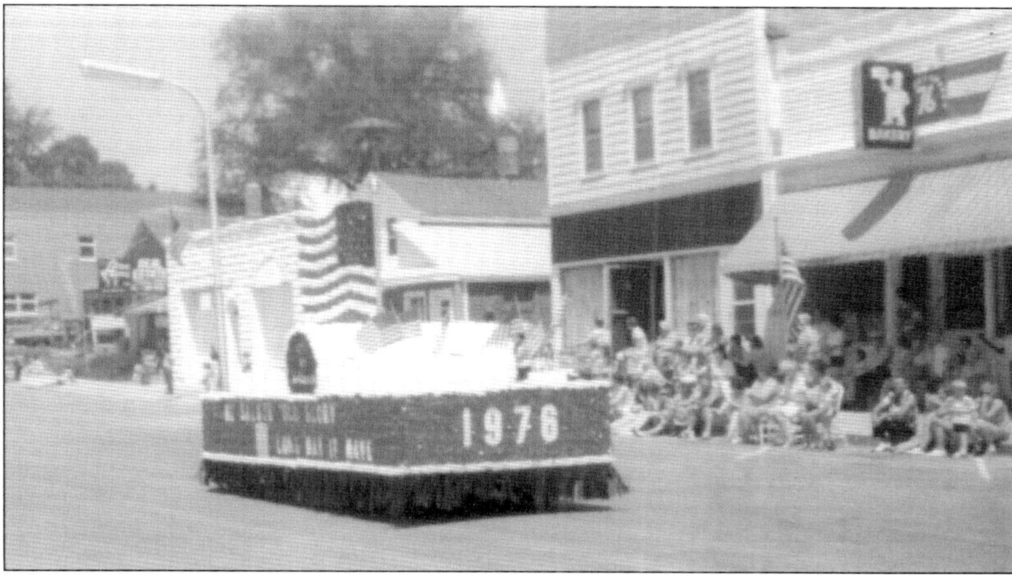

In June 1976, Markesan was added to the roster of bicentennial cites by the American Revolution Bicentennial Committee. In order to be listed as one of these cities, there were criteria that had to be met, and a committee also needed to be formed to organize and carry out the events. This photograph shows the bicentennial committee's float for the parade held during the bicentennial celebration.

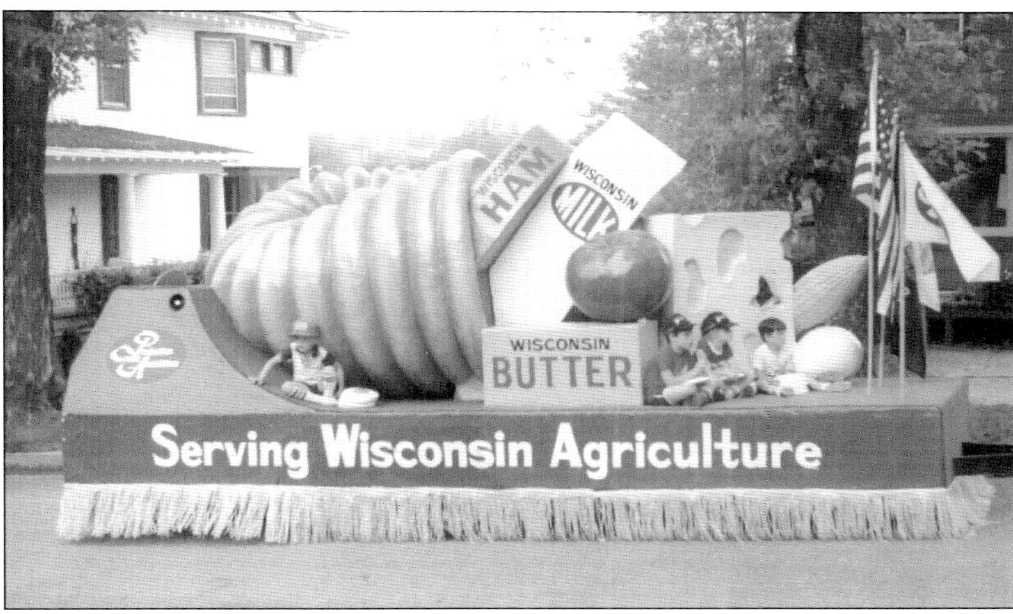

Another celebration that took hold in Markesan in the 1960s was June Dairy Queen Dollar Days, when celebrations of the dairy industry were held. Local stores would run specials, picnics and contests were held, and a parade featuring local businesses and organizations was put on. By the 1970s, it was just known as June Dairy Days, and it remains one of the biggest celebrations in Markesan and the surrounding area. Here is one of the many floats that have participated in the June Dairy Days annual event.